THE BLACK MIGRATION

THE BLACK
MIGRATION

The Journey to Urban America

by

George W. Groh

WEYBRIGHT AND TALLEY
New York

Published in the United States by
Weybright and Talley
750 Third Avenue
New York   New York   10017

1-17-72

To *George S. and Dorothy Groh*

ACKNOWLEDGMENTS

Numerous people have helped importantly with this book. My particular thanks to the following:

My wife, Lynn, who typed the manuscript and assisted in many ways.

Truman M. Talley, who suggested some of the basic approaches to the study.

Mrs. Helen Smith, who collaborated closely in the research and interviewing devoted to the study of Newark as a ghetto city.

Francine Krisel, who made valuable research and interviewing contributions to the general work.

Mrs. Ada Lyons, who assisted in the researching of census reports and other government documents.

I am indebted also to many who shared knowledge and experience acquired through years of work with race and poverty problems. Among these were Randolph Blackwell, director of Southern Rural Action Project at Atlanta, Georgia; the staff of Southern Regional Council at Atlanta; the members of Crawfordville Enterprises, particularly Calvin Turner and Robert Billingsley, at Crawfordville, Georgia; the members of Southwest Alabama Farmers Cooperative Association, particularly Joe Johnson and Freeman Berry, at Selma, Alabama, and Albert Turner of Southern Christian Leadership Conference at Selma.

The case study of Newark as a ghetto city was greatly facilitated by the generous cooperation of a street group called Hopers, led by Frank Grant. I am grateful also for cooperation extended by Donald Malafronte, former administrative aide to Mayor Hugh Addonizio, and to Samuel Shepherd, the administrative aide to Mayor Kenneth Gibson.

My thanks, also, to James Haughton and Joe Carnegie of Fight Back, a Harlem organization which seeks to end discrimination in the construction business. They provided much material and generously offered some of the pictures used in this book.

The people cited are, of course, not responsible for any of the conclusions reached in this study. The viewpoint is the reporter's own.

Permissions

The author wishes to thank the following persons and publishers for permission to include copyrighted material:

Association for The Study of Negro Life and History: for Letters published in the *Journal of Negro History* during the first Great Migration.

CBS Broadcasting: for quote from CBS News of Black America Series, "The Heritage of Slavery." 1968.

Chicago Daily Defender: for material quoted from early issues.

Harcourt Brace Jovanovich, Inc.: for *Black Metropolis: A Study of Negro Life in a Northern City* by St. Clair Drake and Horace Cayton.

Harper & Row, Publishers: for passages from *An American Dilemma* by Gunnar Myrdal.

John Oliver Killens: for quote from *Black Man's Burden.*

Alfred A. Knopf, Inc.: for an excerpt from *Democracy in America* by Alexis de Tocqueville.

New Community Press, Inc.: for a table from *Hunger, USA,* © 1968.

Oxford University Press: for *Strange Career of Jim Crow* by C. Vann Woodward.

Paul Reynolds: for a quote from *12 Million Black Voices* by Richard Wright.

Rutgers University Press: for material from *The Tenement Landlord* by George Sternlieb, © 1969.

Time, Inc.: for material paraphrased from "In a Grim City, a Secret Meeting with Snipers," by Russell Sackett, LIFE Magazine, July 28, 1967, and for material paraphrased from "The Killing of Billy Furr," by Dale Wittner, LIFE Magazine, July 28, 1967.

The Twentieth Century Fund: for a table from *The Advancing South: Manpower Prospects and Problems* by James G. Maddox, et al.

The University of Chicago Press: for material from *Deep South, A Social and Anthropological Study of Caste and Class* by Allison Davis, et al, © 1941.

University of North Carolina Press: for material from *Preface to Peasantry* by Arthur F. Raper, © 1936.

Table of Contents

Tables

THE BLACK MIGRATION

Overview

THE LAST MIGRATION

Then:

*Lord in Heaven! Good God Almighty! Great Day in the Morning!
Our time has come! We are leaving! We are angry no more; we
are leaving! We are bitter no more; we are leaving! We are leaving
our homes, pulling up our stakes to move on. We look up at the
high southern sky and remember all the sunshine and rain and we
feel a sense of loss, but we are leaving. We look out at the wide
green fields which our eyes saw when we first came into the world
and we feel full of regret, but we are leaving . . . we feel glad, for
we are leaving . . . .*

—Richard Wright, talking of escape from
a southern plantation fifty years ago.

And Now:

One out of seventeen represents miserable odds.
—A black youth describes the chances
of escaping today's ghetto.

America's cities have served historically as great arenas in
which newcomers struggled for a foothold. The contests were
brutal, the human cost incalculably high, but up to now it has
always been an ordeal relieved by hope.

For more than a century the drama was one of emigrants
fleeing the social failures of other lands. That story is now a folk
legend about ourselves, and thus hugely sentimentalized. It was

1

never a sentimental experience for those who took part; but still, it worked. Each succeeding group was able in the course of two to three generations to force its way into the larger society.

Today the cities are again engulfed by new arrivals. The participants this time are black Americans, in flight from our own social failures. About seventy-five years ago they began streaming out of the cotton fields, seeking escape from sharecropping, from Jim Crow, from all the inequities of a system that reduced them to serfs. For a time they dreamed that the way North was a freedom road, a "justice ticket." The vision withered but still they flocked to the cities, because they had no other choice. Mechanization was forcing them off the farms.

Recent decades have brought the full crest of the wave. In 1940, or just a generation ago, black Americans were still heavily concentrated in the rural South. Today nearly half live in northern cities and three-fourths are urban dwellers, whether North or South. About 12 million blacks are huddled in the wretched inner-city ghettos. They constitute what may well be the last migration, the final test of a basic American proposition. As of now, the results are shattering.

The ghetto areas are literally falling apart. They are strewn with at least half a million housing units that are unfit for human habitation, and the blight is spreading.

The ghetto unemployment rate is more than double that of white city dwellers. The subemployment rate—the number who drift from one fringe job to another—is three times as high.

Worst of all, the ghettos are breeding grounds for generations of disaster still to come. The black child has about one chance in four of beginning life without a father. At about age six, when he enters school, he encounters his first and most critical failure. Throughout school he falls steadily behind; when he graduates from high school, if he graduates, he is about three years below the general performance level. Long before he is grown, he is in deep trouble with himself and with society.

The casualty rate among such youth was described by one of

the survivors, a young man named Earl Vessup. He testified at a New York state legislative hearing, speaking on behalf of a student aid program, and he told what it is like to grow up black on the ghetto streets.

"Out of seventeen fellows from my block who graduated from high school, five are in jail, seven are dope addicts or on the way, four were in the Army—one of whom was killed in Vietnam. I am the only one attending college.

"One out of seventeen represents miserable odds," he added, "but even that slim chance of working out of poverty will be gone if . . . the budget cuts are approved by the legislature."

Those odds are a bad risk for the country, too, and all the much-publicized poverty programs have had but minor effect. The richest, most powerful nation on earth seems unable or unwilling to cope effectively with one of its basic problems. The extent of the failure was underlined in 1967 when some forty communities were convulsed by riots. At this writing the explosions have subsided, but the fuse is smoldering again, and no one can safely predict when, whether, or in what form the next violence will erupt.

What has gone wrong? Why should this last migration be so full of travail?

One answer is obvious: the migrants are black. The society is obsessed with race; the color question intrudes on all the problems of jobs, housing and education and, beyond that, it permeates human attitudes, warping the responses of both whites and blacks. We shall be in trouble with one another until that poison is finally worked out.

Another harsh truth is that long subjugation left its mark on the migrants. Many of them came to the cities bearing heavy burdens of poverty and ignorance, frustration and despair. That this heritage was imposed does not alter the fact; the manner in which an injury is sustained bears no relationship to its crippling effects.

A third factor is that black migrants had the bad luck to come late. There was a time when the cities needed endless quantities of cheap, unskilled labor, but that era is forever past. Over the last two decades more than 97 percent of all employment increase has taken place in the professional, white collar and skilled workman categories. In the cities today, indeed in the economy at large, there is simply no place for a man whose previous experience consists of swinging a hoe.

The consequences of technologic change are sharply etched in a Department of Labor report for the years 1960-67. In that brief period, more than 450,000 black farm workers were squeezed off the land, displaced by machines. During those same years other machines eliminated some 130,000 jobs from the urban market for unskilled labor. Thus the dilemma of our times: amidst an affluent, expanding economy we have hunger in the rural South, and soaring welfare rolls in the urban centers. In New York City alone, the number of welfare clients exceeds the population of fifteen states.

Finally, migration pressures have coincided with a long period of grievous urban neglect. For more than a quarter of a century we have devoted the national resources to such vast commitments as World War II, the restoration of Europe, the cold war, the conflicts in Korea and Vietnam, the exploration of space. It has left very little for the urgent necessities of our crowded and decaying cities.

The staggering imbalance is demonstrated in Cleveland, where the city government gets only 2.5 cents out of every tax dollar that its citizens pay. The ratio varies in other communities, but everywhere the circumstances are the same: the federal government preempts most of the tax revenues, the states take a large slice of what is left, the suburbs drain off still more, and the cities are left to deal with massive human problems. Thus the ghettos fester and spread, the municipal services crumble, and the discontented inveigh with mounting fury against city officials who are helpless to meet their needs. During the long, hot, always dangerous summers the cities turn on the hydrants, hoping to cool it one more time.

What has gone wrong? The answer would appear to be: nearly everything. Richard Wright, himself a black migrant, said many years ago that "Perhaps never in history has a more utterly unprepared folk wanted to go to the city." For recent migrants it must be added that perhaps never was the city less prepared to receive them.

The problems are so numerous and so overwhelming that despair has become almost a fashionable view. Historical perspective suggests, however, a more open assessment. The ghettos have been festering for decades and racism has been a raw wound on the body politic since the society began. Nothing new in that. What is rather new is national awareness that we are in grievous trouble. The chronic conditions have flared into crisis, and that may well be a healthy sign.

The black Americans are not more deprived now than ever before; they are only more visible. And more vocal. The migration has swept up a long dispossessed people and deposited them on urban doorsteps where they can no longer safely be ignored.

The recognition of crisis does not guarantee resolution. It is a necessary first step. There are other factors which indicate that these turbulent years could mark the beginning of change.

Most encouraging is the recent evidence that large numbers of blacks are beginning to move upward through the economic strata. Between 1960 and 1970, black employment was up 67 percent among skilled craftsmen and foremen, up 131 percent among professional and technical people. The number of black families with middle class incomes more than doubled in that short span.

It cannot be assumed that since some are moving up, others will. For the black field hand who is abandoning his rural shack today, for his city cousin who lacks a high school education, for all the millions trapped one way or another in the substratum of

poverty, the obstacles remain immense. Even so, the recent upward surge is a remarkable event, and it has been achieved
among a people who are largely first or second generation urban
arrivals.

Another sign of the times, not always agreeable to the white
majority, is the prevailing black mood. It is proud, angry, assertive, defiant. Hair straighteners are out and Afro-American hair
styles are in. Black is beautiful. Black power is the goal and
white allies are barely tolerated, if at all. It is often an abrasive
mood—it will become more so if whites do not move over and
make room—but it provides a powerful ferment for a depressed
people struggling to rise.

In sum, we are in the midst of wrenching change. That condition is always trying, and usually dangerous, and a walk down
any ghetto street would dispel the illusion that solutions will be
easy, or painless, or even bound to succeed. There is, however,
some stirring of hope, and that makes it worth the risk, for up to
now, real hope has been the element most often missing from this
climactic migration.

Part I

THE HERITAGE

Chapter 1

ONE MORE BALE

What did you think we were before you began to think of us as human beings?

Well, in a way, we thought of you almost as a very superior pet.
—A deep South dialogue between
black and white.

A TREK from a southern cotton field to a northern city entails a journey of some five hundred to a thousand miles. In other ways not so easily measured, the distance is enormous. An Alabama field hand can board a bus and be in Chicago twenty-four hours later; in that quick spin of the clock he is confronted with jolting changes in the style of life, the ground rules of survival, the whole pattern of existence.

The migrants have been making such a journey while trudging another, much longer road. They have been traveling from slavery, toward freedom. Toward, but not yet to; a century and more after Emancipation they are still seeking basic human rights which most Americans take for granted.

The two journeys have influenced each other in important ways. In exchanging the plantation for the city the migrants stepped out of an almost feudal past, and into the clamorous industrial present. The urban massing of a thus uprooted people

9

created the opportunity, indeed the necessity, for a mobilization of black demands.

By the same token, city life has made demands on the migrants. Many found themselves thrust into situations for which they were wholly unprepared. It was not just a case of poor education, or lack of industrial skills. The migrants were a deprived people in a much deeper sense. They were products of a society which had long denied them both the rights and the responsibilities of freedom.

In the rural South, the old South that is now vanishing, race repression went hand in hand with an intricate master-servant relationship which embraced every area of life. A large measure of dependency was conferred on blacks in exchange for total submission. It was not a bargain that the black could take or leave. He was bound over in many ways to his white overlord, a figure he referred to as "Mr. Charlie" or "The Man."

Mr. Charlie owned the land. He decided who could work a piece of ground, and who couldn't, and on what terms. As often as not he owned the plow and tractor, furnished the seed and fertilizer, and advanced the money which tided the black tenant over from one harvest to the next. And he kept the books.

It was a closed system, tightly controlled by both law and custom. Economically, it amounted at best to dubious paternalism, at worst to harsh exploitation. In every human sense it was disastrous. One view of the consequences—a white planter's view —was presented with stark candor on a CBS-TV documentary.

The planter was Norwood Hastie, a man steeped in the white tradition of the old South; he is an eighth-generation representative of a family that has owned land around Charleston since 1672. He was interviewed by George Foster, a CBS reporter who is black. There ensued this remarkable dialogue:

FOSTER: What do you think are the differences between the races?

HASTIE: I think there's a refusal to accept responsibility. I think there's a lack of motivation. I've tried here to promote people to foremen, superintendents, but they just refuse to do it. They just don't want the responsibility. They don't worry like the—the white man. If they have troubles, they go to sleep, and wake up the next morning and that trouble is over.

FOSTER: Is it possible that white people have something to do with the lack of ability for blacks to assimilate into this culture?

HASTIE: Absolutely. The white man has certainly been prejudiced. And to quite an extent, unfair. But customs die awful hard . . . . Everyone knew years ago that the Negro would have to be given equality. But in the South, knowing Negroes as we think we do, we realized it would take time. It's been compared to straightening teeth. It takes a slow steady pressure. You can't do it with a hammer. And white people's attitudes will change in time. I'm a lot more liberal than I was five years ago, and I know I'll be a lot more liberal five years from now.

FOSTER: What has tended to make you more liberal?

HASTIE: Well, realization that the Negro is a human being like anyone else.

FOSTER: Mr. Hastie, what did you think we were before you began to think of us as human beings?

HASTIE: Well, in a way, we thought of you almost as a very superior pet. Something—or rather, someone, we had to take care of. Because we had to do so much of their thinking for them. We had to do almost everything for them, except living their own lives. Anything outside, we had to do for them.

Such was the system, as seen through the eyes of a white proprietor. The view has the merit of being bluntly stated. The blacks, of course, saw it differently. Their outlook is conveyed in a folk tale heard time and again along the dusty back roads.

The tale involves a sharecropper who is traditionally identified by first name only. We'll call him Joe. In good years he raised ten or twelve bales of cotton, and in bad years only seven or eight, but the result seemed to have no effect on his fortunes. At the annual accounting he always wound up in debt. One year he decided to test the system.

When the harvest came Joe produced seven bales. Mr. Charlie appeared and went through his usual ritual with pencil and paper. "Well, boy," he said, "it's not too bad. What with the expenses, and the money I advanced you, plus last year's debt, and the interest and all, it works out close. Mighty close. One more bale and you'd be dead even."

Joe favored his employer with a disarming smile. "Boss, I've been with you many a year, and you know I wouldn't cheat you. No, sir. But I was funning you a little. I've got another bale. It's stashed out yonder, in the weeds."

Mr. Charlie was only mildly annoyed. "Doggone it, boy," he said, "You've put me to a lot of trouble. Now I have to figure the whole thing over again." When he had adjusted his calculations he said, "Well, now, there were some items I near forgot, like charging you a little something for the use of the plow. But no matter. It all balances out. You still owe me one more bale."

All over the South one can find black farmers who say that something like that happened to them, or to someone they knew. They append a long list of other grievances: that the cotton gins paid a white price and a black price, that the merchants and money lenders had white and black terms, that even the county agricultural agents offered separate and unequal white and black services.

There are, then, two views of the southern experience. They differ sharply as to whether the white overlord did nearly everything for his black subjects, or nearly everything to them. They agree, however, on a critical point. It lay in the white power to do nearly everything.

As a social and economic system it was bound to be ruinous. Individual plantation owners were honest or otherwise, according to inclination, but there was nothing to compel honesty when dealing with blacks. Individual black farm hands were industrious or not, again according to private standards, but there was no incentive for initiative and hard work. They could envision no basic improvement in their lot.

For a full century the system prevailed. Now it is changing. The sharecropper is now a vanishing breed, the system which produced him is disappearing too, and all the old relationships are shifting. Farm technology, urban migration and a black resistance movement of massive dimensions have contributed to a new South that is still taking shape. That will be discussed later in this report. The old South remains relevant because for generations it was the formative black experience, and it casts a long shadow over the ghetto today. A history of the migration must therefore begin with the special circumstances which shaped black destiny in the South.

The black experience on emerging from slavery amounted to an outsized rendition of "one more bale." They arrived as a people at what should have been a time of fresh start, only to find themselves still bound to the servitude of the past.

The abolitionist Wendell Phillips complained that the Emancipation Proclamation "freed the slave but ignored the Negro." The criticism can be extended to nearly every aspect of the largest, most difficult social transition ever attempted in the United States. Between 1863 and 1865, some 4 million slaves were abruptly freed. They had no resources, no skills except the most menial, and no practice at managing their own affairs. They constituted a third of the South's population and they were set loose without plan or preparation in a countryside laid waste by war.

The things done and not done at that juncture were to have a

critical effect on the black future. Particularly the things not done, or not even considered. The nation had been so consumed by the Civil War that it had given almost no thought to the perplexing questions of peace. Only a week before he died, President Abraham Lincoln was still toying with the idea that perhaps the freed slaves could be waved away, by persuading them to migrate *en masse* to Africa or South America. He asked ex-Union General Ben Butler to survey the logistics of the scheme, and got back the report that it was already much too late to disentangle the black and white threads in the national fabric.

"Mr. President," reported Butler, "I have gone carefully over my calculations as to the power of the country to export the Negroes of the South and I assure you that, using all your naval vessels and all the merchant marine fit to cross the seas with safety, it will be impossible for you to transport to the nearest place . . . half as fast as Negro children will be born here."

Some northern radicals wanted to confiscate the Confederate plantations, equip every freedman with "forty acres and a mule," and so establish at a stroke a sturdy, independent peasantry. But that plan went against a national reluctance to dismember property, and was never seriously considered. In the end, President Andrew Johnson inherited the unresolved problem and waved it away in his own fashion, by turning it back to the South.

The South was in utter chaos, its currency worthless, its commerce destroyed, and its fields idle for lack of laborers. The price of defeat had included the loss of slaves valued at $2 billion. It was scarcely possible to hire the freedmen as paid workers, even if the former masters had been of such a mind; very few of them were left with cash enough to meet an extensive payroll. As southern whites struggled to rise from such ruin, their first impulse was to impress the blacks into service again, this time in a form of peonage.

To the economic motive was added fear; the whites expected a wave of black vengeance which never materialized and they thought that they had to suppress the blacks or themselves risk being overwhelmed. The Jackson, Mississippi, *Daily News* expressed the view of many: "We must keep the ex-slave in a position of inferiority. We must pass such laws as will make him *feel* his inferiority."

Within six months the South was doing just that, as one state after another adopted the Black Codes. Some of the codes were thinly disguised as measures for the regulation of farm labor or the control of vagrants; some were openly labeled as applying only to blacks. All were addressed to the proposition that blacks had to work for whites in a servile capacity.

In Louisiana, farm laborers were bound to the land with a law requiring them to sign annual contracts. They were allowed subsistence rations, but all cash payments were withheld until year's end, and any money due them was forfeit if they quit. If they claimed sickness and were judged malingerers, it cost them double the time lost. Additionally, the employer could fine them as much as a week's pay for disobedience, impudence, or leaving the premises without permission.

Mississippi decreed similar enforced contracts, and specified that deserting black workers should be arrested and brought back at their own expense. The sheriff's costs were set at $5.10 a mile, to be paid by the employer and charged against the worker's future earnings; at the prevailing black wage of $1 to $2 a week it meant that a ten-mile flight could cost a man six months to a year of hard labor.

South Carolina ruled that blacks must obtain a special permit to engage in any occupation except farm work or domestic service. The prescribed relationship was underscored by a stipulation that in making contracts "persons of color shall be known as *servants* and those with whom they contract shall be known as *masters*."

Legal coercion was reinforced with terror. General Carl Shurz made a special investigation for President Johnson and reported that, "Some planters held back their former slaves on their plantations by brute force. Armed bands of white men patrolled the country roads to drive back the Negroes wandering about. Dead bodies of murdered Negroes were found on and near the highways and by-ways.

"The emancipation of the slave," he added, "is submitted to only in so far as chattel slavery in the old form could not be kept up. But although the freedman is no longer considered the property of the individual master, he is considered the slave of society."

The repression aroused northern radicals and brought on the brief spasm called Reconstruction. It lasted in various states from three to ten years. Whatever its defects, it decidedly improved the lot of the former slaves. They acquired a political voice, with numerous black leaders serving in state legislatures and Congress. They obtained the beginnings of mass education. They got only token economic aid (The Freedmen's Bureau expended $15 million in seven years, a per capita allotment of 53 cents a year) but even so, some blacks were able to establish a precarious foothold as small farmers.*

More critical than Reconstruction was the period that followed. The South was groping its way toward a new order, and for some twenty years the black fate hung in the balance. In *The Strange Career of Jim Crow* the historian C. Vann Woodward

---

* Other aspects of Reconstruction are beyond the scope of this report. Suffice it to say here that the era has been damned for corruption and waste, and praised for introducing a more egalitarian concept of government.

On the positive side, Reconstruction produced in the South some of that region's first free schools and hospitals, and the first general acknowledgment that government was responsible for services previously consigned to the *noblesse oblige* of aristocrats. It was, of course, expensive. Mississippi's tax rate rose 1,300 percent in five years, but then the previous rate had been only ten cents on $100.

argues with impressive evidence that this was a hinge moment, a time when things might have turned either way.

As Woodward demonstrates, it was a mixed, unstable era. In some localities blacks voted, held office, sat side by side with whites in restaurants and streetcars. In other localities they were shot for asserting such rights. There was a great deal of lynching —100 to 200 cases a year—and some pitched battles between the races. For all the violence and tension, however, the door to genuine freedom seemed briefly open, or at least ajar.

For the most part, the blacks kept their foot in the door through a tacit political bargain. They traded their votes to their former masters, the big landowners, in exchange for protection from the mob. Thus in South Carolina the first post-Reconstruction governor was Wade Hampton, a former Confederate general, who won election on a platform of race reconciliation. One of his campaign booklets was entitled *Free Men! Free Ballots!! Free Schools!!! The Pledges of Gen. Wade Hampton . . . to the Colored People of South Carolina. . . .*

An optimistic witness to events was Union Colonel Thomas Wentworth Higginson. He was a staunch abolitionist, one of the "secret six" who conspired with John Brown before Harper's Ferry, and he had organized and led a black combat regiment during the war. When the Reconstruction troops were withdrawn, he toured the South to see for himself how things were going. Higginson viewed his old Rebel foes through "tolerably suspicious eyes," but came away agreeably surprised. He found southern civil rights compliance at least equal to that of New England, and he thought race progress was insured by the South's huge bloc of black voters.

"The southern whites," he said, "accept them precisely as Northern men in cities accept the ignorant Irish vote—not cheerfully, but with acquiescence in the inevitable; and when the strict color-line is once broken they are just as ready to conciliate the

negro as the Northern politician to flatter the Irishman. Any
powerful body of voters may be cajoled today and intimidated
tomorrow and hated always, but it can never be left out of sight."

In 1885 a northern black journalist named T. McCants Stewart conducted a kind of one-man "Freedom Ride" through the
South to test continuing performance. "I put a chip on my shoulder," he wrote, "and inwardly dared any man to knock it off." At
Petersburg, Virginia, he walked "bold as a lion" into a railroad
station dining room and sat at a table occupied by whites; he was
prepared to protest rebuff but instead was politely served. From
Columbia, South Carolina, he reported that "I feel about as safe
here as in Providence, R. I. I can ride in first-class cars on the
railroads and in the streets. I can go into saloons and get refresh-
ments even as in New York. I can stop in and drink a glass of
soda water and be more politely waited upon than in some parts
of New York."

After several weeks of such experience, Stewart discontinued
his reports on the journalistic grounds that good news had
become no news. "For the life of me," he wrote, "I can't 'raise a
row' in these letters. Things seem (remember, I write *seem*) to
move along as smoothly as in New York or Boston. . . . If you
should ask me, 'watchman, tell us of the night' . . . I would say,
'The morning light is breaking.' "

Looking back, Stewart's prophecy has a haunting ring. The
position he thought almost secure was about to be lost; three-
quarters of a century would pass and a tremendous struggle
would be waged before a black man in that region could again
assume his right to such an elementary privilege as ordering a
glass of soda.

The Supreme Court played a considerable role in setting back
the clock. Congress in 1875 had passed a sweeping civil rights
act, one broad enough to have settled that question for all time.
The Court in effect annulled the law, declaring that while states
couldn't discriminate, individuals could, and by 1896 the Court

had come around to a segregation rationale of "separate but equal."*

At about this time the blacks lost also the general political support they had received from the North. That was due partly to a shift toward North-South reconciliation, and partly to the growth of a national white supremacy attitude engendered by overseas expansion. As America acquired Hawaii and the Philippines, a lot of northern whites began to see the race question in a wholly new light. The *Nation* described the new territorial subjects as "a varied assortment of inferior races which, of course, could not be allowed to vote." And the *Atlantic Monthly* drew the obvious inference: "If the stronger and cleverer race is free to impose its will upon 'new caught, sullen peoples' on the other side of the globe, why not in South Carolina and Mississippi?"

The final blow to blacks was the collapse of their tenuous alliance with southern conservatives. That happened when the Populists appeared, preaching a doctrine of agrarian radicalism, and espousing a coalition of the white and black poor. Populist leader Tom Watson asserted that "The accident of color can make no difference in the interests of farmers, croppers and laborers." He promised blacks that "if you stand up for your rights and for your manhood, if you stand shoulder to shoulder with us in this fight," the People's party "will wipe out the color line."

The coalition flourished briefly, then fell apart. The Populist backbone was made up of poor, uneducated whites, highly susceptible to appeals of hate and fear, and the Conservatives exploited that by race-baiting the movement. Meantime, the Conservatives continued to manipulate the black vote, in many cases by intimidation and fraud. Repeatedly the Populist hopes were

* The long hiatus in civil rights is illustrated by comparative dates. After the Federal Civil Rights Act of 1875, Congress did not touch the subject again until 1957, an interval of 82 years. The Court acceptance of "separate but equal" was in force from *Plessy v. Ferguson*, 1896, to *Brown v. Board of Education*, 1954.

buried by election returns from heavily black districts. In frustration and rage the Populists turned to race-baiting, too. The
blacks were caught in the middle, the object of a white contest as
to which white faction could belabor them most.

Strong opposition to black equality had existed all through the
era of tentative freedom. Now, with the balancing forces swept
aside, the extremists had their way. A mania of race repression
swept the South, cities and states vying with one another to see
which could pass the most restrictive laws.

Some southern whites viewed the spectacle with dismay. The
Charleston *News and Courier*, the South's oldest newspaper, de-
rided a proposal for segregated railroad cars, saying, "As we have
got on fairly well for a third of a century . . . without such a
measure, we can probably get on as well hereafter without it." In
satiric tone the newspaper went on to visualize the absurd lengths
to which a segregation philosophy would eventually lead:

"If there must be Jim Crow cars on the railroads, there should
be Jim Crow cars on street railways . . . on passenger boats. If
there are to be Jim Crow cars, moreover, there should be Jim
Crow waiting saloons at all stations, and Jim Crow eating
houses. There should be Jim Crow sections of the jury box, and a
separate Jim Crow dock and witness stand in every court—and a
Jim Crow Bible for colored witnesses to kiss. It would be advisa-
ble also to have a Jim Crow section in county auditors' and
treasurers' offices for accommodation of colored taxpayers. The
two races are dreadfully mixed in these offices for weeks every
year, especially about Christmas. . . . There should be a Jim
Crow department for making returns and paying for the privi-
leges and blessings of citizenship."

It was intended as ironic thrust, but the real irony was that in
a few years it almost all came true. All except the Jim Crow
witness stand, which was somehow overlooked. Things had gone
full circle; as in the days of the Black Codes the law was em-

ployed not just to render the black man inferior, but to make him *"feel* his inferiority."

By the early 1900s the full paraphernalia of segregation and all that went with it was well established. In human terms, the black children born at the dawn of freedom were middle-aged when they found themselves bound over to a second kind of "peculiar institution." The consequences for them, and ultimately for the country, were to be immense.

Chapter 2

DOWN SOUTH

It's a question, who will do the dirty work?
—An Alabaman describes the
plantation system.

SEGREGATION and discrimination did not originate with the Jim Crow laws. Rather, the laws established as fixed, official and all-embracing a de facto white policy which in many southern areas had already existed to a considerable extent. It is true also that race factors were entwined with other deep-rooted problems which went beyond segregation. Nonetheless, the imposition of official repression was a traumatic black experience, and it marked a major turning point in their southern development.

For some thirty years after the Emancipation, blacks had been emerging slowly from the morass of slavery. In such social areas as education, their position was improving. Politically, their influence had waxed and waned, but they had retained some bargaining power at the polls. They were acquiring a stake as small landowners. They were still the poorest people in a poor region, attempting with immense difficulty to climb from the pit, but their prospects seemed at least moderately hopeful. Then came the rigid repression and all progress was slowed to a crawl, halted or reversed. There followed a half century of stagnation in which the social and economic problems became deeply entrenched. Throughout the South generally, and in rural areas especially, the conditions thus created persisted unchanged and almost unchallenged until the upheavals of recent times.

The right to challenge was, of course, stripped away. That was essential to general repression. Mississippi inaugurated the policy, adopting a state constitution which disfranchised blacks in 1890. Seven other states—South Carolina, Louisiana, North Carolina, Alabama, Virginia, Georgia and Oklahoma—followed suit with constitutional disfranchisement between 1895 and 1910. Tennessee, Florida, Arkansas and Texas accomplished the same purpose by piecemeal rigging of the election laws.

Senator Benjamin R. (Pitchfork Ben) Tillman of South Carolina described the cruder methods employed to drive blacks from the polls: "We have done our level best; we have scratched our heads to find out how we could eliminate the last one of them. We stuffed ballot boxes. We shot them. We are not ashamed of it."

Virginia's Carter Glass typified a more sophisticated approach. He was a prime mover in the state's 1901-02 constitutional convention, specifically convened to disfranchise blacks, and someone asked if the aim was to be accomplished by discrimination and fraud. His reply: "By fraud, no; by discrimination, yes. . . . Discrimination! Why, that is precisely what we propose. That, exactly, is what this convention was elected for—to discriminate to the very extremity of permissible action under the limitations of the Federal Constitution, with a view to the elimination of every Negro voter who can be gotten rid of. . . . It is a fine discrimination, indeed, that we have practiced in the fabrication of this plan."

Throughout the South the "fine discriminations" proliferated: the restricted primary, the grandfather clause, the poll tax, the innumerable other regulations carefully contrived to filter out black voters while letting white voters through. The legal obstacles were reinforced by terror—a black who stubbornly insisted on voting was a marked man—and if all else failed, the county registrar could be counted on to guard the polls through selective interpretation of a good character or a literacy test.

The principle of the tests is illustrated in a folk tale. The story goes that a black teacher who had graduated from Harvard presented himself to a Mississippi registrar. He was told that by law he would have to demonstrate his ability to read and understand. He proved inconveniently proficient in English, and was then shown texts in Latin, Greek, French, German and Spanish. He read them all. Finally the registrar held up a page in Chinese, saying, "What does this mean?" The applicant replied, "It means no Negro will vote in this election."

The effects were decisive. In Louisiana, for instance, there were 130,344 black voters in 1896, slashed to 5,320 by 1900, and to 1,718 in 1904; a former 56 percent white voting majority was thereby converted to 98 percent. Mississippi created a white majority where a black majority had existed before; by 1898 only 3,573 black voters were registered in the state out of a potential 150,000.

The political rights thus stolen were not regained until very recent times. In 1940 only 2 percent of eligible southern blacks were permitted to vote in major elections. There was a slow recapture of lost ground in the 1940s and 1950s, due chiefly to court fights led by such groups as NAACP, but it required the tumultuous and bloody civil rights campaigns of the 1960s to firmly reassert the black political presence in the South. In 1968 a milestone was reached on the road back as 51 percent of eligible southern blacks trooped to the polls.

A crucial effect of disfranchisement was the loss of leverage with the custodians of local government. The sheriff, the tax assessor, the road commissioner and the school board official were under no obligation to black constituents. The results were clearly evident in the neglect of such vital services as education.

The freed slaves had achieved a considerable educational surge during the years immediately following the Emancipation. The 5 percent of them who could read or write in 1865 increased to almost 50 percent by 1900. In the most notable decade, 1870-80, the number of school-aged blacks attending classes jumped from 10 percent to 30 percent. Southern white attendance at the time was only 50 percent of potential and the blacks seemed on their way to achieving parity. But the thrust was brief and fell far short; by the turn of the century black schooling had been relegated to minor and perfunctory attention.

It was a case of the bottom of the barrel. Most southern schools were markedly inferior to those of the North, reflecting the poverty of the region. Rural schools in the South as elsewhere were far below the urban standard, and most blacks originally were congregated in rural districts. With the factor of separate and distinctly unequal status, the black schools became abysmal. There were times and places in which the typical black school received only one-tenth the funds allocated to a white school down the road.

There is no accurate record of the grade levels achieved in the early periods, but that can be reconstructed in approximate fashion. In the rural South today there is a contingent of middle-aged and elderly blacks who in a sense embody the past. That is, they typify the life patterns which applied to most blacks before the urban migration began. In the 1960 census the education of black farm dwellers was tabulated according to age, yielding a rough profile of the rural past.

By such formulation, a black farm boy born in 1885 can be placed in a school period beginning about 1890. He obtained, on the average, 3.3 years of schooling. Twenty years later his son could expect 4.3 years. For his grandson forty years later the figure was 5.7 years. The gain averaged just a little less than 2 percent a year. Meantime, black rural schooling was creeping up on a much higher white rural standard, but the relative gain was a snail's pace advance of one-third of one percent a year. As late as 1940 the typical black rural male was still not finishing grade school, and he was lagging five years behind his white counterpart. Black females did a little better, but they too were far below the white level (TABLE 1).

TABLE 1

Rural Schooling, Black and White, 1890-1940
Median Years of School Completed By Rural
Farm Americans According to Age

		MALE			FEMALE		
Age	*Approximate Enrollment Period*	*Black*	*White*	*Black-White Ratio in Percentages*	*Black*	*White*	*Black-White Ratio in Percentages*
75 or older	To 1890	3.3	7.8	.42	3.8	8.2	.46
70-74	1891-95	3.7	8.1	.46	4.5	8.3	.54
65-69	1896-1900	3.8	8.2	.46	4.7	8.4	.56
60-64	1901-05	4.1	8.3	.49	5.4	8.6	.63
55-59	1906-10	4.3	8.4	.51	5.8	8.8	.66
50-54	1911-15	4.7	8.6	.55	6.3	9.2	.68
45-49	1916-20	4.9	8.8	.56	6.5	10.1	.64
40-44	1921-25	5.2	9.2	.57	6.9	10.9	.63
35-39	1926-30	5.7	10.5	.54	7.2	12.0	.60
30-34	1931-35	6.2	11.0	.56	7.8	12.1	.64
25-29	1936-40	7.0	12.1	.58	8.2	12.2	.68

SOURCE: U.S. Census of Population: 1960, Final Report PC(12ID), Table 173, U.S. Bureau of the Census. (Approximate enrollment period extrapolated by adding 5 years to date of birth.)

The racial gap in education was actually much greater than the figures indicate, since a school year is not a standard unit of measure. In every qualitative measure—in teacher experience, class size, school facilities and budget—the black schools were woefully inferior.

The greatest discrepancies occurred in the so-called black belts where the Negroes were most thickly concentrated. That, of course, was a commentary on their political impotence. It reflected also some special facts of southern life. The blacks were clustered in areas where the great plantations thrived—a residue of slave economy—and the plantation owners remained heavily dependent on black labor. The white community harbored a strong feeling that education would only spoil a black man for his natural function of work in the fields. An Alabama white put it this way to journalist Roy Stannard Baker in 1907: "It's a question, who will do the dirty work? In this country the white man won't: the Negro must. There's got to be a mudsill somewhere. If you educate the Negroes they won't stay where they belong; and you must consider them as a race, because if you let a few rise it makes the others discontented."

That such thinking was widespread is illustrated by the extreme lengths black belt areas adopted in downgrading Negro education. The United States Bureau of Education surveyed the question in 1917, comparing expenditures for teachers' salaries in southern black and white schools, and correlated the result to the density of black population. The result was a scale sliding dramatically downward as follows (TABLE 2):

TABLE 2
Funding of Black and White Rural Schools

Southern Counties According to Black Proportion in Population	Per Capita Expenditure for Teachers' Salaries		Black-White Expenditure Ration in Percentages
	White	*Black*	
Under 10 percent	$ 7.96	$7.23	92
10 to 25 percent	9.55	5.55	58
25 to 50 percent	11.11	3.19	27
50 to 75 percent	12.53	1.77	14
75 percent and over	22.32	1.78	7

SOURCE: U.S. Bureau of Education, *Negro Education in the United States*, Vol. I, Chap. II. (Derived from *Negro Migration, Changes in Rural Organization and Population of the Cotton Belt*, Thomas J. Woofter, Jr., W. O. Gray, New York, 1920.)

The Bureau of Education spelled out in some detail what was obtained for per capita investments of $2 to $3. More than 70 percent of the teachers in such schools had less than a sixth-grade education. The schools themselves were located in make-shift buildings jam-packed with children. In Alabama, eighty black schools were selected as a cross-section sample; they had an average attendance of 5,832 and a seating capacity of 3,794, or standing room only for more than a third of the pupils.

The 1917 survey coincided with the first large urban move-ment of blacks—the great migration, it was called then—and so black belt school standards were compared also with those of the cities to which blacks were flocking. The migrant child who moved from a black belt rural area to New York City encoun-tered a difference in school quality of more than 14 to 1, as measured in investment per student. If he was a bright child just beginning school, such change represented opportunity, though it was accompanied by stiff challenge. He had to make it without help from his parents; he probably passed their level of learning at the first or the second grade. If the transfer occurred later in his school career he was simply lost. He was too big and too old to go back to the first grade and start over, and he couldn't hope to compete in his own age group. He dropped out, and soon enough he fathered other children who were odds-on to become dropouts, too. The pattern of urban school crisis was thus estab-lished; that it has not been resolved in fifty years is another matter to be examined later.

Over the years the quality of black belt education improved slowly, but in the 1940s black children by the tens of thousands were still attending one-room, one-teacher schools.* Gunnar Myrdal visited many such institutions while preparing his classic report on *An American Dilemma*; the experience so shook him

---

* The gradual demise of the one-teacher school is illustrated in Alabama. In the early 1930s the state had about 3,000 such institutions, not specified as to race. In 1945 there were 1,417, of which 1,157 were black. By 1950 it was down to 806, including 691 black.

that he departed from his usual calm style to observe that he "could hardly believe his eyes and ears." He found that the ordinary indexes of educational efficiency were simply not applicable when attempting to "sound the bottom of ignorance" in such schools.

Myrdal cited as an example, a one-room Georgia school which he inspected. "The students were in all age groups from six to seven years upwards to sixteen to seventeen. There was also an imbecile man of about twenty staying on as a steady student veteran. (The lack of institutions for old Negro mental defectives makes the great majority of them stay in their homes, and the homes find it often convenient to send them to school.) The teacher, a sickly girl of about twenty years old, looked shy and full of fear; she said she had had high school training."

Among the students "No one could tell who was President of the United States, or even what the President was. Only one of the older students knew, or thought he knew, of Booker T. Washington. He said that Washington was 'a big white man' and intimated that he might be the President of the United States. This student, obviously a naturally very bright boy, was the only one who knew anything about Europe and England; they were 'beyond the Atlantic' he informed me, but he thought Europe was in England."

Such schools have vanished now, but the effects have not. The students who shocked and startled Myrdal are today men and women in their thirties and forties. More than half of them are probably scattered through the urban ghettos, for they have lived through the wrenching period when hoe labor was displaced by machines. Whether they moved to the city or clung to the land, it is a fair assumption that most of them can be found now in that human substratum which is hopelessly mired in poverty and ignorance. There are, of course, a gifted few who manage somehow to overcome such beginnings. Anne Moody, the talented author of *Coming of Age in Mississippi*, began school in 1946 in "a little one room rotten wood building" with "big cracks in it." She's now on the staff of Cornell University.

Millions of other black Americans remain trapped. The 1960 census found that among those aged twenty-five or older nearly one-fourth had less than five years of elementary education, of whatever quality. In the northern ghettos, the number so handicapped was about one out of seven. The northern figure was presumably heavily swollen by migration, but to the people involved, the regional distinctions become irrelevant; if they are unprepared they are unprepared. In the South the number who got only half way through grade school came in 1960 to one-third of the adult black population (TABLE 3).

Such was the educational heritage which the migrants brought to the cities. It can be represented as a kind of long term, high

TABLE 3

Adults with Less than 5 Years Education, by Race and Region

Place	Black	White
United States	23.5	6.7
Non-South	14.0	5.5
South	33.5	10.5
Alabama	36.0	9.4
Arkansas	36.4	10.6
Florida	31.7	5.3
Georgia	39.7	10.3
Kentucky	23.7	13.1
Louisiana	40.9	13.5
Mississippi	39.7	7.1
North Carolina	31.9	12.2
Oklahoma	20.0	7.6
South Carolina	41.3	11.6
Tennessee	27.8	12.5
Texas	23.6	12.0
Virginia	29.5	9.3

SOURCE: U.S. Census of Population: 1960, Series PC (11C), Table 47, U.S. Bureau of the Census.

interest social mortgage. It was acquired over the course of a century, and it will be a quarter of a century more before it can possibly be marked paid. It will take at least that long to work through the generations who can never catch up.

The cherished economic dream after the Emancipation was "40 acres and a mule," and the first generation of freedmen made bootstrap progress toward that goal. The census of 1900 reported that 158,000 blacks owned their own farms, and that 28,000 more owned part of the acreage they worked. Together the two groups comprised more than a fourth of all black farm dwellers. That, however, was to prove their relative zenith. During the next two decades additional blacks acquired land, but the gain did not match their rural population increase. After 1920 there was an absolute decline in ownership, which has continued in a steep, almost unbroken line until the present time.

Race repression contributed importantly to the result, but the basic reasons were economic. All through the twentieth century the small-scale southern farmer has been fighting a losing battle. Historically he has lacked enough cash to finance his operations, and so often sold himself into debt peonage at ruinous interest. He also lacked land enough to diversify and so gambled heavily on cotton; it produced a high income per acre when things went well, but it was subject to calamitous price swings. These and other factors produced a steady attrition of the small operators, whether owners or renters, whites or blacks; as in other matters, the blacks were the measure of where the bottom was. Over a span of some four decades more than half the black farm owners were squeezed off the land; for black tenants the casualty rate was about seven out of every eight (TABLE 4).

The demise of the black farmer was hastened by the fact that he worked the smallest and poorest tracts. That in turn was a factor of both his poverty and his race. Even if he acquired the means, he could not buy land wherever he pleased, any more

TABLE 4
Decline of Southern Small Farmers, Black and White, 1910-64

(Figures in thousands, rounded to nearest total; percentages rounded to nearest decimal.)

	1910	1920	1930	1940	1950	1959	1964	Percentage Change
Owners								
Black	175	179	140	142	141	90	71	−59
White	1,154	1,227	1,050	1,186	1,277	857	738	−37
Part Owners*								
Black	43	39	42	31	53	38	31	−28
White	172	152	183	185	280	285	272	+58
Tenants (Including Share-croppers and cash tenants)								
Black	670	704	699	507	399	139	82	−88
White	866	887	1,092	943	531	228	171	−80
All Farm Operators (Including owners, tenants, managers)								
Black	890	923	882	680	553	266	185	−77
White	2,207	2,284	2,342	2,327	2,098	1,379	1,188	−51

* The term "part owner," refers to a system which is known also in the South as owner-renter. The farmer owns some acreage and rents some; he is able to expand and contract operations with a flexibility that affords some relative advantage. With black owner-renters it is typically a case of owning 20 to 40 acres, and renting as much more.
SOURCE: U.S. Census of Agriculture, 1969.

than he can buy any house in suburbia today, or rent any apartment in the desirable section of the city. In *Preface to Peasantry* Arthur F. Raper described the folkways that constricted the choice of the black farmer.

"Negro landownership can be achieved only by means of a most exacting and highly selective procedure; the would-be owner must be acceptable to the white community, have a white sponsor, be content with the purchase of acreage least desired by the whites, and pay for it in a very few years.

"The Negro buys land only when some white man will sell it to *him*. Just because a white man has land for sale does not mean that a Negro, even the most liked and respected by him, can buy it even if he has the money. Whether a particular Negro can buy a particular tract of land depends upon its location, its economic and emotional value to the white owner and other white people, the Negro's cash and credit resources, and, doubtless the most important of all, his personal qualities in the light of local attitudes. He must be acceptable."

Negro ownership emerged most often, Raper added, "On the out-of-the-way, or neglected tracts, in the nooks and corners between creeks and between white communities, and in areas where white community organization is disintegrating."* Such areas, moreover, became harder to find as population growth exerted increasing pressure on the land. Thus the blacks became penned in. The average black farm owner had 70 acres in 1900, but only 62 acres in 1959. Meantime, agriculture had undergone a technologic revolution which forced the farmer to expand or perish; the southern white farmer over the same period had expanded to an average 162 acres.

For all of his problems, the small landowner represented an elite among rural blacks. Below him were the tenants. Only a small fraction of that group—10 to 15 percent at various periods —ever achieved the relative independence of renting for cash and managing their own affairs. The rest existed by one form or another of sharecropping.

Sharecropping has been described as a system which combined the worst features of the laborer's toil and the entrepreneur's risk.

* Raper made the observation on "out-of-the-way places" in 1936, and in 1959 the census demonstrated that it was still true. The tabulation showed that only 28 percent of commercial scale southern white farmers were operating on unimproved dirt roads, compared to 50 percent for black owners, and 60 percent for black renters.

Theoretically, of course, the cropper also shared the hope of profit, but in practice he was a laborer on annual contract at an unspecified and highly speculative wage.

Traditionally the black sharecropper worked about forty acres and received half to three-fourths of the produce, depending on various intricate arrangements as to who furnished what. In effect, then, he was trying to scrounge his living off of twenty to thirty acres. He had to do so, moreover, under a very special set of rules. Until recent times he was often required to make all his purchases through the plantation commissary, a rural version of the company store. If he lacked cash, which was almost always, he was extended credit at exorbitant interest. One study found that the average sharecropper was charged a flat rate of 10 percent for short term advances; on a per annum basis the interest averaged 37 percent. The debts were secured by a lien which usually extended to anything the cropper owned and to all his future produce. Finally, in eleven states it was stipulated by law that he couldn't sell his crop if there was a lien against it, and since he couldn't pay his debts until he sold, that meant he couldn't sell at all. The landlord handled the sale, made the division, and gave the cropper his share. Out of such arrangements grew the folk tale of "one more bale."

When Myrdal visited the South he found that whites, too, had a store of folk sayings and colloquial jokes devoted to the subject of cheating the Negro at settlement time. He concluded that the practice was common enough. That is not to suggest that plantation owners as a class were any more dishonest than the ordinary run of mankind. They differed in having such a safe and easy opportunity to cheat. On occasions when they themselves felt pressed for survival, the temptation was great.

What was perhaps equally important was that the black cropper so often *felt* cheated. Most white Americans have been indoctrinated for generations in work-and-win ideas of industry, initiative, acquisition and thrift. A great many blacks over the same period were absorbing a fixed opinion that whatever their efforts the system was fixed to assure their permanent status as losers.

The conviction of being a loser tends to be self-fulfilling, all the more so when it is well founded in circumstances. Not surprisingly, it became a common white complaint that the blacks were apathetic and listless. They worked well enough if closely supervised, so ran the charge, but when left to their own devices they just didn't seem to care. Actually, much of what passed for apathy was malnutrition and chronic disease, two afflictions that are still endemic among the poor of the rural South. Much also was a sly form of passive resistance. But much of it was indeed apathy: not caring too much was the one luxury afforded by a fatalistic resignation which the blacks adopted as a shield and armor against misfortune.

Under such circumstances many blacks became like conscript soldiers impressed into a service to which they gave token obedience but little else. Some developed the refined and subtle arts of doing just exactly enough to get by. They learned to exploit holes in the system, not for any real gain (there was none to be had) but for the small pleasure and ephemeral advantage of conning their masters. An army expects such attitude in conscripts, and tolerates it within well-established limits, and the old South was much the same. It was understood that the black man had to submit if the white man stole his crop. It was assumed that the black man would steal the white man's chicken.

It is a myth that the blacks were deeply attached to the particular plantations for which they worked. They moved about a great deal in what has been termed a kind of poor man's strike. That was one of the holes in the system; if a cropper grew discouraged with his debt he could sometimes shuck it off by moving on to another location. The former landlord might track him down and try to extract the money, but the cropper's only real asset was his labor, and if he had consigned that to another landlord the whole thing became a lot of bother. If the sum owed was small by a proprietor's standards the affair was often dismissed with a passing complaint as to the black man's irresponsible ways.

About a third of the black sharecroppers moved every year. The white sharecroppers had an even higher mobility rate deriving from the same causes; such differences as existed lay chiefly in the manner of leaving. The blacks, whether in debt or not, were always more constrained in their movements; some vestiges of the old Black Codes lingered on and black croppers never knew what pressures might be applied if the landlord wanted to keep them on the place. In response to such exigency they developed a particular style. When they left a place it was often not in the formal manner of a man quitting a job by giving notice, but rather something closely akin to desertion. They would pack up and leave in the middle of the night. The landlord would learn that the relationship was terminated when he made his inspection rounds and found the door gaping open on an empty shack.*

The transient life of the sharecropper contributed to still other ills. The man who owns a farm home spends his slack seasons tending the place, making it more livable for himself and his family. The cropper had no such incentive. He lived in a miserable hovel, usually a one- or two-room shack with perhaps a lean-to out back. The place was unpainted, uninsulated, and as it warped and weathered it became a sagging collection of cracks and leaks. Very little was done to repair such damage, and long term improvements were simply out of the question.

---

* An attempt to curtail night departures produced in Louisiana the last "black code" legislation restricting the physical movements of blacks. Adopted in 1935, the statute declared it "unlawful for any person to go on the premises or plantation of any citizen between sunset and sunrise and assist in moving any laborers or tenants therefrom without the consent of the owner of said premises or plantation."

The sharecroppers had no means to transform such shacks, and often they neglected even the things they might have done. In plantation country one is struck by the fact that some huts stand in the middle of fields, nakedly exposed to the blazing southern sun. The heat in such places is intolerable, worse inside than out. There are woodlands all about and it would have been a simple matter to transplant a few saplings, providing in time the comfort of shade. Often enough, no one bothered. The landlord had no interest, and the tenant no stake.

In such places squalor is the general rule. There are pathetic and futile attempts to relieve it; in the meanest shacks one is apt to see a flowered wall motto proclaiming "God Bless Our Happy Home." But the furniture is broken, the premises are littered with junk, the sanitary arrangements affront the eye and nose. It all reeks of demoralization and decay.

Slum housing, in short, is no new experience for American blacks. Many have never known any other abode, and the rural condition is worse than the urban. Recent years have witnessed some improvement but in 1966 about two-thirds of all rural and semi-rural blacks were living in substandard dwellings, as compared to one-sixth in the large cities. There is a general and consistent pattern in which the black housing gets progressively worse as the scan moves from larger to smaller social units (TABLE 5).

Closely entwined with every other factor was the peculiar caste system of the South. It was more brutal and repressive than the racism of the North, and yet also more human and intimate. In the urban North, it is rare for white and black to associate on easy and familiar terms; the two races are for the most part abstractions to one another. In the South, the rural South especially, the relationship has always been highly personal, though hedged about with the most stringent rules.

Part of the difference can be ascribed to rural and urban styles. Country life is always more personal. Beyond that, how-

TABLE 5
Substandard Black Housing, Rural and Urban,
1960-66*

	1960	1966
Large Cities (50,000 or more)	25	16
Suburbs	43	29
Smaller Cities, Towns and Rural	77	64
United States	44	29

* The survey covers all "dilapidated" housing, defined as dwellings in which "defects are so critical or so widespread that the structure would require extensive repairs, rebuilding, razing, or was of inadequate original construction." Also included is all housing which lacks one or more of the following basic plumbing facilities: hot running water in the house, flush toilets for private use of household members, tub or shower for private use of household members.
SOURCE: Current Population Reports, Series P-23, No. 26, BLS Report No. 347, Recent Trends in Social and Economic Conditions of Negroes in the United States, July, 1968: a joint report of the Bureau of Labor Statistics and the Bureau of the Census.

ever, a particular kind of white-black intimacy was an integral part of the old southern system. The detailed regulation of that intimacy was precisely what the system was about.

On the plantation the white and the black might live within fifty yards of each other, the one in the big house and the other in the hut, and they knew each other as well as men could when viewing life from those very different vantage points. Their close but rigid relationship was consciously symbolized in the fact that they were on a first-and-last-name basis with one another. It was Mr. Jones, and Sam. If their association was long established the white man might acquire such informal title as Mr. Bob. It was, however, always Mister. No white man could ever lose that title, or black man ever gain it. There were countless other nuances of a similar nature. The black man tipped his hand to his hat when he encountered the white. He did not offer to shake hands. He stood in the white presence unless invited to sit. He went around to the back door when he had any reason to visit the white man's house.

Most whites did not think of these things as humiliation for humiliation's sake. Indeed, the more insensitive did not suspect that humiliation was involved. They viewed it merely as a necessary ritual for establishing the fixed, inviolable line between the master and the servant races.

The other side of the coin was that the masters were supposed to assume special obligations, much as a feudal baron had obligations to his serf. The contract was often honored in the breach, but the "quality" whites did in fact take a proprietary interest in "their Negroes." They were supposed to assist the blacks in time of distress, to intercede for them with the authorities, to offer security in return for subservience. To a black man who knew that he wasn't going anywhere anyway, that bargain had its powerful temptations.

In *Black Man's Burden* John Oliver Killens recalls such atmosphere from his Georgia boyhood. "The pragmatic philosophy of some Negroes, particularly in the smaller southern towns, used to be: 'The way for a black man to get along is to attach himself to some well-to-do *good* white folks. Just one big white folks is all you need. Then don't care what happen, can't nobody do you no big harm. Not the sheriff, police, judge, *nobody*! Not even the Good Lord up on High!' "

Killens appends a folk story passed around among blacks to illustrate the value of the paternalistic connection. It seems that a Georgia black arrived in New York in the midst of the Depression. He was jobless, broke and "too nervous to steal," so he became a beggar. He went up and down Park Avenue, knocking on the doors of great mansions, pleading for a little food or money to tide him over for the day. Time and again he was rejected by northern liberals who expressed formal sympathy and said politely, "Sorry, sir, but we are unable to help." Finally he came to a door where a man heard out his story, laughed good naturedly, and said, "All right, nigger, you know better than to be coming to my front door. Go on 'round to the back and tell Mandy I said give you something to eat." To which the black replied, "Thank you kindly, suh. You the first southern gentleman I met since I arrived in New York City."*

Myrdal described a real incident in similar vein, but with a different bite. The affair involved a depression-era relief agency for blacks that was administered through a southern Negro college. An upper class white woman approached the head of the college, a black man, and asked to see his staff assistant in charge of relief. She referred to the man in question as "Sam."

"Sam who?" asked the president coolly.

"You know who I mean, the nigger who sits at this desk and gives out the emergency relief. I want some relief for my niggers."

The head of the college pretended not to know, and one by one he went down the list naming his staff. "Could it be Mr. So-and-So? Or Mr. So-and-So?" Both parties understood perfectly what the by-play was about, and it left the genteel white lady utterly distraught. She finally broke into tears, crying, "Oh, please give me some relief for my niggers." But she would not say "Mister."

The real point of both stories, of course, is the same. Paternalism went hand in hand with the symbols of obeisance. Looking at it from the detached view of a foreign observer, Myrdal concluded that for many whites the affirmations of caste were more important than any economic advantage they might obtain from exploitation. Put to the choice the whites seemed to prefer indolent, subservient blacks to those who were hard working but independent in bearing and spirit.

---

* Adds Killens: "We used to laugh at this alleged joke, when we had no better sense. In retrospect it was undoubtedly concocted by a southern gentleman from Georgia or Alabama to make the point that the South knew better how to take care of its nigrahs than the North."

"In employment relations," Myrdal found, "the paternalistic pattern tends to diminish the Negroes' formal responsibilities. The Negro worker has less definite obligations as well as more uncertain rights. He comes to be remunerated, not only for his work, but also for his humility, for his propensity to be satisfied with his 'place' and for his cunning in cajoling and flattering his master. . . . He is discouraged when he tries to 'work his way up.' It is considered better for him never to forget his 'place,' and he must scrupulously avoid even any suspicion that he seeks to rise above it. Upper-class Negroes in the South have often confided in me that they find it advantageous to simulate dependence in order to avert hostility from the whites and engage their paternalism. But even if the successful Negro puts on a show of dependence, he sometimes feels that he is less safe than if he had stayed at the bottom. A psychological *milieu* more effective in stifling spontaneous ambition is hardly imaginable."

The pressures were more than just psychological, for physical threat was always present. Periodic lynchings were brutal reminders that blacks were helpless against white assault.* Less spectacular but far more common were the occasions when individual whites threatened, beat or killed blacks for transgressions of the code. Generally the perpetrators of such violence were lower-class whites, but the upper class condoned or at least did not interfere, and the law dismissed it as of no importance.

The manner of such random assault was described to this journalist by an elderly black porter on a train out of Montgomery, Alabama. He was talking about the changing South, how much more hopeful it seemed than the South he had known for most of his days, and then he told a story which in recollection still angered him after forty years.

---

* More than three thousand blacks have been lynched, at least a third of them for minor offenses or for forgetting their "place." The barbaric practice all but disappeared by the late 1940s, then had what might be considered a revival in new form during the tense years of civil rights confrontation.

The incident involved a black man who was out driving with a team of fast horses. Presently he came upon a white couple who were plodding along with a slow team. He stayed behind the other wagon for a mile or so and then, growing impatient, slapped the reins at his horses and drove past. That night the white man came to his cabin waving a gun. "You passed me on the road," he said. "You threw dust in my wife's face. If you ever do that again, I'll kill you."

"You have to understand," the porter said, "that the black man couldn't do anything about that. If he took it to the judge or the sheriff, they'd just laugh it off. They'd say to him, about the white fellow: 'Why, you know that man as well as we do. You know he's a mean man. If he says he'll kill you, he'll kill you. So don't pass him on the road.' "

Often such random affairs were not quite as casual and accidental as they appeared. In *Deep South* the authors Allison Davis and Burleigh and Mary Gardner analyzed whippings administered to blacks for caste offenses. They found behind specific acts a frequent pattern of rising community tensions.

"Periodically there seems to develop a situation in which a number of Negroes begin to rebel against the caste restrictions. This is not an open revolt but a gradual pressure, probably more or less unconscious, in which, little by little, they move out of the strict pattern of approved behavior. The whites feel this pressure and begin to express resentment. They say the Negroes are getting 'uppity,' that they are getting out of their place, and that something should be done about it. . . . Finally the hostility of the whites reaches such a pitch that any small infraction will spur them to open action. A Negro does something which ordinarily might be passed over, or which usually provokes only mild resentment, but the whites respond with violence. The Negro becomes both a scapegoat and an object lesson for his group. . . . After such an outburst, the Negroes again abide strictly by the caste rules, the enmity of the whites is dispelled, and the tension relaxes. The whites always say after such an outburst, 'We haven't had any trouble since then.' "

Violence was not, of course, an all-pervasive aspect of race relations in the rural South. Most people, after all, do not go about assaulting each other with guns and whips. What was pervasive was the black knowledge that it could happen on the least provocation. That effect was intended. Whites of sensibility might deplore individual outrages, and they invariably looked down on the "rednecks" who committed such acts, but there was general agreement that force was necessary to keep the blacks in line.

The effects on blacks went beyond fear itself. They had to cultivate gestures of placation and appeasement, and they had to deal as best they could with the throttled anger which self-abasement inspires. The continual maintenance of such charade exacted a heavy emotional toll.

"The steady impact of the plantation system upon our lives," said Richard Wright in *Twelve Million Black Voices*, "created new types of behavior and new patterns of psychological reaction, welding us together into a separate unity with common characteristics of our own.

"We strove each day to maintain that kind of external behavior that would best allay the fear and hate of the Lords of the Land, and over a period of years this dual conduct became second nature to us and we found in it a degree of immunity from daily oppression. Even when a white man asked us an innocent question, some unconscious part of us would listen closely, not only to the obvious words but also to the intonations of voice that indicated what kind of answer he wanted; and automatically we would determine whether an affirmative or negative reply was expected. . . .

"If a white man stopped a black man on a southern road and asked, 'Say there, boy: It's one o'clock is it, boy?' the black man would answer: 'Yassuh.'

"And if the white man asked, 'Say, it's not one o'clock, is it boy?' the black man would answer 'Nawsuh.'

"Always we said what we thought the whites wanted us to say."

Another way of coping, one which combined self-protection with passive resistance, was not to answer at all. That is, to answer at some length but at no substance. It required an artful ability to play the simpleton. The technique was explained to this reporter by I. B. Hopson, a wise old black man who offered to serve as a kind of guide and interpreter when I was seeking out black farmers along the back roads of Alabama.

"You'll have to be introduced by someone they trust," he said, "and after that you'll have to stand around and be patient until they decide whether to talk to you or not. Otherwise, you won't learn a thing.

"A white man like you," he added, "can drive up in a big car, and stop at a place and ask for someone who's supposed to live around there somewhere. The people you're talking to will look at you with a blank stare, and scratch their heads, and say they don't believe they've ever heard of the fellow. You can point to a shack across the road, and ask who lives there, and they'll say they don't know. If you didn't understand the situation you might go away thinking they're stupid. Well, they're not. They know all right, but they don't know why you want to know, and they don't trust you. Why should they?"

Hopson is an accountant, a former teacher and businessman, and he evolved his own more sophisticated style of resistance. The Alabama climate almost requires a hat, but he has gone bareheaded for years. To Alabama whites, if they thought about it at all, it was an eccentricity, an old Negro's fool notion. To Hopson it was a secret flag, a signal to himself that though he might have to submit he would never acquiesce. He wore no hat so that he could not tip it.

All that represents the old South that is gone now, or nearly gone. The back-roads farmers may cling to some of their defensive folkways, but they are nonetheless organizing openly in the face of white resistance. Hopson still goes with his snow white hair bared to the sun but it has become a sentimental custom; he ran up his public flag years ago when "the Movement" came to Selma and he threw open his office as headquarters for the protest marchers.

All over the South there were always blacks who held out against all the pressures, and when their time came they put together a movement that surged back and forth across the region for more than a decade. The action has shifted now to other questions, and so the historical significance of that era tends to be underestimated. The southern blacks did not dispel racism or abolish poverty, but then no one else has managed that; what they did accomplish was to trample down most of the official superstructure of a caste system which had seemed fixed and unshakable. Neither the black nor the white South can ever be the same after that experience.

The observations here have been addressed to another time, still of recent history, and still much alive in the memories of men. For more than half a century millions of blacks were required to exist under circumstances in which submission and passivity were literally a way of life, a way of survival. That, as much as poverty and lack of education, was part of the burdensome heritage they carried with them on the road to the city.

Chapter 3

BIRTH OF THE GHETTOS

I should have been here twenty years ago. I just begin to feel like a man. It's a great deal of pleasure knowing that you have got some privilege.
> —A black migrant exults at the urban prospect.

There is nothing in the make-up of a Negro, physically or mentally, which should induce anyone to welcome him as a neighbor.
> —The Property Owners' Association prepares to resist.

T HE urban migration of blacks, like that of whites, has been a movement rooted in economic necessity and population pressure. In the case of blacks, the population about doubled in two generations after the Civil War. The land could not sustain such numbers, and by the 1890s a drift to the cities was well under way.

Race factors soon imposed a migration pattern. Blacks and whites were both moving from southern farms to southern cities but the black rate was fractionally lower. Meantime, both groups began flowing also to the larger northern cities, and that exodus became predominantly black. Jim Crow was clearly an element. From 1900 to 1910, years in which segregation became entrenched and intensified, the blacks left the South at a proportionate rate seven times as high as whites. In every decade since the black South-to-North movement has exceeded the white at rates ranging from two to nine times (TABLE 6).

TABLE 6
*South to North Migration, Both Races,
1900-1970*

		Net Migration in Thousands	Percentage Migrating by Racial Base Population	Black-White Ratio in Proportion
1900-10	Black	−213	−2.8	7 - 1
	White	−60	−0.4	
1910-20	Black	−572	−6.9	2 - 1
	White	−626	−3.5	
1920-30	Black	−913	−10.8	3⅓ - 1
	White	−626	−3	
1930-40	Black	−473	−5.4	3⅓ - 1
	White	−482	−1.9	
1940-50	Black	−1689	−18	9 - 1
	White	−553	−2	
1950-60	Black	−1512	−15.9	No Ratio
	White	+330	+1	
1960-70	Black	−1400	−13.7	No Ratio
	White	+1800	+5	

SOURCES: Data for 1900 to 1960 from census studies tabulated in *The Advancing South: Manpower Prospects and Problems*, by James G. Maddox with E. E. Liebhafsky, Vivian W. Henderson and Herbert M. Hamlin, The Twentieth Century Fund, New York, 1967. Data for 1960-70 from preliminary census estimate, March 3, 1971.

Mecca was relative. In the North the blacks were barred from most industries by a combination of union and management policies. When they obtained plant entry it was usually in a precarious role as strikebreakers. More often they worked as maids or butlers, janitors or waiters. Even so, it was often the "talented tenth," the most educated and ambitious, who trekked North in the early years.

There developed distinct migration routes which followed natural lines of travel. Blacks from the Mississippi River basin headed for St. Louis or Chicago, spreading to other inland cities. Migrants along the Atlantic seaboard moved up the coast, congregating in New York and Philadelphia. The general patterns thus established still persist in large measure today.*

More than a million blacks were living in major urban centers in 1910, and the demographic balance was shifting toward the North. The transition, however, was still slow-paced. New York had one of the nation's largest, fastest-growing black settlements, yet it was absorbing only 3,000 migrants a year into a total population of nearly 5 million. For most other big cities the influx was averaging about 1,000 a year.

In 1915 all that abruptly changed. Agricultural disasters helped to prepare the way—floods and boll weevil devastation produced hard times in the South—but the larger impetus came from World War I. Industry boomed, the pipeline of European immigrant labor was all but choked off, and blacks began streaming in to fill the vacuum. The next census found black population up two-thirds in New York, one-and-a-half times in Chicago, three times in Cleveland, six times in Detroit. The "great migration" was under way (TABLE 7).

The mass movement was both foreseen and promoted by the Chicago *Defender*, a leading black newspaper of the day. Editor Robert S. Abbott of the *Defender* decried the war as "bloody, tragic and deplorable," but added that "it is an ill wind that blows no one good. . . . Factories, mills and workshops that have

---

* Migrants are drawn to areas where friends and neighbors have preceded, and so old routes tend to perpetuate themselves in an era of easier and more flexible travel. The point was noted by a Georgia civil rights leader who paid a visit to Newark. He said he could distinguish "whole counties" from Georgia that flocked to Newark during the most recent migration wave.

TABLE 7
Birth of the Ghettos

Region	Cities	1910	1920	Increase	Percentage Increase
			Chief urban centers of black population, 1910-20. Order of rank by region as of 1920		
NORTH	New York, N.Y.	91,709	152,467	60,758	66.5
	Philadelphia, Pa.	84,459	134,229	49,770	58.9
	Chicago, Ill.	44,103	109,458	65,355	148.22
	Detroit, Mich.	5,471	40,838	35,097	611.3
	Pittsburgh, Pa.	25,623	37,725	12,102	47.2
	Indianapolis, Ind.	21,816	34,678	12,862	59.0
	Cleveland, Ohio	8,448	34,451	26,003	307.8
	Cincinnati, Ohio	19,639	30,079	10,440	53.2
BORDER	Washington, D.C.	94,446	109,966	15,520	16.4
	Baltimore, Md.	84,749	108,322	25,573	27.8
	St. Louis, Mo.	43,960	69,854	25,894	58.9
	Kansas City, Mo.	23,566	30,719	7,153	30.4
SOUTH	New Orleans, La.	89,262	100,930	11,668	13.1
	Birmingham, Ala.	52,305	70,230	17,925	34.3
	Atlanta, Ga.	51,902	62,796	10,894	21.0
	Memphis, Tenn.	52,441	61,381	8,740	16.7
	Richmond, Va.	46,733	54,041	7,308	15.6
	Norfolk, Va.	25,039	43,392	18,353	73.5
	Jacksonville, Fla.	29,293	41,520	12,227	41.7
	Louisville, Ky.	40,522	40,097	−435	−1.1
	Savannah, Ga.	33,246	39,179	5,933	17.8
	Nashville, Tenn.	36,523	35,633	−890	−2.4
	Houston, Tex.	23,929	33,960	10,031	41.9
	Charleston, S C.	31,056	32,326	1,270	4.1
	Total	1,060,510	1,508,061	447,551*	42.2

* The urban gain for northern and border cities was 344,527, representing only 60 percent of the blacks who left the deep South in the same period. Most of the remainder settled in small towns and some found work as farm hands. In the years since, the urban pattern of migration has become much sharper: more than 98 percent of all northern blacks are now metropolitan dwellers.

been closed to us, through necessity are being opened to us. We are to be given a chance. . . . Prejudice vanishes when the almighty dollar is on the wrong side of the balance sheet."

Labor agents began scouring the South in search of black workers. Some agents dispensed train tickets—"justice tickets" they were called—as an inducement to migrate. There were instances of mass transport, the railroads and steel mills dispatching special trains which rolled through the South picking up any able-bodied black who would climb aboard.*

Alarmed at the labor drain, the South created obstructions, harassing agents and intimidating migrants. Police made the rounds of railroad stations, arresting as vagrants those who attempted to leave. The labor agents were discouraged with cumbersome regulations and heavy fees; in Alabama the combination of state and local fees averaged more than $1,000. The city council of Macon, Georgia, set the fee at $25,000, and stipulated further that agents must be recommended by ten local ministers, ten manufacturers and twenty-five businessmen.

All such measures were like trying to dam a river by decree. Blacks by the thousands believed that their moment had come, and nothing could check their rush to the cities. The *Defender* urged the migration on, organizing a Great Northern Drive; copies of the paper were passed around hand-to-hand all over the South. Many wrote to the *Defender* asking job placement help and they poured out in their letters the varied emotions that propelled the migration.

Pent-up resentment was a big factor. "We are humane but we are not treated such we are treated like brute," wrote a prospec-

---

* Justice tickets were used earlier to recruit black women as domestics, but the practice did not become widespread until the era cited.

In most cases the tickets were not free. The cost of transport was charged against future wages, and the migrant consigned his baggage to the labor agent as a guarantee of repayment. The system was subject to many abuses.

tive migrant from Alabama. Another in Mississippi said "I want to get my famely out of this cursed south land down here a negro man is not good as a white man's dog." And from Louisiana: "I am tired of bene dog as I was a beast and wee will come at wonce."

Many saw the move as a way to open doors for the next generation: "Having a very smart boy in his studies I wish to locate where he could receive a good education. . . ." "I want to come north where I can educate my 3 little children also my wife. . . ." "I wants to get in a good place whear I can educate my children. . . ." "i no i am south rais man i want some places to send my children to school. . . ."

Most powerful of all was the economic motive. The factories were paying four and five times the wages southern blacks were accustomed to earning, and the *Defender* was bombarded with letters like these: "I will go to pennsylvania or any state or N J or Ill. or any wheare that I can support my wife." "I would like to make some of the good pay for God knows we need it."

To the blacks who trooped North the high hopes seemed justified, at least for a time, and the reports they sent back gave fresh momentum to the movement. The *Journal of Negro History* published a collection of those letters, covering 1916-18; they reflect an era when many migrants viewed the city as a place bright with promise.

A black newcomer in Philadelphia wrote to a southern friend: "I havent heard a white man call a colored a nigger . . . since I been in the state of Pa. I can ride in the electric street and steam cars any where I get a seat. I dont care to mix with white what I mean I am not crazy about being with white folks, but if I have to pay the same fare I have learn to want the same acomidation."

From an industrial suburb of Chicago another migrant wrote home to say: "Now it is tru the (col) men are making good. Never pay less than $3.00 per day. . . . I do not see how they pay such wages the way they work labors. they do not hurry or drive you. . . . I wish many time that you could see our People up here as they are entirely in a different light."

Still another wrote that "I should have been here 20 years ago. I just begin to feel like a man. It's a great deal of pleasure in knowing that you have got some privilege. My children are going to the same school with the whites and I don't have to umble to no one. I have registered—Will vote the next election and there isn't any 'yes sir' and 'no sir'—it's all yes and no and Sam and Bill."

Such were the visions of the first mass migration. Jobs, equality, personal dignity and a future to build all seemed within reach. The symbolism of promised land infused the movement with religious fervor, expressed in the biblical imagery of Flight out of Egypt and Going into Canaan. One party of Mississippi blacks held a prayer meeting to mark the exact moment of deliverance. When their train reached mid-point on an Ohio River bridge they stopped their watches, knelt to offer thanks, then gave voice to a jubilant hymn, "I Done Come Out of the Land of Egypt With the Good News."

The joyous bridge crossing occurred in 1917, and the people involved were bound for Chicago. Two years later that city exploded in a fearful race riot. Thirty-eight persons were killed, more than five hundred were injured, and the smoke from burning buildings hung for days over a tormented city. Afterwards the Chicago Commission on Race Relations poked through the debris and issued a report that could stand with only minor editing as a commentary on the urban race crisis today.

The experience in other cities was much the same. Between 1917 and 1919 more than two dozen race riots erupted across the country. When the explosions subsided it became apparent that the race problem was taking a new form. The ghettos had been spawned.

The ghetto is not just a slum, but a slum set aside as a place of black habitation. In the succinct street-corner definition of one inhabitant, "It's where blacks are, and whites aren't." Before the great migration that arrangement did not exist. The earlier black urban settlers met with housing discrimination to be sure, and most were under economic handicap as well; as a result they were generally shunted into the poorer areas. They were not, however, closely restricted along racial lines. Typically the black pockets were scattered through the city, and the so-called black belts were often merely mixed areas in which the black presence was prominent.

The migration shattered such patterns. It came down to the fact that northern whites would accept black neighbors in small numbers, but not *en masse*. As the influx grew, neighborhoods were fenced off by means ranging from real estate covenants to violence. The swelling black stream was forced into tight channels, the newcomers crowding by necessity into areas where the color line had already been broken. That invariably set off a flight of whites, so that former mixed neighborhoods were rapidly ghettoized. The process is vividly illustrated by consecutive census reports from Chicago. In 1910 the blacks were scattered through three-fourths of the city's 431 census tracts, and most lived in predominantly white neighborhoods. The tracts with the highest black concentrations yielded percentages ranging from 21.8 to 61 percent. Ten years later most of the migrants were living in black neighborhoods; the concentration in the principal tracts ranged from 76.6 to 86.6 percent.*

The herding of newcomers into ghetto enclaves was accompanied by a general squeeze against those blacks who had already established long residence. The presence of a single black family

---

* The urban housing pattern cut across sectional lines. Myrdal observed that southern cities with small black populations maintained relatively open housing, while enforcing the rigid segregation which then applied in other matters. When southern cities experienced massive migration ghettos emerged in a fashion similar to that of the North.

in a tenement block became to whites a threat of inundation, and they took vigorous action to forestall the danger. Thus in 1910 about one-third of Chicago's blacks were living in neighborhoods that were 95 percent white. By 1920 the number so situated was only one out of 15. In 41 of the census tracts all black residents were driven out.

A good many blacks found themselves caught in the middle. The poverty-ridden, ill-educated migrants did create slums almost everywhere they clustered. The already established blacks —the old settlers as they called themselves—didn't like slums any better than the middle class whites. When they tried to escape, however, they found that the bars were raised against them, too. In the polarized atmosphere color had become the sole criterion.

One violent confrontation began in middle-class Chicago sections known as Kenwood and Hyde Park. Black home owners established entry there, only to encounter fierce opposition from the Kenwood and Hyde Park Property Owners' Association. In 1918 the association announced its intention to "make Hyde Park white." The campaign began with offers of thinly disguised bribes. It was assumed publicly that the blacks would be happier in a more congenial neighborhood; there was talk of helping them find new homes and lending them a little money to get reestablished. When that didn't work, thirty-five block captains were appointed to marshal community pressure. But the blacks still wouldn't budge, and the expulsion drive began to take on an ominous note.

"The depreciation of our property in this district has been two hundred and fifty million dollars since the invasion," The Property Owners' Journal declared. "If someone told you that there was to be an invasion that would injure your homes to that extent, wouldn't you rise up as one man and one woman, and say as General Foch said: 'They shall not pass'?"

And later: "To damage a man's property and destroy its value is to rob him. The person who commits this act is a robber. Every owner has the right to defend his property to the utmost of his ability, with every means at his disposal."

And still later: "There is nothing in the make-up of a Negro, physically or mentally, which should induce anyone to welcome him as a neighbor. The best of them are insanitary . . . ruin alone follows in their path. . . . Niggers are undesirable neighbors and entirely irresponsible and vicious."

It was never established whether the association acted on the principle of any means at its disposal. But somebody so acted. There were fifty-eight bombings in twenty months, starting in Kenwood-Hyde Park and flaring out to cover most of the city. The terror was directed at blacks who settled outside the ghetto, at whites who rented or sold to them, at banks and real estate firms which played any part in such transactions. Other organized intimidation was mounted by "athletic clubs," composed of young toughs who roamed the streets to beat up Negroes.

All that was prelude to the riot. It began on a hot July day when a black youth swam across an imaginery racial line which divided a beach. He drowned as white boys tried to drive him back with stones. Riot broke out on the beach and spread through the city, lasting for six days. The wounded were so numerous that one ghetto hospital ran out of beds and stretchers and stacked the waiting casualties on the floor. A thousand people were left homeless as arsonists on both sides set fire to neighborhoods.

Such was Chicago's introduction to the ghetto era. It was more violent than most, in keeping with that city's raw traditions, but it was by no means unique. St. Louis two years earlier had experienced an even more savage battle. And all across the country other, lesser outbreaks flickered like heat lightning, warning of a gathering urban storm that has not yet passed.

The Chicago affair produced the first example of what has come now to be a standard sociological document: the riot report. It was a sensible, balanced account, citing such causes of conflict as race prejudice, job and housing inequities, police practices and the problems inherent to migration conditions. One point it didn't stress: Chicago, like America, generally had a lot of experience in dealing with both newcomers and minority groups. During the decade just preceding the black wave the city had received 210,000 Russians, 30,000 Italians and 24,000 Hungarians. At the time of the riot the foreign born in Chicago totaled some 800,000, about eight times the number of blacks. The other groups had been absorbed with difficulty enough, but they had been absorbed. The ghetto blacks, then as now, had proved an exception.

Ghetto disillusionment caused many blacks to question for the first time whether they really wanted to be absorbed. That was evidenced in a dramatic mass movement unlike any that had gone before.

Prior to the great migration there had been three principal black organizations, and each had reflected aspirations of the time. The first was the Colored Farmers' Alliance, formed in the late nineteenth century. It claimed more than a million members. It was Populist oriented, devoted to the interests of the small farmer, and more concerned with the price of cotton than with questions of race. It spoke for a people who still thought they had a future on the southern soil.

The National Association for the Advancement of Colored People appeared in 1909, as a response to mounting segregation pressures. It concentrated on civil rights, believing that race problems would dissolve when blacks obtained full status as citizens.

Close behind came the National Urban League, founded in 1910. It began as a social work agency, addressed to questions of jobs, housing and education; as the name implied it saw the black man surmounting his difficulties by climbing the traditional industrial ladder.

The three organizations differed in approach and analysis but at base they were much alike. All were typically American in outlook, sharing a spirit and purpose common to many another group in the nation's experience. They expressed a root conviction that if the system were properly shaken and prodded it could be made to work.

And then came Marcus Garvey. His theme was stark and clear: the black people had no further business to conduct with the United States of America.

A Jamaican by birth, Garvey appeared as a New York street-corner orator in 1916. Blacks at first dismissed him as an eccentric but within a year they were beginning to listen; in just two years more he forged the largest black movement the country had ever seen. He urged his followers to abandon the United States, return to Africa, and join there with all blacks to forge a mighty empire. Within that framework he anticipated and topped just about everything that black nationalists are saying today.

Race pride? Garvey glorified all things black, and converted to black any symbol that suited his purpose. Jesus Christ was a black. History was a pageant of black triumphs that would be repeated:

"Was not the Negro a power, was he not great once? Yes, honest students of history can recall the day when Egypt, Ethiopia and Timbuctoo towered in their civilizations, towered above Europe, towered above Asia. When Europe was inhabited by a race of cannibals, a race of savages, naked men, heathens and pagans, Africa was peopled with a race of cultured black men, who were masters in art, science and literature. . . . Why, then, should we lose hope? Black men, you were great once; you shall be great again."

And if whites resisted: "The thing to do is to get organized; keep separated and you will be exploited, you will be robbed, you will be killed. Get organized and you will compel the world to respect you. If the world fails to give you consideration, because you are black, because you are Negroes, four hundred millions of you shall shake the pillars of the universe and bring down creation."

He carried his plan far enough to organize his own army, and his own steamship line to conduct the exodus. He acquired by his own estimate six million followers, and his bitterest critics conceded him at least one million. The knowledgeable James Weldon Johnson assessed his influence by observing simply, "He stirred the imagination of the Negro masses as no Negro ever had."

The movement collapsed in a few short years, as it was bound to do; his schemes were hopelessly grandiose. It has been debated since whether he was mountebank or visionary. Probably he was a visionary, but the question does not really matter. The episode was significant not for the man or the movement but for the mood. Garvey told blacks that they had been betrayed, that they would always be betrayed in the white man's world, and in the anguished ghettos millions heard and believed. A half century later echoes of that bitter cry are being heard again.

The riots, the Garvey movement, the 1920-21 recession all came and went, and blacks continued to flock to now solidified ghettos. They had no better choice. The 1920-30 migration was more than 900,000, some 60 percent higher than the previous decade. In Harlem 118,792 white people trooped out of the area in ten years, and 87,417 black people trooped in. In all the big ghettos the black predominance was fast shifting toward a figure of 90 percent.

It was the jobs that drew and held them. The bulk of the black workers had by now found their way onto the bottom of the industrial ladder. With a few notable exceptions they didn't gain real entry to the important unions, and that was to cost them later when they tried to move off the bottom rung.

In 1929, of course, the bottom dropped out, and the blacks were the first to know. If a really shrewd financier had been reading the Chicago *Defender* he might have got out of the market just in time. "Something is happening in Chicago," the paper asserted in January, 1929, "and it should no longer go unnoticed. During the past three weeks hardly a day has ended that there has not been a report of another firm discharging its employees. . . ."

The *Defender* had maintained a relentless campaign for continued migration, and now for the first time it began advising southern blacks to stay home. The logic was impeccable. If white Chicago was running short of money, black Chicago was about to go broke.

During the Depression there were times and places in which half the ghetto residents were living off relief. Northern and southern relief standards were as inequitable then as now, and there were fears that the entire black South would trek North in quest of welfare checks. It didn't happen. Depression migration fell to the lowest point in thirty years. Then World War II set the factories booming again, and migration rose to the highest point ever reached.

By the mid-1950s the war booms had run their course but the migration had not; it was holding at near-record levels of some 150,000 people a year. A new element was involved. Technology was forcing out those who still remained on the farm, and they were arriving in the cities to find that machines had replaced manual labor there, too. The ghettos, and therefore the cities, were headed for crisis.

Part II

THE CRISIS YEARS

Chapter 4

THE RURAL EXODUS

I don't know how they stay alive.
—A rural black leader
talks of his people.

THE South in recent years has been profoundly shaken by
two shock waves of change. One was a clamorous public event, a
social and political upheaval that could be heard in the sound of
black feet marching. The other wave ran quietly beneath the
surface but it, too, had a distinctive sound, the clanking sound of
farm machinery doing work which human hands had always
done before.

The juxtaposition of forces has created for rural blacks a
harsh paradox. They acquired a political voice at almost precisely the period when they lost such tenuous economic status as
they ever had. Thus it was that poverty grew worse and migration swelled through all the years when civil rights demonstrators were winning important victories. Over the last two decades
more than two-thirds of all black farm families have been forced
off the land, contributing some two and a half million people to
the migration stream. The relentless attrition still dispossesses
tens of thousands a year.

The southern countryside is littered with eloquent reminders

63

of the great exodus. Along a typical stretch of Alabama road this reporter counted a dozen abandoned shacks in a mile. Some had been burned to clear the ground and were represented only by crumbling chimneys and heaps of ash. Others just stood there, desolate and empty. It was as though the populace had fled before invading tanks. These people, however, were driven out not by tanks, but by tractors and cotton-picking machines.

Mechanization is not an event which yields to exact dates, but in the case of cotton farming the general sequence is clear enough. Prior to World War II, the South carried on such agriculture by means essentially unchanged from centuries past. The plowing was accomplished by a man and a mule. After that came the interminable hoe labor of chopping away the weeds. Then, at harvest time men, women and children moved stoop-backed through the fields plucking the soft, sticky bolls. It required a long day's work to pick 200 pounds.

The first radical departure was the adoption of tractors, a development which coincided roughly with the 1940s and 1950s. Alabama, for instance, had some 7,000 tractors in 1939. The number increased in five years to 15,000, in ten years to 45,000 and in fifteen years to 65,000. Throughout the South in the early 1950s horses and mules were disappearing from southern farms at the rate of 100,000 animals a year. In 1955 the agricultural experiment station at Stoneville, Mississippi, dismantled its mule shed as token that an era had passed.*

A tractor covers in a day the ground that takes a mule the better part of a week. Planting labor was enormously reduced. The next big breakthrough was the use of flame throwers and chemical applications for weed control. Plant breeders developed special varieties of cotton, with the bolls appearing well up on

---

* During the Poor People's March on Washington a southern delegation employed a mule caravan as traditional symbol. They had a hard time finding available mules.

the stalk, so that a flame thrower could flick beneath and sear the weeds. And there went the man with the hoe.

In the late 1950s the cotton-picking machines rumbled into the fields. They could pluck the delicate bolls almost as adeptly as the human hand, and a great deal faster and cheaper. Ten years ago such machines were picking about 2 percent of the South's cotton. Today they are picking more than 80 percent.

Mechanization of tobacco farming has followed a similar but slower course which is only now entering the final phase. The harvest is still gathered by hand, and it provides peak seasonal employment for about 100,000 workers. Their days are numbered. A tobacco-picking machine is scheduled for commercial debut at about the time this book appears.

In sum, the industrial revolution has arrived in the rural South, and the plantation which once maintained a hundred workers now needs the labor of only five or six. Moreover, the advancing technology has been accompanied by a major shift in the whole pattern of southern farming. Between 1940 and 1955 about 40 percent of the former cotton acreage was converted to other uses, notably timber and pasture which require almost no labor at all.

For the South as a whole, such change represents progress. The region is shaking off a blighted agricultural economy which provided, at best, institutionalized poverty for most of its workers. Nonetheless, the passing of even a wretched system can be a disastrous event to those who are ill-prepared for transition. So it has been for most farm blacks. Once they were exploited but functional. Now they are simply obsolete.*

The hardest hit are farm hands who work for a daily wage.

---

* The blacks, of course, are not the sole victims of changing farm patterns. The rural poor total 12.5 million, of whom some nine million are whites.

White rural poverty is likewise heavily concentrated in the South, notably Appalachia. Other stricken rural areas include parts of California, Arizona, and Nevada, plus sections of the upper midwest and upper New England.

Despite mechanization a large number still cling to that occupation, for they know no other. The most recent comprehensive
survey was made in 1965 and found a non-white (predominantly
black) field labor force of 923,000. The total included 691,000
adults, with the rest juveniles ranging down to age fourteen.
Dependent young children were not tabulated but rural families
are large; at a conservative estimate the number of people involved at least equals the combined ghetto populations of Detroit, Watts and Newark. Their condition can only be described
as desperate.

About one-fourth of the farm labor blacks subsisted on family
incomes of less than $1,000 a year, according to the 1965 report,
and 60 percent had incomes of less than $2,000. The means by
which they reached the higher bracket is itself a commentary on
their way of life.

In the families best situated, the man and wife both worked in
the fields in season, and both filled in with other jobs at slack
periods. Typically, she found occasional employment as a domestic, and he odd-jobbed as gardener, ditch digger, whatever he
could pick up. Together they managed 269 working days in the
year, and obtained from all their occupations a combined income
of $1,640. It amounted to $31.50 a week, but they didn't get it
weekly. They had to contrive a budget from ill-spaced, unpre-
dictable paychecks.

At the next level down were families entirely dependent on the
earnings of the male head. The average man obtained 124 days
of seasonal farm work, receiving $795. About half of these men
found outside jobs, raising their annual incomes to an average
$1,232. The range for such households was thus $15 to $24 a
week.

At the bottom were families supported by female breadwin-
ners. Rural poverty disrupts families, too, and so the field labor
force numbered more than 60,000 black women who were heads

of households. The women averaged $202 a year from agricultural labor, $408 a year if they had additional jobs. Four to eight dollars a week.

The bottom level seems a statistical improbability. It is a human improbability as well, but tens of thousands must struggle for existence on such terms. This reporter asked an Alabama black leader, "How do they live?" His answer: "I was born and raised on a back road, I've known the country people all my life, and even I don't know how they stay alive." At a community meeting a woman answered the question with, "Some people are starving. I don't mean just hungry. I mean starving."

The small farmers are only slightly better off. The 1964 agricultural census listed some 184,000 black farm operators, both owners and renters, and together with their wives and children they numbered 822,000 people. That's enough to refill an entire East Coast string of ghettos including Atlanta, Washington, D.C., Pittsburgh and Boston. They are being squeezed into just such places by inexorable economic laws.

The small farmers can't afford to modernize—a tractor costs as much as a Cadillac—and they can't compete by the old methods. Their operations in any case are simply too marginal to offer an economic base. The Department of Agriculture figures as rule of thumb that a small farmer must sell four dollars worth of produce for every dollar he puts in his pocket. The black farmers had an average sale of $2,700, yielding a net of some $675. Additionally, about two-thirds of them eked out a little extra income, averaging $1,766. For the typical farm operator, then, the range of family income was $13 to $47 a week. The great majority of them are literally dirt poor.

Finally, there is a huge pool of rural poverty diffused through the little towns and hamlets which dot the southern countryside. This overlaps the farm problem, because many of the townspeople do field work when they can get it. In terms of residence the last count yielded more than three and a half million black rural poor, and two-thirds of them were town dwellers.*

The black belt small towns were never thriving, but in times past they served as market places for a poor but numerous peasant class. If a single plantation hired a hundred full-time workers that represented a farm hand income of nearly a quarter of a million dollars, all of it was immediately consumed, and channeled back through the local stores. Now more than half the workers are gone, those who remain are only half employed, and the machines that replaced them consume only fuel. Add all the other factors that are drying up little towns throughout the country and black belt hamlets become desolate indeed.

The small-town populations are heavily unbalanced, overladen with the elderly, the enfeebled, the ill-educated, all the people left behind. That increases the burdens of poverty and inertia. The community leaders, both black and white, complain particularly about losing almost all their young. There is a saying that the youngsters go forth from high school commencement clutching two prized pieces of paper, a diploma, and a bus ticket out. Some don't wait for the diploma.

Such is the swamp of rural poverty. For years a steady stream of migration has flown out of it, only to drain into ghetto swamps at the other end. Rural expulsion, not urban attraction, has long since become the controlling factor in the black trek to the cities.

Herding the rural poor into cities is not an official government program, but it might almost as well be. The effect of both national and local policies is to exacerbate the rural problem,

* The Department of Health, Education and Welfare defines the poverty line by a sliding scale according to circumstances, with periodic adjustments for cost of living changes in the consumer price index. As an example, recent calculations placed the poverty threshold at $2,906 a year for a typical farm family of four, and $3,410 for a non-farm family of four. The statistics on non-farm poverty make no allowance for the huge cost of living difference in such widely varied environs as New York City and an Alabama village. The effect is to underestimate the number of non-farm poor.

contributing immense pressure to the flow of forced migration. Thus farm subsidies take acreage out of production, magnifying unemployment. And welfare benefits are so unevenly distributed that the dispossessed crowd into urban centers in search of relief.

Some of these results are inadvertent, the consequences of pursuing one goal at the expense of another. That's largely the case with farm policy. Some other aspects reflect the nation's failure to see itself as a whole. We have had a generation and more of intense migration, over a period marked also by the innumerable social experiments of the New Deal, Fair Deal, New Frontier and Great Society, and in all that time the government has never addressed the fact that North Carolina poverty winds up as a crisis on New York streets. That kind of national absent-mindedness contributes heavily to the welfare disaster. And finally, the refusal to deal with rural poverty must be ascribed in some measure to deliberate intent. In an era of sharply polarized race conflict some southern communities have lost all interest in alleviating black distress. A good many southerners take wry satisfaction at the thought of handing the problem over to northern cities.

A fairly common southern reaction can be capsuled by comparing two migrations. Fifty years ago, when black labor was an economic asset, departing migrants were pulled off the trains. Today the blacks are viewed as a social and political threat, and officials sometimes respond to demonstrations by passing out handbills on the superior welfare advantages to be found in the North.

Welfare discrepancies are large enough to constitute a powerful migration motive. The most important welfare category is Aid to Families with Dependent Children (AFDC). It accounts for more than two-thirds of all welfare cases, and is financed by a federal-state arrangement with the level of aid geared to local contributions. In 1968 the Department of Health, Education and Welfare reported that monthly AFDC payments per dependent child averaged $42 in the nation, but only $22.50 in southern states. At the extreme ends of the spectrum Massachusetts paid $67.85, Mississippi only $8.50. If a woman with six dependent children moved from Mississippi to Boston she increased her monthly welfare income from $51 to $407.10 (TABLE 8).

TABLE 8

Welfare Standards, Selected States

Average Payments per Person in Aid to Families with Dependent Children, 1968			
Southern States		*Selected Northern States*	
Virginia	$31.85	Massachusetts	$67.85
Kentucky	28.95	Connecticut	67.45
N. Carolina	27.85	New York	64.75
Tennessee	26.15	New Jersey	59.60
Georgia	24.50	Wisconsin	55.85
Louisiana	23.60	Minnesota	55.50
Florida	22.20	California	48.40
Arkansas	19.25	Michigan	46.75
Texas	18.85	Illinois	46.55
S. Carolina	18.35	Ohio	38.00
Alabama	15.35	Pennsylvania	37.75
Mississippi	8.50	Indiana	32.20

SOURCE: Department of Health, Education and Welfare.

It must be added that southern states are saddled with an outsized share of the poverty load, and they have to support it from a much lower tax base. Nine of the ten poorest states are southern. As ranked from the bottom in per capita income these ten include Mississippi, South Carolina, Arkansas, Alabama, Kentucky, Tennessee, Louisiana, South Dakota, North Carolina and Georgia. The South in general accounts for only a fourth of the nation's population, but half of the poverty, and 97 of the 100 poorest counties are clustered in the Old Confederacy. Mississippi alone is plagued with 24 of the poorest counties (TABLE 9).

TABLE 9
Profile of the Poorest Counties

SELECTED CHARACTERISTICS BY MEDIUM AVERAGE
AND MEDIUM RANGE

*(Average and range both compiled from
medium figures for counties involved)*

Location by State	Poorest Counties	Annual Income Per Capita, Family	Unemployment	Education	Population Characteristics
Alabama	8				Population Size:
Alaska	2				Average: 14,606
		Per capita			
Arkansas	8	Average: $633			
		Range: $435-			Range:
Georgia	9	$886			2,443-
			Average:		54,464
Kentucky	22		5.523%		
					Rural
Louisiana	1	*Family*	Range:		Proportion:
		Average: $1,736	.5%-		Average:
Mississippi	24	Range: $1,260-	21.3%		42.74%
		$1,956		Average:	
N. Carolina	3			7.3 school	
				years	Range:
Tennessee	11				.1%-
					47.5%
Texas	6			Range:	
				5.2-	
Virginia	1			8.9 years	
					Non-White Proportion:
					Average: 38.89%
					Range: .1%- 81.3%

SOURCE: *Public Assistance in the South*, a Special Report of the Southern Regional Council, Nov., 1966, Atlanta, Ga. Based on data from Department of Health, Education and Welfare.

When aid programs are prorated against the resources the problem is seen in a different light. At a recent report, Mississippi had a per capita income of $1,438 and committed to welfare a community average of $3.11 for every $1,000 in personal income. That's about par for the national course and topped the proportional efforts of such well-to-do states as Connecticut and New Jersey. Alabama communities contributed an average $4.33 per $1,000, ranking ahead of Michigan and Illinois. Some southern programs are miserly by any standard—Virginia sets aside for its poor 82 cents out of every $1,000—and then again Oklahoma is the nation's most generous state (TABLE 10).

Welfare effort, then, has no sectional pattern. It's a highly random affair, varying widely from state to state, and it bears only the most incidental relationship to need, benefit levels, or the ability to pay. It adds up to the fact that a poor state can reach deep into the barrel, and still come up with not nearly enough to go around. Louisiana, for instance, makes a proportionate effort almost half again higher than that of New York, and yet the dependent Louisiana child receives only a third as much aid.

TABLE 10

Welfare Effort by Ability to Pay, All States

State	Expenditure Per $1,000	Per Capita Income (and Rank by Wealth)
THE TEN HIGHEST		
Oklahoma	$10.33	$2,083 (37th)
California	8.17	3,103 (6th)
Colorado	7.32	2,566 (18th)
Louisiana	7.05	1,877 (44th)
Massachusetts	6.52	2,965 (9th)
Minnesota	5.41	2,375 (25th)
New York	5.13	3,162 (4th)
Rhode Island	4.80	2,541 (20th)
Washington	4.70	2,635 (13th)
North Dakota	4.38	2,133 (34th)

TABLE 10 (*continued*)

State	Expenditure Per $1,000	Per Capita Income (and Rank by Wealth)
THE TEN LOWEST		
Virginia	.82	2,239 (30th)
Nevada	1.09	3,248 (3rd)
Delaware	1.11	3,460 (1st)
Indiana	1.28	2,544 (19th)
South Carolina	1.52	1,655 (49th)
Florida	1.78	2,250 (29th)
Tennessee	1.90	1,859 (45th)
Montana	1.99	2,252 (28th)
Arizona	1.97	2,233 (31st)
Maryland	2.06	2,867 (10th)

Other States in Order of Effort, with Rank by Wealth

Alabama	4.33	(47th)	New Mexico	3.75	(38th)
Arkansas	4.28	(48th)	Iowa	3.66	(24th)
Kansas	4.05	(27th)	Missouri	3.50	(17th)
Illinois	3.84	(7th)	West Virginia	3.45	(40th)
Wisconsin	3.82	(21st)	Idaho	3.35	(39th)
Michigan	3.30	(11th)	Vermont	3.03	(36th)
Kentucky	3.24	(46th)	New Hampshire	3.01	(23rd)
Oregon	3.14	(15th)	Connecticut	2.83	(2nd)
Mississippi	3.11	(50th)	Utah	2.79	(33rd)
Pennsylvania	3.07	(16th)	Nebraska	2.78	(26th)
S. Dakota	2.77	(43rd)	Wyoming	2.51	(22nd)
Maine	2.76	(35th)	Ohio	2.46	(12th)
Georgia	2.74	(41st)	Texas	2.44	(32nd)
Hawaii	2.67	(14th)	N. Carolina	2.30	(42nd)
New Jersey	2.60	(8th)	Alaska	2.12	(5th)

Per capita income figures and ratings are for 1964, the state and local welfare expenditures represent 1965.

SOURCE: *Public Assistance: To What End?* A Special Report of the Southern Regional Council, Nov., 1967, Atlanta, Ga. Based on data from the Department of Health, Education and Welfare.

The federal government makes the gap still wider by keying its payments to those of the state and local units. In theory, matching funds are supposed to provide an incentive, and the scale is adjusted according to local need. In fact, the adjustments are not realistic and the poorest communities pass up many benefits because they can't meet the matching requirements. As a peculiar result, the federal program serves local governments in an approximate order of inverse need.

The states are in turn just as haphazard in their dealings with cities, towns and counties. Overall, the states return nearly $3 billion a year to local governments for welfare purposes; it amounts to a sixth of all state expenditures, and figures out to an average per capita assistance of $14.70. The average is misleading, however, being swollen by a few large donors. Actual per capita state aid ranges all the way from California's $48.77 to Arkansas's four cents. More than half the states fall below the $5 line, and thirteen states dump the entire welfare burden on local units. Mississippi with twenty-four of the poorest counties and Kentucky with twenty-two both adhere to the philosophy of complete local responsibility.

Such is the national non-policy on welfare. It resembles a crazy quilt assembled by a room full of seamstresses, each applying pieces at random without reference to each other and with no common notion as to the size, shape, design or function of the intended article. Inevitably there are big holes in it, places either inadequately covered or not covered at all. One such place is Tunica County, Mississippi. It's the nation's poorest county, and as such it provides a scale model view of both rural collapse and welfare failure.

Tunica County had, at last count, 16,826 people, with a black-white ratio of more than four to one. About two-thirds of the residents are farm dwellers, and the rest are scattered through little hamlets of a few hundred each. The hardcore unemployment hovers around 5 percent, but the real problem lies in the kind of employment the 95 percent have. They subsist in the hand-to-mouth rural fashion already described, and more than three-fourths of them fall below the poverty line. In most cases, way below. The median family income is $1,260 a year, or $24.23 a week. The typical county family could double its income and still be poor.

Poverty in Tunica County is quite often a fatal disease. It assumes, of course, all sorts of medical disguises, such as malnutrition and consequent lowered resistance to infection, and it is revealed most starkly among the very young. One of the critical phases in a child's development is the postneonatal period, from the second to twelfth months. Tunica's postneonatal death rate is 31.5 per 1,000—about five times as high as the national average. Some other medical consequences may be in a way even more tragic. The evidence strongly suggests that in many children the malnutrition may produce irreversible brain damage.

The county is unfortunate above all in the kind of disaster from which it suffers. It is located on the banks of the Mississippi River, and if it were overwhelmed by some wild surge of the river the problem would command attention. If marooned children were crying for food, if the aged were slowly starving in villages awash from flood, then helicopters would bring help in a hurry. But chronic disaster has no such drama, and very little appeal, and so Tunica County is left to manage as best it can. It receives no help from the state. From the federal government it receives matching funds. The result at last report was a county welfare budget of $374,404.40.

If Tunica County spread its welfare largess evenly among all its poor, it could provide to each an annual dole of $29.78. About eight cents a day. That, of course, would be absurd, and so the county doesn't spread it evenly. Tunica's poor number about 13,000, and a little over 1,000 of them are on welfare. The rest are on their own.

Tunica's circumstances are by no means unique. The one

hundred poorest counties contain altogether more than one and a half million people, the poverty rates range from half to three-fourths of the residents, and the welfare programs in most cases reach only 10 to 20 percent of those in urgent need. And even those get very little.

No one really knows how much the welfare discrepancy acts as a direct stimulus to migration. The question is complex and controversial: if a family moves from Mississippi to New York and goes on welfare that doesn't prove that they moved for welfare. In fact, some fragmentary findings indicate that the newly arrived migrant usually scuffles around in the city for two or three years before he shows up on the welfare rolls. Other evidence suggests that the rural poor are not at all sophisticated about the intricacies of the welfare system. But they do know when they're not eating, and, if they get hungry enough, a lot of them hit the road toward the places where they've heard the money is. Between 1960 and 1968 the national AFDC (dependent child) rolls rose by 1,600,000, and nearly half of that increase took place in New York and California.

One obvious solution would be a single-standard welfare program, and by its nature that would almost certainly require the federal government to take over complete financial responsibility. The President's Advisory Commission on Rural Poverty estimated that all rural poor, both black and white, could be boosted above the poverty line by an additional outlay of about $5 billion a year. The sum amounts to one-half cent on the nation's personal income dollar. To close the gap for urban poor would cost another $7.5 billion a year, or $12.5 billion total.*

Officials of the Nixon Administration are reported to agree privately on the logic of a national program, while balking at the cost. At this writing, the Administration has proposed a compromise in which the federal government would guarantee a four-

* Of the projected sum, about $9 billion would go to white poor, about $3.5 billion to non-whites.

person poor family a subsistence level of $2,400. The scheme does not envision that the government would dispense that amount to all the families involved. Rather, the federal program would serve as a backstop, providing whatever funding proves necessary for families who fail to reach $1,600 under the hodgepodge of existing programs.

The plan is open to several cogent objections. It goes only a short way toward relieving the inequitable burdens of rich and poor communities, and it may well prove insufficient to halt the rural exodus. It may also tempt some communities to abandon now existing marginal efforts, allowing the federal program to pick up the difference without in any way improving the lot of those dependent on aid. Finally, and above all, it has drawn sharp criticism on the grounds that by the government's own definition of poverty this is a half-measure. Nonetheless, the proposal represents a first hesitant step toward accepting the proposition that poverty must be dealt with in terms of some basic national standard.

Another type of aid involves a complex of food programs. It reaches only half of the 25 million poor, and it provides only a meager supplement for many of those who are enrolled.

No one knows the extent or severity of malnutrition among the poor. The lack of data is itself one index of how much the problem has been neglected. Only recently, after much prodding, the Department of Health, Education and Welfare began a general survey of the question. Meantime, however, there are samplings from congressional hearings and foundation studies, and they show clearly that for many of the poor, hunger is a chronic condition.

Ironically, it appears to be most acute in rural areas. About a fourth of the rural poor have incomes so low that if they spent every penny on food they could not reach the diet level which the Department of Agriculture describes as adequate. The villagers suffer particularly, but even the farm dwellers are caught in such a cycle of poverty that they often wind up ill-nourished. Many don't keep cows for milk or hogs for meat because they can't afford the initial outlay. Most have no means for preserving perishables.

Among such people the mainstays of diet are rice, flour, hominy grits, occasional salt pork. It exacts a heavy toll of health and energy and has particularly disastrous effects on the young. In a study sponsored by the Southern Regional Council, a team of eminent physicians toured the Mississippi Delta and submitted an angry report as follows: *

"We saw homes with children who are lucky to eat one meal a day—and that one inadequate so far as vitamins, minerals or protein is concerned. We saw children who don't get to drink milk, don't get to eat fruit, green vegetables, or meat. They live on starches—grits, bread, flavored water. . . . We saw children fed communally—that is, by neighbors who give scraps of food to children whose own parents have nothing to give them.

"In sum, we saw children who are hungry and who are sick— children for whom hunger is a daily fact of life and sickness, in many forms, an inevitability. We do not want to quibble over words, but 'malnutrition' is not quite what we found; the boys and girls we saw were hungry, weak, in pain, sick; their lives are being shortened; they are, in fact, visibly and predictably losing their health, their energy, their spirits. They are suffering from hunger and disease and directly or indirectly they are dying from them—which is exactly what starvation means."

The medical investigators added that one mother of a poor family described it all in one poignant sentence: "These children

* The report was the work of the following physicians: Dr. Joseph Brenner, Medical Department, Massachusetts Institute of Technology; Dr. Robert Coles, Harvard University Health Services; Dr. Alan Mermann and Dr. Milton J. E. Senn, Yale University Medical School; Dr. Cyril Walwyn, Medical Advisor to Friends of the Children of Mississippi, and Dr. Raymond Wheeler, chairman of the executive committee, Southern Regional Council.

go to bed hungry, and get up hungry and don't ever know nothing else in between."

The federal government gives away surplus commodities to the poor, sponsors an alternate food stamp plan for discount buying of groceries, and finances school lunches. Why then should Mississippi children go hungry? Why should anybody? There are two basic answers. First, the food programs are paltry as measured against the need. And second, local officials have sometimes seemed bent on deliberate sabotage.

In 1967, some 500 counties had declined to apply for the program. The list included a third of the nation's 100 poorest counties. Civil rights groups brought law suits and other pressures and today almost all counties are finally enrolled. In many places, however, the program remains in the hands of administrators who are hostile to such aid. In Georgia a local official told the state welfare director, "It would just mean a lot of niggers lined up for food and that's all there is to it."

Local obstruction is not, however, the chief problem. The larger failures must be laid at the federal door. The food distribution programs are just not designed to do a real job. In Mississippi, for instance, every county participates, and yet in that state hunger abounds. Many of Mississippi's poor have never laid hands on a food stamp or a surplus commodity.

In Tunica County, the nation's poorest place, 53 percent of the destitute receive aid from the food program. That's very good, as the averages go. Of the state's twenty-three other poorest counties, three have food participation rates of over half the poor; for the remaining twenty counties the participation ranges down to 15 percent. Elsewhere it drops a lot lower than that; in Beaufort County, North Carolina, 59 percent of the people are poor, but only 1.2 percent of the poor are on the program.

Those who do qualify do not necessarily enjoy a substantial gain in nutrition. A Department of Agriculture study in two Mississippi Delta counties found that surplus commodity recipients, food stamp recipients and non-participating poor were at nearly the same level of nutrition, or rather, malnutrition. The difference was that participants achieved diet deficiency at a considerable saving.

The Delta nutrition study was for 1965 and it must be qualified with the notation that the food programs have since been somewhat improved. In the case of surplus commodities there has been a gradual expansion of benefits over the last decade; in 1960 the recipient got a monthly five-item, twelve-pound package which has been increased to twenty-four items and thirty-eight pounds. Such foods as fruit juice, canned vegetables and evaporated milk have been added to a list originally heavily weighted with dry beans, flour, cornmeal and lard. Even so, it remains true that commodity packages provide only a third of diet's bulk needs, and the makeup of the package is not even ostensibly related to the requirements of diet balance. What it's related to is the well-being of the food industry. The Department of Agriculture buys and stores the food to keep prices up, and the poor are fed such items as may fall into the surplus bin.

Food stamps provide in theory a much better approach. The participants shop for food of their choice, using discount stamps underwritten by the federal government. The discount schedule is complex, depending on region, family size and income; as illustration, a $10-a-week southern family of four can get $60 worth of groceries for $20. On paper it seems sensible enough. The law, however, contained the most incredible vagaries, not the least of them being the proposition that the poorest of the poor have the least need for food.

The need level was arrived at through a quite remarkable bureaucratic exercise. The Department of Agriculture sent its agents into the field, interviewed various-sized families at various low-income levels, and established for representative groups a food budget requirement based on what they were spending at the time. Naturally, the very poorest were spending the least and that became their norm, establishing the quantity of stamps they were entitled to buy. The department statisticians apparently lost sight of the fact that the norm was what they were trying to change.

A still more serious drawback is the distribution system. In the typical setup the stamps are disbursed through the county welfare office, and for the government's administrative convenience, the poor are required to purchase the coupons in lots covering two to four weeks at a time. The $10-a-week participants can seldom manage that, and they quickly fall out of the program.

Beyond all that is the fact that the stamps just don't go far enough. Typically, they cover only two-thirds of the food requirement, and even at the discount price the participants must spend 35 to 50 percent of their total income to achieve a minimum diet. By comparison the typical middle-class budget allocates about 18 percent for food.

The school lunch program is still another chronicle of failure. That, too, is operated by the Department of Agriculture, and there's nothing wrong with the nutrition level. The failure lies in the fact that it reaches only a third of six million school children from the poorest families.

Sometimes the youngsters get left out because their schools have no program. Sometimes there is a program, and a subsidy arrangement for the poor, but still they get left out because the specifications don't quite cover their contingency. How that can happen was graphically presented by Dr. Raymond Wheeler who appeared as guest expert on the CBS-TV documentary "Hunger in America." Dr. Wheeler was interviewing a rural Alabama boy, a lad named Charles, and there ensued a dialogue as follows:*

* "Hunger in America," CBS-TV, May 21, 1968. Reporter Charles Kuralt, written by Peter Davis and Martin Carr, produced by Martin Carr, executive producer Don Hewitt.

DR. WHEELER: How old are you?

CHARLES: Fourteen.

DR. WHEELER: You go to school?

CHARLES: Yeah.

DR. WHEELER: Do you get breakfast at home before you go?

CHARLES: Yeah. Some mornings we have peas.

DR. WHEELER: You have peas?

CHARLES: Yeah.

DR. WHEELER: Well, when you get to school what do you have to eat there?

CHARLES: Nothing.

DR. WHEELER: Isn't—is there any place at school where you can buy something to eat or get something to eat? Do they—do they cook a meal for you there?

CHARLES: Yeah.

DR. WHEELER: Well, why don't you have some?

CHARLES: I don't have any money to buy it.

DR. WHEELER: How much does it cost?

CHARLES: Twenty-five cents.

DR. WHEELER: It costs twenty-five cents to have something to eat at school?

CHARLES: Yeah.

DR. WHEELER: Well, what do you do while the other children are eating?

CHARLES: Just sit there.

DR. WHEELER: Where do you sit?

CHARLES: I sit where all the children be seated.

DR. WHEELER: How do you feel toward the other children who are eating when you don't have anything?

CHARLES: Be ashamed.

DR. WHEELER: Why are you ashamed?

CHARLES: Because I don't have the money.

Not all rural programs suffer from such parsimony. Over a ten-year period, 1957-67, the federal government spent more than $55 billion to maintain farmers and prop up the food industry. If those large sums didn't make much dent on rural poverty it's because the money didn't go to the poor. It went to the rich, and to the middle class.

The biggest and most expensive venture is the subsidy arrangement in which farmers are paid not to grow food and other commodities. That runs better than $3 billion a year. Most of it is given as aid to middle-class farmers, but about a billion a year goes to those who range from the substantially solvent to the downright rich.

About 90,000 farmers of quite comfortable means receive annual subsidies of $5,000 or more. A select group of some 16,000 receive $25,000 and up. Formerly there was also a very select circle of big farm corporations which were each paid a million dollars or more a year. Congress has imposed limits now, establishing a ceiling of $55,000 per farmer per crop, but even so, the nation continues to spend vastly more for empty fields than it allocates for empty stomachs. The average unemployed farm hand receives in food stamp aid only $1 for every $50 that the average middle class farmer receives for not growing food. Between the farm poor and rich farmers the aid disparity is more than five hundred to one. A report issued in 1968 as Hunger, U.S.A., illustrated state-by-state how Congress and the Department of Agriculture collaborate in care of the farmers, and neglect of hungry (TABLE 11).

Probably the poor would complain of such welfare division even if the big subsidies didn't come out of their pockets. As it stands, they can contend justly enough that they are being strained heavily to support the system. For one thing, the direct and intended result of the subsidies is to force food prices up, and that hits the hungry where they live. For another, the aim is accomplished by taking acreage out of production, and that hamstrings the man who is trying to earn a living by farm labor. Currently some 35 million acres are lying idle under subsidy contracts.

It may well be that some type of farm subsidy is required in

TABLE 11

Farm Subsidies and Food Supplement Programs, Comparative Costs

U.S. DEPARTMENT OF AGRICULTURE PAYMENTS TO SUBSIDIZE FARMERS AND FEED THE HUNGRY—BY STATES REPRESENTED ON THE SENATE AGRICULTURAL APPROPRIATIONS SUBCOMMITTEE

State	Senator	Population	Total Agricultural Payments for One Year to Producers Receiving $5,000 or more from Federal Government	Total Food Assistance Monies for One Year	Percent of Population Receiving Agricultural Payments of $5,000 or more	Percent of Population in Poverty
Alabama	Lister Hill	3,266,740	17,646,689	8,331,193	.048	39.1
Arizona	Carl Hayden	1,302,161	38,224,264	3,879,900	.035	21.3
Florida	S. L. Holland	4,951,560	6,645,323	4,412,800	.0065	28.4
Georgia	R. B. Russell	3,943,166	21,250,326	4,593,804	.05	35.6
Louisiana	A. J. Ellender	3,257,022	21,986,600	5,304,747	.048	35.6
Mississippi	Eastland & Stennis	2,178,141	68,393,171	19,776,848	.16	51.6
Nebraska	R. L. Hruska	1,411,330	35,836,429	957,631	.31	26.1
New York	J. K. Javits	16,782,304	857,624	21,100,400	.0006	13.8
N. Dakota	M. R. Young	632,446	31,160,615	1,011,428	.62	28.8
S. Dakota	K. E. Mundt	680,514	13,787,046	1,283,800	.25	33.5
Texas	R. W. Yarborough	9,579,667	249,247,483	7,487,621	.02	28.8
Vermont	G. D. Aiken	389,881	000	589,800	.0	23.1
Wisconsin	Wm. Proxmire	5,951,777	3,210,990	2,977,117	.009	17.4
Wyoming	G. W. McGee	330,066	3,375,283	506,835	.112	16.5

SOURCE: Hunger, U.S.A. A Report by the Citizens Board of Inquiry into Hunger and Malnutrition in the United States, New Community Press, Washington, D.C., 1968.

the general national interest. The observations made here are addressed to the question of a balanced policy. Surely, that is lacking. The poor are hungry, and the rich are paid huge sums to not raise food. The society is confronted with desperate problems in the explosive ghettos, and the government is going to great expense to drive more people into those wretched warrens. In the zealous concern over surplus commodities we have helped to create surplus people.

On the "Hunger in America" documentary referred to earlier a black woman named Mrs. Carlile described all this as seen from the bottom. She and her husband and their fourteen children and grandchildren were hanging on in a sharecropper's shack. They were farmers no longer allowed to farm, and so they went hungry with a fertile earth beneath their feet. They were too poor to take advantage of aid to the poor. Mrs. Carlile had no statistics at her command, and her horizon stretched only to the edge of the field, but she knew exactly where she was at and what that was like. In a dialogue with Dr. Wheeler she summed it up about as well as any study commission ever has:

DR. WHEELER: Mrs. Carlile, why don't you raise your own food?

MRS. CARLILE: Well, we raise what we can. We raise that okra, we raise all stuff like that in the garden, when we can, but not no corn. That's the only food we can grow.

DR. WHEELER: Why no corn?

MRS. CARLILE: Because we don't have no corn acres.

DR. WHEELER: What do you mean?

MRS. CARLILE: The landlord said he sold the corn acres to the Government. And we can't have no corn.

DR. WHEELER: So then who plants the corn?

MRS. CARLILE: Don't nobody plants none. Just the land for the corn it lays up and it's nothing.

DR. WHEELER: The land's there.

MRS. CARLILE: That's right.

DR. WHEELER: But nobody plants it.

MRS. CARLILE: That's right. Can't plant it, when you sell it to the Government. Whoever sell it get a check off it. Can't raise nothing on it. Just have to stay there. I've always been raised on corn. Having corn raised hogs, chickens, turkeys. But I can't raise them 'cause I don't have food to feed them. I can't raise corn and I can't buy it.

DR. WHEELER: Now that you can buy food stamps, aren't you able to get more food for your family?

MRS. CARLILE: I can't buy them every two weeks because I don't have the money. I don't have the thirty-three dollars every two weeks. I don't have anybody to get it from. My husband don't make but three dollars and a half a day for the city and that's all. He don't make over twenty, twenty-two, or twenty-three dollars a week and I couldn't get the food stamps. They sets the price what they want you to pay and if you ain't got that price, why, you don't get no food stamps. But I just have to go along with it because I can't do no better.

To Mrs. Carlile it seemed improbable that all her troubles were the result of accident or oversight. There had to be some reason for it, and she thought she knew what the reason was:

MRS. CARLILE: None of them white people—they don't care how you live. You can work for them all right but the livin' problems, they don't care too much for it.

DR. WHEELER: Why's that?

MRS. CARLILE: They don't treat us like they used to treat us. They did used to treat us a lot better than they do now. But they don't do it, and I imagine—I feel like it's because the children go to school together and do a little voting, something we never have did. . . . And the younger group can speak a little more clear and a little more for themselves than we used to could. That's why the young people is leaving, leaving home, going North. . . . But, see, the older people, we still here in it. We ain't like the young ones. I figure they don't care whether we go or stay.

DR. WHEELER: Why do you think they don't care?
MRS. CARLILE: I know they don't care. I don't have to think
they don't care. I know they don't care.

It's difficult to quarrel with Mrs. Carlile's analysis. And yet,
curiously, it is possible to tour the South and come away feeling
hope. The reasons lie not in what is but what might be, and in
the kind of people who are trying to make it happen.

Some remarkable leaders have emerged from the southern turmoil. They are civil rights veterans for the most part but they
have long since moved on to broader political and economic
action. Some of them are running farm or factory cooperatives.
Some are building power bases in city halls and courthouses
where a few years ago they couldn't register to vote. But they
don't talk much about black power. Green power interests them
more.

They are tough and practical men, and they have witnessed
just about every kind of disaster, and they remain hard to dis-
courage. They have a vision. They think they can turn the rural
South around.

Whether they can or not remains to be seen. They are in any
case trying, and that represents something new in most of the
places where they work. It is worth pausing to inspect their
efforts before moving on to the ghetto scenes. The success or
failure of these new style rural progressives may, in fact, have
quite a lot to do with how the cities fare in the 1970s.

Chapter 5

THE CO-OP
MOVEMENT

The answer is not in Chicago.
> —Southern blacks define
> a position.

"WE can't cuss white people anymore. It's in our hands now."
That's Charles Evers talking, and what's in his hands is Fayette, Mississippi. He's the first black mayor in Mississippi since Reconstruction.

Only a bold and resourceful man would want the job. Fayette is a two-stoplight town (pop. 1,700) but within those small confines it distills and concentrates all the problems of the region. A third of its adults are functionally illiterate. Two-thirds of its young men are so physically or socially debilitated that they can't meet the draft board standards for military service. And, of course, nearly all of its people are poor. There are only three poorer places in the nation.

As though that were not enough, a violent shadow hangs over Evers. His brother Medgar was a civil rights martyr, shot down from behind, and his own life has been threatened repeatedly. He routinely carries a gun.

He's a rough-edged, combative man but he bears no grudges, not even against Mississippi. A few years ago after losing a congressional election he startled his white opponent by walking into the latter's headquarters, sticking out his hand, and saying: "Congratulations. I'll do anything I can to help you. Just remember, we're all Mississippians."

When he was elected mayor the village whites wouldn't attend his inauguration but he addressed them in absentia, beginning his speech with "Grandsons of former slaves, and grandsons of former slave owners." He reassured the whites that "We won't treat you the way you treated us." And then he assured them that "You aren't going to treat us that way any more."

Evers has neatly reversed an old southern attitude. He understands his white folks. Indeed, he likes them. They need a couple of lickings, he says in effect, but after that he expects that blacks and whites can get along fine.

He is not obsessively concerned as to just when that understanding comes about. When the whites are ready, he's ready. Meantime he's got important things to do. Fayette needs schools, hospitals, parks and above all industry payrolls. To Mississippi whites, Evers may seem a radical, but when he goes on national tour he is a chamber of commerce promoter trying to corral a textile mill or a chemical plant. Fayette desperately needs something like that.

Rarefied idealists might write Evers off as a man already corrupted by the establishment. He would no doubt reply that he was never corrupted by that kind of idealism. He sought power in order to use it and he represents a constituency that can't afford a lofty alienation. "The time for raising hell has about passed," he told a reporter recently. "We got to do our fightin' on the inside with the ballot and the dollar. We can't lose our cool and destroy what we've gained. Oh yes, we've accomplished something. And we're gonna be part of this country—nobody can stop us."

All over the South there are others like him. Not exactly like him, of course—men of his size and style don't come in bunches —but one encounters many who share a common outlook and tone. Some of them are gaining power. In less than four years the number of southern blacks holding political office has risen from 72 to more than 400.

How much can they accomplish? No miracles, but then part of their strength is that most of them don't expect any. They've traveled too hard a road to have easy illusions. They are visibly changing the South, however, and they take pride in their hardearned gains. "Those cats up North don't know anything but *burn*," an Alabama black told this reporter. "We're way ahead. We're building."

Such observations should not suggest that southern blacks are euphoric, or easily mollified with a few crumbs from the national table. The rural South in particular stands in need of immense transformation, and no one knows it better than the people on the ground. Why, then, should some of the most desolate places produce men who still have faith in progress? Several answers seem in order.

One reason is that rural problems are inherently more soluble than those of the city, simply because rural life is scaled to far more manageable human dimensions. If Mayor Evers can install a single fair-sized textile plant in Fayette he may raise the average family income as much as 400 percent. Mayor Kenneth Gibson in Newark can envision no such solution for his city's crowded ghetto.

Another factor is that hope seems related not so much to absolute conditions as to relative change. Southern blacks measure their position in terms of where they're at, but also where they've been, and they can see movement. They can at least express their aspirations through their own leaders and for many of them, that's new. The momentum thus acquired will not last indefinitely—not unless it yields tangible results—but for the present it is a critical element.

And finally, the southern blacks have behind them the special experience of the civil rights struggle. Frantz Fanon has advanced the now familiar theory that colonial or subject people must purge themselves of self-doubt and submission through the bloody catharsis of revolution. Certainly it is true that a revolution can stir passionate commitment, raise up heroes, and create useful myths. The long march for civil rights seems to have had the same effect on many southern blacks, producing not only the moral but the emotional equivalent of war.

All through the South one meets quite ordinary men who have known their extraordinary moment. They were well up front the day the Selma marchers tested will and courage against tear gas and billy clubs. Or they faced down Bull Connor and his police dogs at Birmingham. Or they took their stand at one of the hundreds of lesser known encounters that were just as brutal, and just as important to the people involved. Such veterans have gone on to become community leaders in the new era, and one does not hear from them any echo of the ghetto cry about the need to establish manhood. They have settled that point to their own absolute satisfaction.

All this has created a breed of men who are proud, tough, highly political, and above all, humanistic. They see their enemies as human, too, the product of circumstance, and in their self-confidence they are able to extend a measure of tolerance. They hate poverty, and discrimination they will not accept, but as to race prejudice, that's the white man's hang-up—and the white man will just have to get over it the best way he can.

They believe that whites can make it, at least in the South. After all, the races have long lived in intimacy there, however peculiar the rules, and so it's just a question of whites accepting the fact that the rules have changed.

Of course, not all southern blacks would subscribe to those attitudes. Neither races nor regions can be categorized under a single label, and the southern experience has brought forth a full range of black response from apathy to commitment to total rejection and nihilistic rage. There remains, however, a distinct southern style; it's in the optimistic tradition of Populist striving and it draws strength from a deep attachment to the native soil. *New York Times* reporter Joseph Lelyveld discussed the point with Evers, observing: "You've always said you think Mississippi will one day be way ahead of the country [in race relations]."

Replied Evers: "I know so."

He may be right. In any case, new forces are loose in a region long resistant to change.

The other main thrust among southern blacks comes from the formation of co-ops. Groups have sprung up in Alabama, Mississippi, Louisiana, Virginia, Georgia, the Carolinas. Most of them are rural ventures, either farm or village, and all are addressed to a grass roots struggle for economic survival.

The co-ops make candy and toys, stitch quilts, operate woodworking shops, raise hogs, market truck crops and run communal farms. One of the most ambitious efforts is a community operated textile mill. Thanks to foundation backing and federal loans some co-ops have expanded into considerable enterprises.

The leaders are black, but whites are often present as friends of the movement, and race attitudes among the participants are about as relaxed as one can find in America today. There is, however, plenty of conflict. That's usually furnished by the local white community and it is not surprising. Visit a co-op and you'll often find that the area has been the scene of a hard-fought civil rights confrontation. Frequently, that's how the co-op began, and the old segregationist foes continue to view it with deep suspicion long afterwards. The old-line southern whites are nursing psychologic wounds, still adjusting to the shock of change, and besides they really can't believe that all those rabble-rousing radicals have suddenly developed a passionate interest in growing cucumbers. They just know it's a front for something.

In fact, the co-ops are just what they seem. Civil rights has become a secondary question, poverty is the big issue now, and

the activists have turned to do-it-yourself experiments in the rehabilitation of blighted areas. Of course, there are political implications—common economic interests are easily converted into a
political base—but right now most co-op leaders are playing that
aspect down. They have a tough struggle on their hands, and
they don't want to stir up more opposition than they've already
got.

Now and then a quixotic note appears. One black sweet potato
co-op fell briefly under the influence of a white New Left roman-
tic; he propounded the doctrine that grading produce for quality
was a capitalist device to defraud the people. That was an expensive fling. Another co-op became so imbued with communal
spirit that the president provided blank, signed checks for the
convenience of the staff. That, too, proved costly. Most of the
mistakes, however, can be marked off as the kind that might be
expected from enthusiastic amateurs. Co-op founders are by nature visionaries and risk-takers and such qualities do not always
combine with a tidy approach to double entry bookkeeping.
Moreover, these ventures are operating of necessity in places
which private enterprise has abandoned as hopeless. Inevitably,
many co-ops flounder from crisis to crisis. The encouraging news
is that somehow most of them stay alive.

The more realistic leaders do not see the cooperative as a
panacea. Here and there if things go well a co-op will survive
and flourish and offer its workers a decent living. For the larger
task of rebuilding the region, the co-op resources cannot possibly
suffice. The men involved know that, but still they regard their
work as far more than a token effort. They see themselves as
constructing pilot models, demonstrating to both government
and business what can be done. They believe that sooner or later
the country will have to make some real attempt to solve the
problem. When that time comes they intend to have some blue-
prints ready.

One of the biggest and most interesting of the co-ops is an organization called SWAFCA. The name has an exotic ring; from the sound it might be some militant secret society, perhaps with an African connotation. Actually, however, SWAFCA stands, quite prosaically, for Southwest Alabama Farmers Cooperative Association. Its business is truck farming, and it radiates out from Selma, Alabama, to embrace a sprawling ten-county area of Alabama's black belt.

SWAFCA could stand well enough as a case history of the cooperative movement. It was born out of the tumult of the Selma-to-Montgomery march in 1965. It has since survived investigations, boycotts and endless harassments, and along the way it has grown from eight hundred to two thousand members. Most of its participants are family heads, which means that it's helping to support some twelve thousand people.

It has been assisted by about $1 million in federal grants and loans. That sounds like a considerable sum until it's broken down. Over the period covered it came to about $500 a year per member, or about a tenth of the subsidy that is routinely paid to middle-class farmers.

SWAFC's economic role is simply stated. Intensive truck farming brings in a high cash return per acre, and so offers survival to those who can provide a little land and a lot of labor. In the SWAFCA plan each member works his own tract, employing the co-op for mass marketing of produce and the wholesale purchase of seed and fertilizer.

As a practical matter a hard working family can handle three acres, turning the earth to successive same-year crops of cucumbers, peas and turnips. They may raise as much as 60,000 pounds of produce, and earn from it $3,000. The goal seems modest enough but it amounts to double the accustomed income of most co-op members. It represents also a degree of independence from the big landowners. The latter became the critical

point after the Selma march, as landlords began evicting the
blacks in economic reprisal. That's when and why SWAFCA was
formed.

One of the founders was Joe Johnson. He had been active in
voter registration, and it had nearly cost him his life. He was
confronted in the fields one day by a gun-waving white neighbor
who threatened to blow out his brains.

"I just stood there," Johnson says of that affair, "and I looked
at him awhile, and then I walked on off. The way I felt at that
particular moment I didn't care whether he killed me or not."

Johnson is also a firsthand expert on the subject of rural poverty. He is a man in his early fifties and he is struggling to raise
the last of his eight children on a tenant farming income of less
than $500. He owns neither automobile nor telephone. Despite
those handicaps he proved such a natural leader that he was
named the co-op's first president. When the other members
needed to reach him they left word with his brother Mike who
lives some two miles away.

The communications problem was by no means confined to
Johnson. The first board of directors numbered twenty men, and
nineteen of them lacked phones. Yet they put together an organization covering more than 10,000 square miles.

The director with the phone was Freeman Berry. He cannot
read or write. He observes that "my schooling was in the fields."
When he was six years old he began plowing behind a steer,
using a special harness rigged by his father, and he has been
plowing for sixty years since.

He has taught himself the things he had to know. He learned
to print his name, so that he could obtain a driver's license, and
with the aid of dominoes he became adept at doing arithmetic in
his head. He recalls proudly that once he handled a church
collection and when some question arose as to the amount he
was able to figure it faster in his head than the bank teller could
do it with pencil and paper. His other pride is that in his prime

he could pick three hundred pounds of cotton a day, half again more than an ordinary man.

He is also the father of twenty-two children, including "eight in the house." He has raised all the others while saving enough to acquire a seventy-acre farm. Recently he presented his wife Tina with their finest possession, a kitchen and bathroom with hot and cold running water. Before that the huge family made do with the outhouse, the pump and the zinc tubs for bathing.

Mrs. Berry was in the Selma demonstrations. When she joined a beleaguered voter registration line at the courthouse it was the first time she had ever entered that building except to pay taxes. Berry didn't march or demonstrate but when SWAFCA began he volunteered. He put 3,000 miles on his old truck and wore out a set of tires as he drove up and down the black belt spreading the word.

Some civil rights organizers pitched in to help with the recruiting. One of those was Albert Turner, the thirty-two-year-old state director of Southern Christian Leadership Conference. Turner is a rare type, a college-trained son of a black belt Negro farmer. As one of the educated few he could have escaped, but he chose instead to fight it out on his home ground. He became an unpaid, unofficial consultant to the fledgling co-op.

And then there was Shirley Mesher. She is not of the local community, and her presence is especially rankling to SWAFCA's foes. Miss Mesher is white. She is a young woman from Seattle, a one-time public relations agent and high fashion merchandiser, who came to Selma "to furnish a body for the march." It proved so profound an experience that she stayed on to work with the black community.

For a time she picked cotton in order to meet the people and learn their problems. She often conducted impromptu organizing sessions in the fields. Now she's a woman of all work in SWAFCA's operation, but she's not on the payroll. She shares the lot of the black poor, living from one family to another.

Miss Mesher is a hard-nosed idealist, or realist-idealist as she puts it, and she disclaims any self-sacrificing motive. "Money," she says, "I can always make. I'm doing this because I need to do it."

The local whites in Selma do not believe Miss Mesher. They are quite sure she's a white panther.

SWAFCA was formally launched in January, 1967, and it's been a battle ever since. The first big round was over money. The O.E.O. offered an initial grant of nearly $400,000 but the late Governor Lurleen Wallace stepped in to block the funds. Every senator and congressman from Alabama threw his weight against the project. The O.E.O. wavered for months, then finally overrode the objections, but meantime SWAFCA almost died aborning. It was a question of fertilizer. Each member needed about $40 worth to prepare the fields, the co-op possessed neither funds nor credit, and while the government hesitated, the season was rolling around. In desperation SWAFCA negotiated some small foundation loans and plunged ahead.

There was a close race to raise the money, and then a scramble to find someplace to spend it. No one in Selma would sell to SWAFCA. Finally they located a small rural dealer who indicated wary interest in the transaction. Turner recalls it as marking the moment when Alabama Negroes flexed an economic muscle and made it felt.

"We walked in waving a check," he says. "We told that cat we had twenty-five thousand dollars for fertilizer and we were gonna buy it somewhere. The man decided he'd better talk."

Berry remembers the same turning point from a farmer's view. "It was time to start working the fields," he says, "and that's something that can't wait. The members were getting very shaky. I kept going around, telling them to hang on a little longer, we were going to make it. Some, I know, did not believe me. Then that first big carload of fertilizer rolled in, and they began to believe."

About ten weeks later, cucumbers were rolling in by the ton. SWAFCA by now had a packing shed, a ramshackle rented building equipped with a borrowed conveyor belt machine for sorting and grading. The facilities were so swamped that some staff members worked twenty-four-hour shifts, getting the stuff out before it spoiled.

Local packers wouldn't buy their produce, and so they trucked it to northern markets. Then suddenly at the height of the season they were almost wiped out. All their orders were cancelled. A local processor had called his trade associates to claim unfair competition. He claimed that the farmers were under contract to him.

It hit on a Monday morning, at a time when SWAFCA had a semi-trailer almost loaded and ready to go. Co-op salesmen tried desperately to locate a diversion market, but the response everywhere was the same. The pickle industry had closed ranks. The load of cucumbers sat in the yards, rotting under a blazing sun. Turner tells what happened next:

"We got on the phone, and we did what we know how to do best. We called all our brothers in civil rights. We called the FBI, the Justice Department, the Department of Agriculture. We talked about anti-trust suits, and we promised to raise a stink that would be smelled a lot farther than those cucumbers. In five days we broke that boycott wide open.

"It was expensive," he adds. "We lost thousands of dollars on the spoiled produce, but we gained respect. Those packers found out that we can reach some people who have long arms."

That was the first year. The second year they had crop failures, always a hazard in farm enterprises, and they endured flank attacks from political foes. The third year brought difficulties of their own making. They had applied for an $850,000 federal expansion loan and a government auditor checked their books. He found that an office employee had apparently diverted money to a highly questionable account. SWAFCA fired the man, and was able to reclaim all but a few thousand dollars, but even so it was a hard blow. The co-op's opponents made maximum use of the scandal. What was worse, the auditor declared the bookkeeping and general office procedure to be a shambles. He recommended that the government refuse further assistance.

William Harrison, a farmer and schoolteacher, is now SWAFCA president, and he has stepped in to take personal charge of the office. He concedes mistakes, and says they are being corrected. He adds, "We have been through crisis before, and we are still in business. We'll stay in business. We are going to make it." And quite possibly they will. They are over-expanded and under-capitalized, and they are engaged in a high-risk business, but they have some assets, too. Chiefly they have a determination and resilience which has already carried them farther than anyone thought they could go.

All that struggle and effort have been expended to raise their people to a level which is just about at the poverty line. To SWAFCA's members, however, that seems well worth it. Mere poverty is better than hunger. Freeman Berry says of the co-op: "If the black people will just stick together, and pull together, and work together, SWAFCA is the best proposition in this county since I've been old enough to remember."

Adds Turner: "Our goal is to keep these people down here, where they know how to live. If they have to walk away from the farm, it's very sad. They don't know anything, they have never done anything, except follow a plow. The answer is not in Chicago."

Other co-op groups are attempting to establish village industries. That effort is potentially addressed to an even larger segment of the rural poor. The approach is exemplified in the work of Randolph Blackwell, the organizer and driving force behind a string of such ventures.

Blackwell is a big, handsome, articulate man who has been involved with the problems of race and poverty almost all his life. His father was a Garveyite, and he recalls that it was a black Christ whose likeness looked down from a wall of the family home. At thirteen he was distributing handbills on behalf of a local black political movement in Greensboro, N. C. As a young man he taught at an Alabama Negro college, and there led one of the early sit-in demonstrations. He marched at the side of the late Dr. Martin Luther King, Jr., as a top-echelon staff member of SCLC, and he has ridden through a hail of bullets while directing a voter registration drive in Mississippi. He can't recall how often he's gone to jail, but he offers an offhand guess that it comes to eight or ten times.

Today Blackwell is conducting rescue operations for the rural poor of both races. Essentially he acts as a kind of broker in ideas and money. He puts together economic self-help programs, recruits local leaders as managers, and drums up government or foundation grants to get them well started. When he feels that an enterprise is sufficiently launched he turns loose of it and moves on to repeat the process somewhere else.

He operates out of a threadbare little two-room office at Atlanta, Georgia. The sign on the door reads Southern Rural Action Project. It's a small organization, existing unsteadily on contributions and lecture fees, and the office staff has been reduced in lean periods to Director Blackwell and a temporary secretary. SRAP has managed nonetheless to generate some impressive examples of rural action. A visit to the office conveys some of the style and manner in which it is done.

When this reporter called, the organization was in the midst of financial crisis. A major backer was phasing out, and it was an open question whether or not support could be found in time to keep things going. The secretary-receptionist had quit, because she couldn't stand the suspense that was regularly associated with payday. A temporary replacement had been installed at the front desk, but she had been there only a day or two, and she was still ill-informed as to what SRAP was about. In response to all questions she nodded toward an open-doored inner office where Blackwell sat with phone to ear, behind a desk awash with correspondence and memos.

If he was unnerved by the difficulties, he didn't show it. He waved the reporter in and proceeded to conduct an instructive one-man seminar on rural circumstances. It was late in the afternoon, but he talked on for an hour or more past closing time, and all the while his phone kept ringing steadily. Invariably it was someone with a problem. Blackwell would push some documents across his desk to occupy his visitor, and then lean back in his chair and handle the phone with the air of a man who enjoys solving problems.

One call involved a rural housing program that Blackwell was trying to promote. It was a turn-key project, an approach that mixes public and private elements. The idea is that the govern-fent builds a housing unit, turns it over to an indigent family, and then meets mortgage payments out of money that would be spent anyway on welfare rent supplements. The householder shares some of the expense and is held accountable for upkeep of the premises; if he fails that obligation, he loses the place and someone else gets the chance. Blackwell argues that such method is cheaper in the long run, that it combats the neglect and abuse which often afflict public housing, and that it creates stability by giving the poor some stake in society. He was trying to sell the federal government on an 800-unit demonstration model in Hancock County, Georgia.

The news that day was bad. One of SRAP's friends in Washington was trying to push an application through the federal maze, and he had called to say that housing officials were balking. The problem of the moment was that the project's local sponsors had failed to specify elaborate construction codes. Blackwell swiveled in his chair, listening impatiently, and then interjected: "Now look," he said, emphasizing his words in the distinctive southern cadence, "We are talking about Hancock County, Georgia. It's 'way down in the piney woods. They don't have plumbing codes down there. They don't have electrical codes. If they had a code, they wouldn't have anyone to enforce it. There's only two or three people in that courthouse, and one of them sweeps it out." There was a sputter of objections over the line, and Blackwell sighed. "All right," he said, "I'll go down there and see if I can get some building codes on the books. You talk to your people in Washington. Try to persuade them that they'll have to be a little more flexible if they want to get things done."

Flexible is the word for Blackwell's operation, and he's imbued with a single-minded determination to get results. In the case of rural housing, he has since abandoned any immediate hope of federal aid, having come to the reluctant conclusion that Washington has no real interest in the matter. He has, however, an alternate approach. SRAP is currently sponsoring poor people's construction firms which utilize new building techniques to provide low-cost housing. Plants tailored to that purpose are currently operating in Wilcox County, Alabama, and Mt. Bayou, Mississippi, with another scheduled for Worth County, Georgia. The houses produced are basically brick-faced prefabricated units; a four-bedroom model can be built for $8,500, and has been appraised at a market value of $14,000.

The house in question meets modest middle-class standards, which means that it is immeasurably better than most of the rural poor have ever known. It can be financed for less than $50 a month. But even that outlay, of course, requires a dependable income. To achieve such an end, SRAP has gone into half a dozen communities to establish local industries.

The industries are primarily textile mills, and most are co-ops, though both those factors are incidental to the over-all approach. "It can be any one of a thousand income-producing things," says

Blackwell. "The main idea is to produce income. Real income—not grants. You run to the end of grants. The enterprise has got to compete, show a profit, and make enough to support its people. We refuse to touch a project here if it doesn't have a real possibility of continuing existence."

The co-op emphasis does not preclude private industry. SRAP has been a prime mover in forging a textile manufacturing association whose member plants are about half co-op and half privately owned. The common denominator is that all are small mills operating in poverty-ridden rural communities. The theory is that a loose knit merger will improve their economic position, and therefore their employment potential. Thus no one of the plants is large enough to afford a salesman. By pooling orders they can maintain a sales force, and bid jointly on big contracts. Similarly, they can hire a production engineer to serve their common needs. They can share expensive, specialized equipment by shuttling it back and forth as occasion requires. There are eight small mills involved, scattered through South Carolina, Georgia and Alabama, and Blackwell believes that association benefits can triple their payrolls.

Southern Rural Action Project seeks also a working alliance between the black and white poor. A victory for that policy occurred after Blackwell set up a textile co-op for poor blacks at Crawfordville, Georgia. Word of it got around to Blue Ridge, Georgia, a community of poor whites, and the people there asked Blackwell's help in establishing a plant of their own. It was perhaps the first time in Georgia history that whites solicited the leadership of a black man. The Blue Ridge co-op was successfully launched, and later its members showed their gratitude. They had acquired by then some experience at a specialized textile operation, and when Crawfordville picked up a contract of the same nature the Blue Ridge co-op sent some people over to demonstrate the techniques involved. To Blackwell, and to co-op leaders generally, this gesture represents something more than sentimental affirmation of race brotherhood. If the white and black poor can be united in common interest, they will constitute an important coalition for change.

SRAP can be described then as color blind, non-ideologic in the broad sense, and devoted to the old-fashioned idea that the best solution to poverty is gainful employment. "We want our people to turn away from the traditional welfare concept," Blackwell says. "We want them to demand real opportunity. And we are saying to government, to business, to foundations, to anyone who cares: 'There is a community of decent, hard-working people who are starving to death. If you will assist us, we can make that community fruitful.' We believe we can offer some attractive models."

SRAP puts its philosophy to hard tests. It goes into places few others would touch. One example is the textile mill which Blackwell helped to launch at Crawfordville, in Taliaferro County, Georgia.

Taliaferro County is another of those disaster areas. The average adult resident has less than a grade school education, and about a fourth are in the category of zero to four years. When a recent survey was taken, not a single county resident was attending college. It's among the 100 poorest counties in the United States, with a median family income of $35 a week. The population is down to some 3,000, which is less than it had when it was founded in 1865. At the last tabulation it was still losing people at a rate of some 200 a year.

It is also a place heavily mortgaged to all the traditions and myths of the old South. Confederate Vice-President Alexander Stephens had his plantation here and his mansion still stands at the edge of Crawfordville, carefully preserved as a museum and shrine. When civil rights came to Crawfordville the resistance was as harsh as any in the South. The town's whites still nurse emotional scars from that battle. The blacks have gone on to other things.

The drama of Crawfordville is embodied in the person of Calvin Turner. He's lived every part of the modern story, including the migration. As a young man he went to Chicago and took a job in a starch factory. He made more money than he ever had before but he gave it up and returned home for a country man's reason. He thought Chicago was a terrible place to raise children.

Turner became a teacher at the local black school and then was fired for organizing a voter registration drive. It touched off a protest which escalated into demands for school desegregation. The fight was bitter, all the more so because it was conducted in a little crossroads town where the participants on both sides had known each other all their lives. The whites waded into the demonstrators with clubs. The blacks threw their bodies in front of the whites-only school bus, men, women and children lying down in the road to block its passage.

It dragged on into a two-year siege. Turner recalls it as "two years of hunger and fear. Times when there was no food in the house. Times when the lights were turned off, and no money to turn them on." Many a night he sat in a darkened house with his wife and children, waiting for the bomb or bullet that never came. He felt that he could not show even such small sign of weakness as seeking refuge in another house.

"They were bound and determined to run me out," he says. "And I had made up my mind that I would not run."

SCLC supported the Crawfordville movement and offered Turner a staff job. That's when he made a really tough decision. He turn it down.

"If I had gone with them," he said, "I'd have become just another outside organizer. Not that I have anything against that, but I didn't feel I had any special talent for it. Whatever strength

I have is on my home ground. This is my place, and these are my people."

Eventually the blacks won their school fight, though it proved an ironic victory. The whites packed all their youngsters off to a private school, and the blacks took over an officially "desegregated" public school. Turner went on to a second and more difficult fight, an effort to do something about Crawfordville's wretched poverty.

With the aid of SCLC he set up a small company engaged in silk screen printing. That's a technique for printing words or symbols on such items of apparel as school jerseys. It was, says Turner, a shade tree operation. In southern parlance, that's an outfit that could be housed comfortably under a tree. The capitalization was on that order, too, and in about six months it folded.

SRAP stepped in then with some new money that Blackwell obtained from private foundations. It was shoe-string financing, $10,200 to start, and on that the Crawfordville poor launched the desperately optimistic venture of a textile mill. It's a story heard often on the co-op circuit; they gambled that once started, they could pick up support enough to keep going until they made some money.

The initial work force consisted of Turner and twenty-six women. The women were mostly middle-aged with previous experience as domestics and field hands; none of them had ever worked in a plant before. "We said to one of them, 'You're going to be the floor lady,'" Blackwell recalls. "She had never seen the machines. We said to another, 'You're the inspector.' She had never heard the word."

For a plant they had a big, rambling old log building which stands about a mile or so down the road from the Stephens mansion. Like the mansion it is a symbol of the old South. The other old South. Blackwell says of the building's history: "Back about fifty years ago when the Negroes had no school they went back in the woods and built one for themselves out of hand-hewn logs." It served as a schoolhouse until the 1950s, then stood abandoned until they moved the plant in.

They hired a textile expert as consultant and trainer. He expected the training to take at least six weeks but after two weeks they were filling some small orders. Within two months they had landed their first sizable contract.

They won their gamble with time, stretching out a series of small loans and grants until the O.E.O. came through with some financial support six months later. The O.E.O. application was endorsed by two otherwise disparate public figures who agreed that people in Crawfordville had to make a living somehow. The cosigners: Governor Lester Maddox and the Rev. Martin Luther King, Jr.

The O.E.O. allocated some $212,000: about half of it to finance additional equipment and training and the remainder for a community development program. Turner became director of community development and Robert Billingsley stepped in as plant manager. Billingsley is another ex-school teacher who came up through the civil rights route.

When this reporter paid a call, Crawfordville Enterprises was about eighteen months old. It had expanded to some sixty employees, the biggest payroll in the county by far, and they had opened a second operation, a woodworking plant for men. It was housed in a converted barn, with the office stashed away in what had been a corn crib.

The textile mill was about to evolve from the primitive stage. They were planning to leave the log house for a new cement building they were putting up on a fifty-two-acre plot. They had dreams of turning that into a combined housing development and industrial park.

The Community Development program had provided them with Head Start and day-care centers for young children, and Upward Bound for would-be college students. The town had retained a third of its last high school graduating class, the best record in years, and three or four of their young people had gone off to college.

It would be agreeable to leave the story there: a bootstrap saga in which the poorest of the poor achieved through great effort their modest dream. However, a telephone check a year later disclosed that things hadn't gone that well. The woodworking plant didn't make it. The textile plant was not flourishing. They had committed the errors of optimism, expanding too fast, underpricing some contracts, and overestimating the speed with which they could bring all their workers up to full industrial efficiency. They had reorganized again, passing from SRAP's aegis to the status of an SCLC foundation, and they were still precariously dependent on grants. They had cut their payroll back to about what it had been at the start. They were in a sense starting all over again, though they were still the county's leading industry.

If Crawfordville cannot be called a success story, neither is it a failure. They have kept hope alive, and some of their people are working. In Crawfordville, that's a gain.

Some other bootstrap efforts have flourished. In Lincolnton, Georgia, SRAP helped to launch the Twilight Sewing Plant, a cooperative enterprise of the Twilight Improvement Association of Lincoln County. The name is explained by the association secretary, Norris Gumby, who observed: "For years the Negro has been living in darkness. Now there is some light, at least enough light for us to see the way. Sort of like at twilight."

The Lincolnton co-op seems to be over the hump. They are meeting production quotas, hiring forty or fifty people, and making money. They have a contract with one of the nation's major clothing distributors.

The co-op movement is viewed by some observers as a new capitalism, a device that will allow the poor to become not just wage earners but shareholders in the industrial system. That small miracle is happening here and there but as to a general co-op solution, this reporter is not that optimistic. At least not under present conditions. It requires quite remarkable efforts to bring it off.

The movement is nonetheless important, if only for its stubborn adherence to an idea of large sweep and dazzling simplicity. Namely, that if an economic base is needed and does not exist, it is possible to create it.

The general society has, of course, long operated on this principle. The co-ops are merely trying to extend it.

As a case in point, the government decided some forty years ago that society had a stake in the continued existence of a 180-acre family farmer. It was easily accomplished, by granting him a subsidy that offset his disadvantage in the market place.

The government has not discerned any social advantage in the continued existence of a thirty-acre family farmer. That occurred to Freeman Berry, who cannot read or write, and to Joe Johnson, who has no telephone, and together they and some others like them put together an organization that might save a thousand farmers or so. With luck they'll make it. If they could trade benefits with the middle-class farmer they wouldn't need the luck.

In similar fashion the government has long since discovered how to create, sustain or encourage an industry whenever that is thought to be in the general interest. It's done with land grants, tariff protections, tax concessions, cost-plus contracts, outright subsidies, special arrangements of every kind. In a word, money. It has been applied to aerospace industry, defense industry, oil industry, transportation industry and innumerable others.

Economic advantages are not created in order to sustain villages as part of a balanced national whole. New industry, private or co-op, could be channeled to stricken areas readily enough if the incentives were there. As it is, Blackwell is trying to accomplish it with a telephone, a typewriter, a gift of persuasion and a

considerable fund of ideas. On occasion he induces the government to back him up with small grants or loans.*

The irony is that eventually society is forced to deal with
the human consequences, and does expend considerable sums.
The effect, however, is always too little, in part because it is too
late. If rural industries were financed at anything like $3,000 a
year per poor family served, it would be a pretty plush operation.
When the city sustains a welfare family on $3,000 a year it is a
disaster.

The lack of a rural policy precludes urban solutions at almost
any price. Blackwell puts it thus: "If we spend billions on the
cities, and if we ignore the rural scene, then the bigger the
program the more it must be self-defeating. It can only draw more
and more poor people into the slums.

"The cities can't stand that kind of pressure," he says. "The
poor people can't stand it either."

* In the first 5 years of the War on Poverty the O.E.O. supported rural
co-ops with loans totaling $14.7 million. Private loans were also made to permit
capital improvements in farms and business ventures. The program reached
about one percent of the rural poor.

The first black slaves arrived on our shores before the *Mayflower*. Through more than two-thirds of the nation's history the black Americans were bought, sold, and even raffled off like so much livestock. (*Above*, a New Orleans horse-and-slave raffle, date unknown, courtesy of the New York Historical Society. *Below*, a slave gang passing the national capitol, an illustration appearing in *Popular History of the U.S.*, by William Cullen Bryant and Sidney Howard Gay, 1888, Library of Congress print.

Reconstruction's failure was summed up in two *Harper's Weekly* wood-cuts published fifteen years apart. In 1867 the print above was captioned, hopefully, "The first vote." In 1882 Thomas Nast drew the illustration below, captioned "One vote less." The campaign of terror which drove black voters from the polls was described bluntly by Senator Benjamin (Pitchfork Ben) Tillman of South Carolina. "We shot them," said Tillman. "We are not ashamed of it."

Mob violence became a general instrument for forcing black freedmen into new forms of subjugation. *Harper's Weekly* illustrated one of the first outbreaks: a New Orleans riot in 1866. A decade later the publication depicted persecuted blacks streaming out of the South in the first exodus, bound for Kansas. The inset drawing compares the migration to the earlier slave flights. (*Courtesy of the New York Historical Society*).

The conditions of rural serfdom were in some respects worse than slavery, for the plantation owner no longer had a proprietary interest in his laborers. The Florida slave cabins shown above were still being used in the 1890s, and they provided better shelter than a typical sharecropper's shack of the 1930s. (*Slave cabins courtesy of the New York Historical Society. South Carolina shack photographed by Carl Mydans, 1936, Farm Security Administration Collection, Library of Congress*).

Segregation evolved as an intricate caste system which defined the roles of the master and the servant race. It could be used to deny blacks a bottle of soda—or an education. The youths shown here in a one-room rural Georgia school are now middle-aged men. (*Storefront photographed by Bob Adelman at Sumter, S.C., 1960. School photo by Jack Delano, 1941, Farm Security Administration Collection, Library of Congress*).

About 1890 blacks began moving to the cities, sharing the slums with the immigrant poor. Jacob Riis photographed the scene above in a New York "black and tan dive" about 1899. (*Courtesy of Museum of the City of New York*).

During World War I the black urban movement swelled to "the great migration" and it was greeted by riots in a score of cities. The black man being stoned to death was one of thirty-eight killed in the Chicago riot of 1919. (*Courtesy of Chicago Historical Society*).

Over the last thirty years the blacks have continued to flock North at a rate of about 100,000 a year. The family above is shown leaving a South Carolina farm home in 1941. The woman waiting in the depot joined the migration in the 1960s. (*Photo above by Jack Delano, Farm Security Administration Collection, Library of Congress. Below, Bob Adelman*).

The migration continues today almost as great as before, but ghetto fertility has become now the larger cause of black population growth in the cities.

The ghetto birthrate is about half again higher than the national average. The population pressure is continually creating new ghettos, like this Bedford-Stuyvesant section of Brooklyn. (*Bob Adelman*).

In the rural South blacks were exploited for their labor. When they came North they found themselves in the worse condition of being unwanted, unneeded. The ghetto unemployment rate is twice as high as the national average, and the disparity for young men is greater still. Sitting on a stoop, waiting for nothing, these young men embody the ghetto's frustration and despair. (*Bedford-Stuyvesant street scene, by Bob Adelman*).

The modern wave of black protest began in the South, and was determinedly peaceful at first. Men marched, singing and praying, enduring assaults from police and mobs, as they sought their elemental rights as human beings. Here blacks withstand a fire-hose assault during a bitter Birmingham, Ala., confrontation in 1963. (*Bob Adelman*).

And then the storm broke. The protests spread from South to North, convulsing the cities in bloody riots. Shown here is the 1967 Newark riot, one of forty major eruptions that occurred that year. The cost in Newark was twenty-three dead, twenty-one of them blacks. The pattern

in other cities was much the same. Blacks attacked property, burning and looting, and whites responded with martial law. The scars of explosion have not healed yet. (*Frank Dandridge, LIFE Magazine,* © *Time, Inc.*).

For two tumultuous decades blacks both South and North have been protesting and demonstrating. Out of it has come the slow forging of Black Power. The picket above compressed his demands into a single eloquent word at the 1963 March on Washington. Below, a Harlem group called Fight Back pickets a New York construction site. (*Above, Bob Adelman. Below, Rhyder McClure, courtesy of Fight Back*).

From the tumult has come also an emerging black pride and confidence which wears many faces. The tangible gains are still limited but even so blacks are beginning to push forward in almost every political and economic area. Black advances in the last decade about equal those of the previous century. (*Photos at top and middle by Rhyder McClure, courtesy of Fight Back. Below, George Gardner*).

In Newark Black Power produced Mayor Kenneth A. Gibson. He regards his city as "a test case. Wherever the cities are going," he says, "Newark will get there first." (*Camera Five*).

Chapter 6

THE CITIES

They riot because they have no hope and nothing to lose.
—Carl Stokes

S INCE 1950 the nation's black population has increased at an average rate of 360,000 a year, and all of it took place in the cities. That is a population stream sufficient to refill the ghettos of Boston every four months, of Newark or Cleveland every year, of Detroit or Philadelphia every two years. The twenty-year increase amounted to three times as many blacks as now inhabit all the sprawling ghettos of New York City.

Rural blacks (farm and small town) started the period with 6.7 million people and ended with 6.6 million, meanwhile maintaining a birth rate sufficient to provide more than three million migrants. The urban population rose from 15 million to 22.4 million.

The city populations were swollen both by migration and natural increase. As late as 1958 the census studies found that half the adult urban blacks were first generation arrivals. That has since shifted dramatically; only a fourth are now new arrivals and ghetto fertility has replaced migration as the chief source of continuing growth. The migration, however, continues almost unabated, adding a still powerful stream.

Late in the 1960s still another movement began as old ghettos burst their seams and blacks began flowing into the suburbs. More than 700,000 people were involved. The pattern of suburban movement is irregular, varying widely from one metropolitan complex to another; the suburbs of New York, Los Angeles and Washington D.C., accounted for a third of the total.

Some of the suburban shift represents blacks escaping from poverty and segregation. Much more of it is simply a case of race and poverty problems spilling over the suburban dams. The ghettos are beginning to export people in the same fashion as the rural South, through economic and population pressures which create an inexorable flow. And the new migrants are finding suburban entry in the same way that earlier waves established themselves in the cities. Black suburban poor wedge in behind the factories, where the highways and train tracks cut through— in all, the least desirable locations. Their arrival stimulates white flight, other blacks move into the vacuum, and a mini-ghetto is formed. Prediction on the short-term evidence now available would be rash but if such trend continues it could well be a major development of the 1970s.*

Blackwell tells a story which catches a human moment in the urban migration. He was in New York City on business one day and he was approached on the street by a gangling, teen-aged

* A new era is reflected also in the NAACP attitude toward suburbanization. Formerly the organization was concerned with entry for the black middle class. Now it is demanding admission of the black poor.

In a recent test action addressed to the question, NAACP threatened to bring suit against the exclusive community of Oyster Bay, Long Island, New York. The point at issue is that Oyster Bay requires every home to be a country estate, set off by several acres of expensive real estate. NAACP contends that this zones out the poor, and thereby interferes with their civil rights.

The threatened suit appears to be a tactical maneuver, aimed mostly at pressuring well-to-do communities into erecting some low-cost housing. The brief, however, raises some large legal and philosophical issues. It could presage a future thorny issue if living space in and around the cities becomes ever more scarce and sought after.

black country boy just off the bus from South Carolina. The
youth had come to the city to live with his father, and he asked
help in finding directions.

"He had with him," said Blackwell, "an envelope bearing his
father's return address in Harlem. The envelope was all crumpled
and stained and yellowed with age. You could see that it had
been tucked away in a drawer for a long time; the postmark
showed that it was seven years old. It was the last letter his father
had written.

"The youth was standing on a downtown street corner,"
Blackwell recalled. "He didn't have any idea that the place he
was looking for was a hundred blocks away. It didn't occur to
him that when he got there he would find a tenement house,
inhabited by transients, with his father long gone, with no one
there knowing who his father was, or where he was, or whether
he was alive or dead. That youngster had no concept of the scale,
the complexity, the *mobility* of life in New York." Blackwell
shook his head at the memory. "I hailed a cab," he added, "and
rode him up to 138th Street, and when we reached the tenement
I pointed to the door and said, 'That's it. Good luck.' It was a
cowardly thing to do, but I just couldn't take the responsibility."

The vignette applies to something more than the difficulties of
one youth adrift in an uncaring city. Over the last generation a
host of rural blacks have arrived in the great urban centers under
circumstances nearly as bleak. In Blackwell's words they have
come "economically and educationally naked. Homesick. Culturally crippled. Ready to rake leaves where there are no trees and
tend yards where there are no yards."

Obviously not all the migrants fit that description, and the
long ghetto travail cannot be ascribed in main part to such circumstances. When the blacks made their first mass trek to the
cities more than half a century ago they were greeted with violence, and their descendants and successors have ever since been
confronted with a huge obstacle of racism. The color line has

barred them in most instances from the union card by which they might have worked a passage from poverty. Until very recently it has shunted into minor business or professional roles those who managed to secure white collar status. It has roped them off into restricted housing areas, always the worst available, to create that prison without walls that is the ghetto.

It remains true that, race aside, the transition from rural fields to urban streets was in itself an undertaking fraught with problems. In many ways it has become more difficult in recent times. Over the last thirty years great numbers of rural refugees have arrived in the city equipped with a grade school education or less, and they have had to compete on a constantly declining market of unskilled blue collar labor.*

The job situation involves a peculiar problem. The modern era of migration has coincided with an economic boom unparalleled in the history of this or any other nation. For a full three decades the boom has rolled on with only brief and relatively minor interruptions. In the last ten years alone the national output of goods and services has almost doubled, from $500 billion to $980 billion. Put another way, the economy grew in ten years as much as it had grown in all the preceding 184 years. It has been, however, a highly specialized growth, one which seemed to provide endlessly expansive room-in-the-middle while almost foreclosing entry from below.

The point is illustrated by inspection of that vital urban job mart, the classified ad section of the Sunday newspaper. On a recent Sunday, the Help Wanted section in *The New York Times* ran to sixty-six pages, totaling some 11,580 column inches. Great swaths of those pages held forth glittering promises of "Challeng-

---

* Some non-racial aspects of rural-urban transition can be seen in Latin America, where dispossessed peons have created large slums around many cities. In Mexico City a medical survey found that the first generation of such migrants suffered a decline from their previous poor standard of living, as measured by nutrition. The second generation recouped the loss, and the third generation began to show gains.

ing Opportunity, Growth Unlimited, $ open." Job-hunting accountants, auditors and controllers could shop that day among 682 column inches of prospective employment. For computer programmers and analysts there were 460 inches of ads, for engineers and electronic specialists 369 inches. A more specialized section ran to more than two feet of type soliciting the services of men capable of directing multi-million-dollar construction projects. There was not, however, a single line which advertised for common labor.

Unskilled men are still employed, of course, but they no longer play a significant role in any major industry. At construction sites, for instance, one used to see muscular workmen wielding shovels, pushing wheel-barrows and hoisting materials. On the big jobs all that is now highly mechanized. Moreover, when the building is completed, mechanization again appears. Elevator men by the thousands have given way to pushbutton self-service systems. In modern buildings even the janitorial chores have been vastly streamlined over the methods of two or three decades ago.

The general demise of unskilled workers is summed up in a survey of factories in thirty-nine major metropolitan areas. The finding: by 1961 the companies were hiring 50 percent more professional people than laborers, and the role of the laborer had been reduced to one job in eighteen. The ranks of the unskilled have since been thinned even more; during the 1960s the number of ghetto men employed as laborers decreased one-fourth, a loss of 70,000 jobs.

The migrants are thus a people twice caught and mangled in the gears of technologic change. Driven from the farm by one set of machines, they have arrived in the city to find other mechanical competitors preempting the work they might have done.

They have found also that industries which might have hired them are deserting the cities. That's due in part to such growing city problems as high taxes and traffic congestion. In part it's simply a reflection of the fact that a plentiful supply of cheap, unskilled labor is no longer an industrial attraction. The net result is that the black poor have bunched up in the cities at a time when 70 to 80 percent of all trade and industrial expansion was taking place in the suburbs.

There is in the economic problem a cruel irony. When other ethnic groups established an urban foothold their labor was harshly exploited. In all the old immigrant ghettos the sweat-shops flourished, extracting grinding toil from men, women and children. The very fact of being exploited, however, gave to the immigrants a latent strength. They were needed. As they acquired numbers and organization they gained bargaining power, because they could always threaten to stop turning the wheel. Today's ghetto poor have no such recourse. They aren't turning any wheels that really matter. That fact may have a great deal to do with the nihilistic rhetoric of some militants. They have concluded that society pays attention only when they threaten to smash the wheel, so that no one can use it.

The bleak portrait just etched does not constitute the whole story. In fact, by shifting the focus it is possible to see the black urban story as one of vigorous upward thrust in recent years. That development began slowly in the 1950s, picked up speed in the early 1960s, and has accelerated markedly over the last five years.

Only a decade ago about two out of five urban blacks were existing below the poverty line. That has been cut in half, to one out of five. Nearly 2.5 million blacks escaped from the bottom ranks of poverty during the 1960s.*

Even more dramatic is the rise of a black middle class. It has largely escaped press and public attention but the middle-income

* The black progress statistics here cited are chiefly drawn from the census special study, "The Social and Economic Status of Negroes in the United States, 1970." Supplemental data is from the 1969 edition of the same report.

urban blacks now comprise a larger group than the hard-core ghetto poor.

Twenty years ago only one black family in fifty received to-day's purchasing power equivalent of $10,000 or more a year. Between 1950 and 1960 this group increased to one out of eleven. It rose again to one out of seven in 1965, and to one out of four in 1970; in the northern and eastern cities it has reached one out of three. It adds up to an increase of some twelve-fold in twenty years, and it is accelerating. The proportion of blacks achieving such income has risen almost as much in the last five years as in the first one hundred years after the Emancipation.

The black-white income ratio is changing, too, though at much slower rate. For a long period blacks averaged just a little over half of white income; their progress depended on what they could extract from that small, fixed share of an expanding economy. In recent times the black share has been creeping up slowly but steadily at about a point a year. Black income in northern and western cities is now about three-fourths of white and one notable breakthrough has occurred. The 1970 census reports provide a profile of young, stable, striving black urban families who are achieving par for the economic course. The group description is age thirty-five or under, husband and wife both present in the household, and both working. In cities of the North and West these people are earning 99 percent of the income enjoyed by their white counterparts. On a national basis both rural and urban the young, two-parent black households have pushed up to 80 percent of comparable white income.

Some of the recent black gains appear tenuous when examined closely, and some contain elements of statistical illusion, as will be noted shortly. Some of the gain, however, is solidly based on progress and change. In the decade just ended the employment of black professional and technical workers soared 131 percent. There was a 67 percent gain among black officials, proprietors and managers, and a 67 percent increase also of foremen and craftsmen. The increase in the combined categories amounted to nearly 750,000 jobs. Such thrust, moreover, is growing stronger. Between 1965 and 1970 black college enrollment nearly doubled, rising from 274,000 to 522,000.

None of this suggests that race prejudice is being rapidly abolished, or poverty dispelled. Nonetheless, something important has happened. Historically, the blacks have long been locked in by a social and economic ice pack that was frozen solid. Now, around the edges, the ice pack is beginning to break up.

Throughout the period of recent advance there remained a hard core of problems which were dissolving either very slowly or not at all. Ghetto unemployment in the 1960s held consistently at about twice the white average, and a third of the employed ghetto men worked at part-time or periodic jobs. There was a rising incidence of families with no wage earners. Welfare rolls were rising, too; in New York the decade produced a staggering case load increase of 600 percent.*

There is in these circumstances no real paradox. The crux of the matter is that the real advances to date have been almost entirely confined to an elite group. These people are mostly young to middle-aged, highly skilled or well educated; they are benefiting from a considerable crumbling of race barriers and they are riding a zestful wave of black pride and power. They account for a hugely disproportionate share of what appears in statistical summaries as a general improvement in the black lot.

Behind them is another group which has experienced gains of a much more tenuous sort. They are middle income, but not middle class. Thus a semi-skilled factory worker and his waitress wife may eke out something approaching an average family income but their position is fragile; it can collapse quickly if either is laid off.

* The welfare increase is more a social than an economic phenomena; it reflects not increased poverty but rather the fact that aid is just beginning to reach many of those in need. We still have a long way to go before touching bottom on that problem. Nationally, less than half the black poor and only one-fifth of the white poor received public assistance in 1969.

At a third level is a large mass that remains stuck about where they always were. They have struggled out of poverty but not very far out; they scratch along as best they can at low-paying, mostly dead-end jobs. They are much the largest of the ghetto groups, and they see no change worth noting in either present comfort or future prospects. And finally there are the poor, officially defined as those who do not make enough to afford adequate diet. They are fewer now, but they still number millions, and their position has become in many cases more desperate than before.

The existence and nature of these strata is sharply illustrated in a special study which the Census Bureau conducted in Cleveland for the period 1960-65. It could be called a three-dimensional report in that it provides decidedly different aspects as one views it from three perspectives.

The first perspective is a broad profile of Cleveland with notations of five-year change. It revealed a city in transition, one which lost nearly one hundred thousand whites while gaining 25,000 blacks. Despite suburban drain-off of the white middle class the city seemed prospering, median family income rising $570 in real dollars. Black income was only 70 percent of white but the blacks, too, appeared to be gaining at a slightly lower rate. Their median family income was up $454 (TABLE 12).

The second perspective examines Cleveland blacks in terms of ghetto and non-ghetto average. Nine predominantly black areas were labeled "the Neighborhoods" and were compared with predominantly white areas which were termed "Remainder of Cleveland." Here we see where almost all the black progress occurred. In the five-year period 19,042 blacks established new residence in the white sector, about doubling their numbers there. These were people on the move, economically as well as physically. They had already achieved middle income, and their income gains in the following years ran about twice as the city's white average (TABLE 13).

TABLE 12
Income Gain of Cleveland Blacks, 1959-65

INDICES OF 5-YEAR CHANGE.*

	1959-60	1964-65
Population	249,364	275,037
Families	56,439	62,129
Median Family Income	$5,055	$5,489
Families Earning $10,000 or More	4,099 (7%)	8,229 (13%)

* Base lines in the report vary slightly, the years 1960-65 being employed for population counts, and 1959-64 for income data. The sums are in adjusted values of constant 1964 dollars.
SOURCE: Current Population Reports, Series P-23, No. 21, "Characteristics of Selected Neighborhoods in Cleveland, Ohio, April 1965," published Jan. 23, 1967.

When we turn to the ghetto blacks the appearance of general progress is almost entirely dispelled. Over the five years their median family income rose $132—or exactly $26.40 a year. The unemployment rate remained at a deep depression level. About a third of the ghetto inhabitants were locked in poverty, and the number of poverty cases was edging up (TABLE 14).

Even the figures just cited do not yield a complete picture of urban poverty, for there are levels in the ghetto, too. When

TABLE 13
Comparative Income Gain of Cleveland's Non-Ghetto Blacks, 1959-64

	1959-60	1964-65
Number	22,409	41,451
Median Family Income	$6,178	$7,285

Non-Ghetto Blacks with Family Incomes of:	1959 Number of Families	1964 Number of Families
$ 7,000-7,999	497	1,075
8,000-8,999	362	921
9,000-9,999	259	844
10,000-14,999	528	2,302
15,000-24,999	101	230

TABLE 14
Cleveland Income Data for Ghetto Blacks

	1959-60	1964-65
Population	227,578	233,660
Below Poverty Line	70,414 (31%)	74,779 (32%)
Families with Incomes Under $2,000	9,270 (18%)	10,242 (19%)
Unemployment Rate For Males in Labor Force	13%	11.2%
For Females in Labor Force	12%	14.5%
Median Family Income	$4,953	$5,085

Cleveland's nine black neighborhoods are considered separately, the 1964 median incomes ranged as high as $6,513 and as low as $2,984. In faithful reproduction of the larger society the more prosperous black neighborhoods have been going up, and the less prosperous down. During the five-year period five of the nine ghetto neighborhoods sank deeper into the poverty morass.

One of the declining neighborhoods is a place called Hough. In Cleveland it's known as "rough Hough," and in July, 1966, the rough edge of it was briefly displayed to the nation. The affair began in a bar when a man asked for a glass of ice water, and was refused. There was a brawl, then a riot. Four hundred policemen were rushed in to quell the disturbance, and when that failed, 1,500 national guardsmen came in behind them. Four people were killed, 46 injured, 187 arrested, and several million dollars' worth of property went up in smoke. The then mayor Ralph Locher expressed surprise and indignation; he called it the work of hoodlums and he suggested that just possibly subversive agents were behind it. An opposite view was offered by Carl Stokes, then a state legislator and now the mayor. Said Stokes: "They riot because they have no hope and nothing to lose."

Hough blew up while the Cleveland report was still in the works. When the data was published it confirmed in exact detail what Stokes already knew. In places like Hough, hope was indeed a scarce commodity, and it was getting scarcer all through the years of supposed progress. Hough's median family income had dropped from $4,732 to $3,966, a loss of $766. The neighborhood's poverty rolls had been swollen by some 3,500 new cases. The number living in poverty had risen to more than 40 percent. Nearly a third of the residents were at the abysmal level of under $2,000 a year.

Cleveland's four other declining ghetto neighborhoods differed from Hough only in minor detail. All were sunk in intractable poverty. All were steadily falling farther behind. The National Advisory Commission has warned that we are moving toward two societies, separate and unequal. The Cleveland report showed how fast that movement is progressing (TABLE 15).

TABLE 15
*The Widening Income Gap Between Inner
Ghetto and Other Strata*

THE DISPARITY BETWEEN HOUGH'S
MEDIAN FAMILY INCOME AND THAT OF:

	1959	1964
Ghetto Average	$ 221	$1,119
Non-Ghetto Blacks	1,446	3,219
White Cleveland	2,257	3,676

The Cleveland study is the only report in depth so far available but there is corroborating evidence which suggests that the pattern found there is typical. In general, progress has been least in the urban core areas which the Census Bureau designates as central cities. That is where the ghettos are. Moreover the huge ghettos in the major cities have been economically the most stagnant. In the period 1959-67 the proportion of central city black poor fell only slightly in New York and Los Angeles and rose slightly in Chicago; the big three together whittled just one percentage point off the poverty ratio in that eight-year span. Even that gain was in a way illusory for the population base was rising and the actual number of poverty families increased in each city. All told, the tri-city poverty rolls were swollen by some 34,000 families, or about 150,000 people (TABLE 16).

TABLE 16
Black Families Below Poverty Line
Three Cities, 1959-67

CENTRAL CITIES OF THE THREE LARGEST METROPOLITAN AREAS, 1959-67

		Number of Families Below Poverty Line	Percent Below Poverty Line
New York	1959	68,000	26%
	1967	80,000	24%
Chicago	1959	55,000	30%
	1967	71,000	33%
Los Angeles-	1959	24,000	24%
Long Beach	1967	30,000	20%
Three-City	1959	147,000	27%
Total	1967	181,000	26%

SOURCE: Trends in Social and Economic Conditions in Metropolitan Areas, Bureau of the Census, Series P-23, No. 27, Feb. 7, 1969.

In 1967 the total of black poor in all central cities stood at some three and a half million. There was no indication that they would be the next to climb from the poverty pit. In 1959 the typical poor family in the ghetto had an income $1,148 below the poverty line. Eight years later the deficit was $1,052. That rate of gain comes to $12 a year, and if steadily maintained would permit such family to edge out of poverty in another 87 years.

The ominous fact is that stagnation and decline coincided with what should have been auspicious years. Conditions in the hard-core ghettos have not responded to general prosperity. The easing of racial barriers has not helped. The much heralded (and hugely over-advertised) anti-poverty programs have made but little dent. The ghetto has remained for great numbers of its inhabitants a dead-end trap, and if a major recession should occur, the prospects of these people would be bleak indeed.*

For decades, ghetto culture has been the subject of endless analysis by sociological probers, nearly all of them bent on finding out why things have gone so badly. Lately there has been a vigorous counterattack by many blacks. It is white middle-class society that is sick, they assert, while the ghetto has life style and soul.

The ghetto does imbue many of its people with a special style, a looseness and resilience which is a way of rolling with incessant punches. A young black Puerto Rican described the strength of it to a reporter from *The New York Times*.

"You know," said the young man, "I'd like to move all the people from Scarsdale, New York, right into my block. I don't believe those people from Scarsdale could take it." Most Scarsdale residents would at the least prefer not to try the experiment.

The life style of the ghetto is the stuff of great drama, music and literature, as is the saga of any people who somehow survive and endure amidst a sea of troubles. There should be, however, no sentimentalizing of the things endured. The subculture of the impoverished slum was a disaster when Charles Dickens described it for mid-nineteenth-century London. It was still a disaster when Jacob Riis examined New York's immigrant slums in 1890. It remains a disaster in the stricken ghettos today.

One of the more ruinous aspects of ghetto life is the shattering effect it has on families. The subject has become highly controversial, though the fact itself cannot be doubted. One view is that racism and all its concomitant effects have undermined black manhood, reducing the ghetto father to an often ineffectual figure. The thesis was advanced more than thirty years ago by E.

*As this manuscript is completed, in June of 1971, a recession is evident. It has added one million blacks to the poverty rolls.

Franklin Frazier, a black sociologist and author of *The Negro Family*. In 1965 Daniel Patrick Moynihan stirred a beehive response when he elaborated the idea and made it the core of his Moynihan Report. Moynihan traced a presumed ghetto syndrome of social and economic collapse and ascribed it to the disintegration of the black family. School failure, narcotics addiction, crime and impacted poverty were seen as a "tangled pathology" deriving in large part from family failure.

The basic thesis is that historically, slavery, segregation and discrimination forced the black male to abdicate his masculine role as chief provider and protector of the family. His poverty completed his psychic ruin. He became ineffectual in the eyes of his wife and children and, worse perhaps, in his own eyes. When he could no longer endure the humiliation and pressure, he deserted, setting a model for his sons. Moynihan believed the pattern had become self-perpetuating among many failure-prone lower-class black males.

"At the heart of the deterioration of the fabric of Negro society," he wrote, "is the deterioration of the Negro family.

"It is the fundamental source of the weakness of the Negro community at the present time."

When Moynihan drew up the report he was alarmed at a sharp rise in the incidence of black families headed by women. Since then the rate has gone still higher. The 1970 census revealed that 28 percent of all black families are now headed by women, a rate just over three times as high as the white 9 percent.

Coincidentally, however, the same census showed that the black poverty rate was 31 percent, or just over three times the white 10 percent.

One can deduce too much from a table of statistics but it does seem a close match—three times the incidence of poverty producing three times the rate of family break-up.

Moynihan notes that when the two races are compared by

class, the black rate of absentee fathers continue higher across the board. There is, however, a decrease of nearly four times in the black rate as the scan moves up the social ladder.

It is a question then of what causes what. Does poverty wreck the ghetto family, or is there a pattern of black familial instability which perpetuates continuous poverty? Whatever the cause and effect there is a huge correlation between the two factors. The 28 percent of female-headed families account for more than half of all black family members living in poverty. They are, moreover, the ones with the least prospect for escape. The mother is much more often than not a member of the underclass, unskilled, and poorly educated; she labors under the double economic discriminations of race and sex, and she must divide her energies between trying to earn a living and care for the children.

Her chances of succeeding in such struggle are bleakly set forth in the 1960-65 special census for Cleveland referred to earlier. In the poorest ghetto neighborhoods, termed the crisis ghetto, the female family heads started the period with median incomes of $2,300 a year. Five years later, after a period of supposed progress, they were down to $1,950 a year, or $37 a week. Considering the price differential they were probably poorer than most of those in Mississippi. Moreover, their numbers had increased by nearly a third.

The I.Q.s of ghetto school children often drop as much as twenty points while attending school. The I.Q.'s value as intellectual yardstick is a disputed matter, but in this case it seems clearly to offer a measure of what is not happening. All other indices point in that direction, too. Typically, Harlem's ghetto children drop as much as two years behind average reading level by the time they reach the sixth grade.

How does a child get to the sixth grade if he's only fourth grade in his reading ability? The answer is that about twenty years ago the New York school system was confronted with the problem of massive failure, and someone came up with a neat sociological solution. A prime purpose of the educational process, it was decided, was to "keep the child up with his peer group." An ex-teacher who is somewhat cynical about the system explains it thus: " 'Keeping him up with his peer group' means one in, one out, keep them moving, and don't ever stop to inspect because the whole assembly line will jam up right there."

Every year, all of the cities turn out swarms of ghetto high school graduates who are not really equipped for the demands of a modern technological society. About half of them are unable to pass the quite functional Air Force examination. The failure has led to furious charges and countercharges as to who is at fault and what to do. Increasingly angry blacks blame the teachers for being racist. No doubt some of them are, but certainly not all; there are by now a good many black teachers and their ghetto students are not doing any better.

The search for solutions has brought the whole school system under fierce challenge. Formerly educators argued the ways-and-means question of how to teach. Now they debate what to teach and, in some cases it seems, whether to teach at all. The new catch word is "relevant." If a child does not score properly on a test it is not the child that failed, or the teacher, but the test. It was not a relevant test.

There is reason enough to question the relevance of much pedagogy. Certainly, too, the schools should be flexible enough to adjust to the needs and backgrounds of the children involved. To this observer, however, there remains the suspicion that relevance is becoming an elegant cop-out, a kind of upper-case "peer group." In sum, a means of making a virtue out of not solving the problem. As an example, the linguist Thomas Kuchman of Northeastern Illinois State College was quoted recently to the effect that standard English is not relevant to black children. They should learn "black English," the speech of the streets, and Dr. Kuchman is not concerned about what that will do to their economic prospects because he doesn't believe they have any. Dr. Kenneth Clark, the black educator-psychologist, and author of *Dark Ghetto*, espouses a contrary opinion that black children can and must have the same kind and quality of education that whites receive.

This reporter does not know the school solution, but will attempt to define at least part of the problem. The failure of ghetto schools is a faithful mirror which reflects the deep anguish of ghetto communities and the grievous neglect of the general society. The anguish is revealed at one New York high school, where one thousand boys and girls, about 40 percent of the student body, are reportedly using heroin. There are schools where teachers spend three-fourths of their time trying to maintain order, and schools where platoons of policemen periodically restore order. We are not likely to see real improvement in ghetto schools until there is some improvement in the quality of ghetto life.

Heroin claims untold numbers of ghetto victims. No one really knows how many, but Dr. Clark has estimated that New York alone contained at least 10,000 addicts with the Harlem rate about ten times as high as the rest of the city.

This reporter recalls vividly an encounter on the ghetto streets. He was a young man, in his early twenties probably, and he was in the midst of extreme withdrawal pains. He danced along with a frightful, jerking gait, body twitching and arms flailing. People along the street looked past him and went on about their business. There is much random cruelty in the ghetto but this was not an act of cruelty. The young man was very sick, and there was nothing they could do. If they called the police he would be taken to a jail cell to endure his suffering there, and so they were willing to let him suffer on the street. As for hospitalization, the cities do not begin to have facilities sufficient for the need.

Occasionally some random accident highlights the street

scenes of the ghetto. Such was the case in the short, desperate life of Walter Vandermeer, a child of Harlem, whose story was told by Joseph Lelyveld of *The New York Times.*

Walter was born to trouble. In the social worker jargon he was a member of a multi-problem family. His mother was a migrant from South Carolina who has had five husbands and eleven children. There were times when the family of the moment lived in a one-room apartment. By age six Walter was sniffing airplane glue. He was expelled from the third grade because of violent temper seizures in which he attacked the teachers, his little fists swinging wildly. There followed a round of institutions and situations: Family Court, a children's center, a special school for disturbed children, a temporary, informal adoption by a motherly neighbor, a school for boys, a half-way house, an upstate institution for problem children, back again to Family Court.

He came to the official attention of the Society for the Prevention of Cruelty to Children, the Department of Social Services and its Bureau of Child Welfare, the Bureau for the Education of Socially Maladjusted Children and the Office of Probation.

Sometimes he just ignored the letters they sent him, or just didn't show up at the place they assigned him. Sometimes his mother intervened to take him out of the hands of this agency or that. There was a stretch of fourteen months when he slept at home only sporadically and attended school for two and a half days.

He was quick and bright, ingratiating, suspicious and wild. When he felt betrayed—and sooner or later that always happened—he flew into one of the terrible tempers. The neighbor who took him in had to rescind the arrangement when her son came home from Vietnam, and Walter hurled a bottle through her window in revenge.

Presently he was in custody again, temporarily billeted at the half-way house while waiting assignment to a school for disturbed boys. He became friends with a counselor and at his urging went back to school for what proved the last time. He was getting to be a big boy, and only reading at the first grade level, but the teacher thought he could catch up. To please the counselor he tried hard. Every afternoon, faithfully, he did his homework before anything else. Then he learned that the half-way house was just a temporary arrangement and he felt betrayed again. When he was sent to an upstate school he ran away four times. After awhile, people quit looking for him. His file went around and around in the city bureaucracy and Walter took to the Harlem streets.

He became a street waif, a child out of a Dickens tale. He had a regular run of places where people allowed him to hang out for an hour or a night. When all else failed he could always sleep on a fire escape. Occasionally he would track down his mother and she would shout at him, "Go home." "Go home, yourself," he would shout back.

He learned the tricks of an apprentice hustler, peddling small items, begging, stealing a little, acting as runner perhaps for small drug transactions. Once he found an empty glassine envelope, filled it with salt, and sold it for three dollars to his brother, an addict.

He became a kind of mascot for a gang of young auto thieves, and for another gang of purse snatchers. Sometimes they would let him go along on their raids. He hung out a lot with addicts, too. Sometimes he would play the role of the young tough and then, suddenly, turn child again. He cried easily when he was being a child. He would call his addict friends "Mommy" and "Daddy" and fantasize a house in which he would set up a family.

He wound up in court again and was nearly sent away to a state training institution. A sister intervened and managed to have that stopped. She knew about state training institutions because she had been to one when she was twelve, the first time she was pregnant. If Walter were sent to a place like that, she warned, the homosexuals would get after him and "mess up his mind."

Somewhere along the way he began taking drugs. Probably he picked it up from a teen-aged girl who would sometimes let him pretend that he was her son. He was afraid of the needle, she recalled later, and would always say, "Wait, let me get myself together."

About this time he got a pair of shoes from a woman on the block who liked to look after him. He told her he was going to save them, to wear when he went back to school. He had taken to dropping in on his little brother's classroom where the teacher would allow him to sit and watch. His brother was helping him learn to read. Then one night he locked himself in a bathroom and tried his still inexpert hand at mainlining heroin. When they found him he was dead of an overdose.

He was twelve years old.

Reporter Lelyveld got hold of Walter's story and wrote an eight-column account. The street waif had become a personage, the youngest known heroin fatality in a drug epidemic that was breaking out among New York's children.

"Walter lived to be thirty in twelve years," said a junkie friend. "There was nothing about the street he didn't know."

"There are thousands of Walter Vandermeers out there," a school official said when asked why no one had taken charge of the boy.

Some others are destroyed in slower, quieter ways. There is the case of twelve-year-old Sharon, a black child from the Bronx. She was difficult to teach, angry and withdrawn. Her composition papers were wild, almost illegible scrawls filled with fantasies of power and revenge. She would become, she predicted, a prostitute, an addict, a murderer. "Kill, kill, kill," the words appeared often in her childish hand. And then one day she turned in a paper in quite different mood. This was the text:

"Family life is not really happy. Reality is hard to find. We are all in a mixed up state of mind. Which brings us problems hard to solve. We are all reaching for help but are slapped down by that brutal hand which suficate us into our own distruction we are brutaly nasty to each other locked in an eternal hell which bring the beast in every god forsaken body. We must still [she means steal] each others happiness in order to breath we are not sane nor insane. We a cannibals saluages [savages?] and scavengers we must portray our ancestors. We must not betray them but we are. oh but yes we are cruel which we point out vague in the beginning of the paragraph
we are helpless."

The teacher doesn't know what happened to Sharon. She was in school for a while, and then not. Children like that come and go. There are thousands of Sharons out there, too.

Chapter 7

THE GOVERNMENT ROLE

Ought not a national urban crisis to be met with something like a national urban policy?

—Daniel P. Moynihan

S O long as present conditions prevail the cities will not solve their problems. They can't. The efforts required would cost large sums, and the urban tills are empty.

The root of the problem is expressed in a simple equation. Out of every three dollars raised from general tax revenues, the federal government collects two. The remaining tax dollar is left to be divided among all the state capitals, city halls and county courthouses in the land.

The federal preemption of tax revenues is often ascribed to the heritage of New Deal and other social welfare policies. In fact, that is not primarily the case. In 1936, at the height of the New Deal, local governments were still the principal agencies of public service, as reflected in tax revenues half again higher than the federal total. The shift to federal dominance occurred during

World War II and has ever since continued as a direct consequence of enormous global commitments.*

For the cities the result has been thirty years of neglect. When combined with a heavy influx of the dispossessed it has produced a predictable disaster. The slums have spread miles wide through the core areas of almost all the great metropolitan centers. Clamorous demands for new municipal services have arisen at a time when even the old services were falling apart. In the typical big city today the schools are crowded and dilapidated, the public hospitals understaffed, the transit systems creaking, and the police and fire protection stretched thin. The parks are ill-tended by day, and hazardous by night, and such routine urban chores as garbage collection and snow removal are frequently neglected to the point of crisis. Such programs as large-scale housing renewal are simply out of the question. Scrape as they will for new revenues the cities cannot cope with their problems, and mayors are reduced to the roles of trustees in bankruptcy.

The migration did not create all these problems. It served rather as an added pressure, one which magnified other stresses already at work. The total effect has been to produce in the cities a major crisis.

The crisis has several fundamental elements. At the root of them all is the fact that the city is the stepchild of the American political system. This has always been true, and it takes on critical dimensions as we become ever more an urban nation.

The cities have literally no constitutional rights. The federal government has its assigned powers in the scheme of things, and the states likewise, and the cities are left to operate in whatever

---

* At this writing the proposed defense budget for fiscal 1971 is some $81 billion, or 37 percent of all federal outlays, and it has been announced as the lowest defense ratio in twenty years.

The relative austerity in the new military budget reflects a redefinition of policy. Throughout the 1960s the Defense Department operated under guidelines requiring constant readiness for the simultaneous conduct of three wars, two major and one minor. The new policy limits stand-by capabilities to one major and one minor war.

haphazard manner the states may decree. More often than not, the state decisions are controlled by legislators who don't live in the city, don't understand its problems, and have no wish to share its burdens.*

What this means in practical terms is illustrated in the case of New York City. It is a community of some 8 million people, a vital center for much of the nation's commerce. Decisions made in its towering skyscrapers affect the nation and the world. And yet as a community it is all but powerless to conduct its own affairs.

Its problems are staggering. Even the little problems become big ones through the sheer size of the operation. As an instance, New York police remove more than 60,000 abandoned, derelict cars from the streets every year, and they tow away more than 100,000 illegally parked cars from the borough of Manhattan alone. The traffic congestion is such that a single double-parked automobile can tie up a street, blocking fire engines, slowing sanitation details to a crawl. And yet New York must ask legislative permission before it can deputize sanitation men to ticket impeding vehicles. It must ask legislative permission before it can shift policemen to a more efficient time schedule.

New York maintains a public payroll of 350,000 employees, and runs on a budget of $6.6 billion a year. It cannot raise its dog-tag fee without the state's permission.

Those are the minor examples of New York's political impotence. A major instance occurred when race confrontation became ensnarled in a school dispute, closing the schools for months and all but tearing the city apart. City hall could only

---

* The failure to assign any specific jurisdiction to the cities was apparently a deliberate omission by the founding fathers. Thomas Jefferson was the chief framer of the Constitution and he considered cities to be at best a necessary evil to be kept in curb as much as possible. In letters to his friends Jefferson wrote: "I view great cities as pestilential to the morals, health and liberties of man. . . . The commercial cities, though by command of newspapers, they make a great deal of noise, have little effect on the direction of government." A lot of harassed mayors today would agree at least with that last clause.

negotiate between the clashing factions. The state had, and finally used, the authority to impose settlement.

New York, in sum, is where the problems are, and the state capital in Albany is where the power is. The same is essentially true for every city-state relationship in the country.

A second element in the crisis stems from the huge spin-off of suburban communities. It used to be that people who worked in a city lived there, and shared a common stake in its well being. Today more than half of all metropolitan dwellers are suburbanites. They surround the cities with ring on ring of satellite communities, often extending for thirty or forty miles in all directions. The result is a tangled metropolitan complex which is at once an interdependent economic whole and a series of disjoined, often mutually antagonistic political units. Daniel P. Moynihan, former director of the President's Urban Affairs Council, has termed this "a fractionating process." It has, says Moynihan, "made it ever more difficult to collect enough power in any one place to provide the rudiments of effective government. As a result of or as a part of this process the central cities ceased to grow and began to decline. The core began to rot."

It is not just power that is fractionated, of course, but also money. The outsized example is again New York City, which provides a livelihood for innumerable commuters. At a conservative estimate they earn from the city well over $65 billion a year, and they support a high level of community services in the suburbs where they live. As for the city and its problems, however, the commuter's daily withdrawal is symbolized by a custom frequently observed on trains running through the ghettos of Harlem and the Bronx. Along a particular section of the route men glance up from their newspapers and card games and reach over to pull the window shades. The gesture, so far as it goes, is entirely practical. The shade offers a measure of protection against flying glass when a rock or missile comes hurtling through the window. The rock and the shade together comprise about the only form of communication now existing between those in the ghetto and those speeding through to the safety and comfort of another world.

The third and most critical element in the urban crisis is a total imbalance in the tax structure. The cities generate huge tax revenues but almost all of it is siphoned off to serve other purposes.

The inequity is all the greater because it is the cities (the towns, too, of course) that perform all the essential day-to-day services. The citizen expects the city to clean his streets, pick up his garbage, safeguard his person, protect his household from fire, educate his children. He is inclined to raise hell if these and many other services are not performed well.

It is at city hall that people clamor when they want a housing ordinance enforced, or a slum cleaned up. It is the city they turn to if they need welfare to subsist. It is the city that is held responsible for nearly every collective need that touches intimately on individual daily lives.

Under the present tax structure the cities cannot perform these functions well. It is coming close enough to the point where the cities can hardly meet their obligations at all.

The average city gets back in direct federal benefits about four or five cents for every federal tax dollar that city people pay. If the indirect benefits are calculated the figure might go as high as ten or twelve cents on the dollar. It is not enough.

From the state government the city sometimes gets back as much as forty to fifty cents on the tax dollar—if the state is uncommonly generous.

The city's own tax-collecting powers are closely circumscribed by law, but more than that, there are limitations imposed by political and economic realities. There is a bottom to the tax barrel somewhere, and the federal and state extractions leave the city very little room in which to maneuver.

Income taxes are steep enough now that only a bold mayor will propose a city addition. The federal government could increase its income tax levy and the citizens would grumble but pay, because federal affairs are distant and complex and people don't quite know how to address their complaint. But they know where city hall is, and the objectors are there in a physical body when any new tax is even suggested.

Similarly, the federal government can tax business heavily and business objects; and then cranks it into the price of the product and things go on about as before. If a city government tries too much of that, business moves.

The cities have settled on real estate as being their principal fief in the tax domain. It has the political advantage of being partially hidden, as much of it becomes disguised in rent. The disadvantage is that it forms a fairly rigid tax base, one which has not kept pace with the rest of the economy. The federal government by contrast has a built-in escalator in its heavy reliance on the progressive income tax. Moynihan has estimated that "for each one percent increase in the Gross National Product the income of the federal government increases one and one-half percent while the normal income of city governments rises half to three-quarters of a point at most."

Inflation has produced a final squeeze. It is a particular problem for city governments because they deal primarily in services. They cannot, like industry, offset rising wages by stepped up technologic efficiency. Industrial workers have at least doubled their production per man hour in recent decades. But teachers have not acquired the ability to instruct twice as many children. Housing inspectors cannot check twice as many complaints. At least not efficiently. Nonetheless, the cities must compete for personnel on a wage market largely geared to industrial scales.

The National Advisory Commission on Civil Disorders (the President's Riot Commission) cited education as one instance of a cost spiral that has brought city governments to the edge of bankruptcy. From 1947 to 1967 the costs per pupil increased almost four times. Other outlays were soaring to similar heights. From 1950 to 1966, the total cost of local government rose about three and a half times, from $17 billion a year to $60.7 billion. Revenues were rising too, but never fast enough to catch up (TABLE 17).

TABLE 17
Rising Costs of Local Governments
(in billions of dollars)

	1950	1966
Annual Expenditures	17.0	60.7
Annual Revenues	11.7	41.5
Annual Deficit	5.3	19.2

Adapted from Report of the National Advisory Commission on Civil Disorders.

Most of the deficit is made up by state or federal aid. The grants, however, never quite close the gap and every year local governments slide deeper into debt by about $4 billion. The state governments are falling behind, too, and so are increasingly reluctant to help the cities. In the years 1950-66, state debts rose from $5.5 billion to $29.5 billion; local government debts climbed from about $19 billion to $77.5 billion.

Throughout this period the state and local deficits ran well beyond that of the federal government. The federal budget has in fact achieved relative stability in proportion to the growth of the country; federal per capita debt has been now up a little and now down with a slight overall decrease ince 1950. State and local per capita debt has been climbing steeply (TABLE 18).

The urban fiscal crisis amounts to much more than mere budgetary dilemma. The cities have been for decades a dumping ground for the poor, and city governments simply do not have the means to deal with the problem. The gap between needs and means cannot be closed under prevailing ground rules. Mean-

TABLE 18

Per Capita Debt, Local, State and Federal
Governments (in dollars)

	1950	*1960*	*1966*	*Dollar Change, 1950-66*
State and Local Governments	$ 159	$ 389	$ 547	+$388
Federal Governments	1,697	1,591	1,633	−64

SOURCE: Health, Education and Welfare Trends, 1966-67 Edition, Part 1, Table S-143, HEW publication, Washington, D.C.

time, the ghetto poor have grown impatient and angry. Nor is the ghetto the only constituency that must be considered. The urban middle class provides the main support for the city's public functions, and no program can be maintained without their acquiescence. They are not now in a very acquiescent mood. They have been paying more and more taxes for less and less public service, and they, too, are becoming impatient and angry. If these tensions and angers become increasingly polarized, the consequences can be very ugly and dangerous. The mood now is dangerous enough.

The urban crisis has been developing for thirty years and in all that period there has never been any attempt at a national approach to the basic problems. Moynihan has posed the problem in the form of a question: "Ought not a national urban crisis to be met with something like a national urban policy?" Moynihan's answer to himself: "The United States does not now have an urban policy. The idea that there ought to be such is new."

The lack of policy should not be confused with a lack of programs. There has been indeed a plethora of programs, all of them tacked on as piecemeal additions to this or that federal, state or city infrastructure. The federal programs alone are so numerous, and so diffused through departments and bureaus, that no one knows exactly how many there are. A common estimate is about four hundred.

The programs do not add up to a policy because there is no clear view as to what the society is trying to accomplish, or by what means. So far as the cities are concerned, the federal government often takes away with one hand more than it provides with the other. Two prime examples have already been cited: the farm program and the jerry-rigged welfare system. The federal highway program is a lesser though by no means unimportant example. Highway systems repeatedly have been jammed through cities with relentless disregard for the urban consequences, and more often than not the neighborhoods affected deteriorated into slums. There are cities in which the highway program has created more slums than urban renewal has cleaned up.

Urban renewal itself has frequently produced more slum pressure than it has relieved. Too often the projects have consisted of razing rundown low-rent buildings and replacing them with middle-class housing; in the process the poor have been shunted from one part of the city to another while the supply of housing available to them became less than before. There is a ghetto conviction that "urban renewal means Negro removal."

Beyond the defects of individual programs there is the root fact that the cities have a low priority among federal concerns. The point is illustrated by the relative federal expenditures for highway building and urban maintenance. The comparisons that follow are for the decade 1957-66; the period is chosen because it represents approximately equal segments of the Eisenhower, Kennedy and Johnson administrations and thus can be viewed as a policy of national consensus during the recent past. The tabulation: federal investment in highway building came to nearly nine times the sums spent on urban renewal and public housing combined (TABLE 19).

In the current era the spending levels have increased but the sense of national urgencies remains much the same. The proposed Nixon budget for fiscal 1971 places urban rebuilding

TABLE 19

Federal Grants-in-Aid to State and Local Governments

COMPARATIVE GRANTS FOR URBAN RENEWAL AND HIGHWAY CONSTRUCTION.
IN MILLIONS OF DOLLARS, FOR 10-YEAR PERIOD 1957-66

	1957	1958	1959	1960	1961	1962	1963	1964	1965	1966
Public Housing	86.7	94.6	110.8	127.2	140.2	154.3	170.4	182.6	207.5	225.5
Urban Renewal	30.3	37.2	77.4	104.4	144.0	169.4	199.3	232.0	314.2	359.9
Highway Construction	954.7	1518.5	2613.9	2941.7	2622.6	2782.8	3022.5	3644.2	4017.7	3975.2

10-Year Totals in Rounded Sums:

Public Housing .... $11½ billion
Urban Renewal .... $12⅓ billion
Highway Construction .... $ 28 billion

SOURCE: Health, Education and Welfare Trends, Tables S-157 and S-158, 1966-67 Edition, HEW publication, Government Printing Office, Washington, D.C.

144

efforts on a par with airport construction, at about $1.5 billion each. Highway construction gets $4.5 billion. It would appear to be our fixed national conviction that a swift and expeditious passage between cities is a matter of more consequence than the quality of the cities themselves.

Some other federal programs are not specifically addressed to the cities as such, but have a critical bearing on urban problems. The anti-poverty effort is a major case in point. It has had a curious history. It rendered poverty a little less pervasive, but a great deal more conspicuous, and it succeeded mostly in rousing the poor without fulfilling their expectations.

President Johnson launched the anti-poverty campaign in his 1964 State of the Union message, declaring: "This administration, today, here and now, declares unconditional war on poverty in America." Even allowing for the inflation factor in political rhetoric that was an unfortunate exercise in hyperbole. In the ghettos and elsewhere a lot of poor people believed that an earnest campaign against poverty was about to begin. When it didn't happen, they were bitter. Later on, a lot of other people concluded that the campaign had been fought, and lost, and they were ready to write it off as a hopeless cause.

Both misapprehensions are understandable enough. For years the nation has been bombarded with thousands of newspaper articles, magazine pieces and television interviews on the War on Poverty. Moreover, there were all those programs: Job Corps, VISTA, Head Start, Upward Bound, Operation Mainstream, Neighborhood Centers, Neighborhood Youth Corps, New Careers, Concerted Employment Program, Economic Opportunity Loans, Model Cities. Surely there was in this mélange something new and big and important. But was there?

Theoretically, the War on Poverty was launched with a first-year appropriation of one billion dollars. Actually, about half of that sum represented old programs shifted to new offices in order to dress things up. The $500 million in new money prorated to about four cents a day for each of the 34 million Americans who were then listed as poor. Four years later the poverty rolls had dropped to about 23 million people and the anti-poverty budget had crept up to almost $2 billion; it amounted to 24 cents a day for each person involved. Anti-poverty workers have a saying, "This is no war. It's a skirmish."

Lack of funds combined with general boondoggling to produce a stillbirth in the program's most ambitious offspring. That was (technically, still is) Model Cities. The original idea was to select experimental urban areas for intensive, all-out assault on all the related ghetto problems of poverty, slum housing, crisis-ridden schools and general social disintegration. Federal, state and city resources were to have been harnessed for a concerted effort, and the ghetto poor were to be drawn in as participants in rebuilding their neighborhoods. Hopefully, it was to have provided laboratory demonstrations of ways and means by which a stricken community could be lifted bodily out of the morass. The society would then have had an informed estimate on what was needed for the total urban task. It might or might not have worked; there is at present no way of knowing because it was never tried.

Model Cities went off the track almost at once when Congress insisted on including 150 cities. Every congressman wanted a piece of it for his district and so it was parceled out, becoming at once something too big to be an experiment and too small to be a program. Several hundred million dollars was then spent in preparing plans, making surveys, setting up staffs. At least fifty cities actually got around to submitting proposals. And then it was allowed to languish. It wasn't abolished, of course—the government almost never does that—but it has been dismissed as a project which can putter along at $300 million a year. Nobody expects any sweeping experiments from that kind of money spread that thin, and the cities are treating it as a little something extra that can be tucked into overstrained budgets. Chicago is using Model Cities grants to spruce up its school janitor service and hire some teachers' aides. Boston is providing free milk to some ghetto children. It's a big come-down from the original bold promise.

Other anti-poverty programs have suffered from a similar diffusion. Job placement and training efforts have reached only a small fraction of those in need, and have been only marginally successful with those reached. In general, the O.E.O. by-passed the knotty problems of mass unemployment to concentrate on involving the poor in community action.

This reporter asked a New York City community action official to estimate how many people the program reached on a typical ghetto block, and what change that had produced in their lives. The answer: "We don't measure it that way. We consider a program successful if we can get people to attend the meetings."

Eventually a lot of people did attend a lot of meetings. The way it usually went, community action groups stirred poor people up to make demands which city hall was then expected to meet. A political cynic might have viewed it as an exercise in taking the credit while passing the buck. If such was the intent, however, it backfired. After awhile community action groups began making demands on federal agencies. A lot of community action energy went into organizing the Poor People's March on Washington.

There is, of course, nothing alarming in the spectacle of people making demands on their government, local or national. What was remarkable was the federal government's role in the matter. First, it announced with grand fanfare promises which it did not keep. Next, it recruited and hired thousands of articulate street-corner organizers who went forth to rouse the poor and make them ready for the War on Poverty. By then, however, things had gone all wrong; we were at war in Vietnam and the government tried to hold the War on Poverty to a vest-pocket operation. It resolutely ignored the rising demands it had helped to stimulate. Within two years the riots began.

It is not suggested that community action precipitated the riots. The forces were much more elemental than that. Nonetheless, the official policies did indeed augment what Saul Alinsky has described as the radical's natural function: to rub raw the sores of discontent.

The Nixon administration has concluded that promises should not be made. The term "War on Poverty" has not been seen nor heard in a government announcement for some time now, and the O.E.O. has been quietly downrated as but one of the minor means by which the nation addresses its poverty problem. The difference in style is sharply etched when one compares two budget presentations. In 1964 the Johnson administration bally-hooed a half-billion-dollar addition to anti-poverty efforts. In 1970 the Nixon budget message reduced the discussion to a few low-key paragraphs and then presented an anti-poverty invest-ment of—it said—$32.9 billion.

What this new approach amounts to is that ballyhoo has been replaced with quiet flim-flam. The $32.9 billion figure was as-sembled by throwing into the pot prorated estimates of what the poor receive from general government operations. Thus the pro-gram was credited with $9.9 billion dispensed to the aged poor in social security. Also, $2.6 billion as their slice of Medicare. And $3 billion in veterans' benefits. If this is a reasonable definition of an anti-poverty program then the official accountants must be charged with oversight: the postal deficit should be prorated, too, providing some calculation of the subsidized letters which ghetto dwellers write to the folks back home in Mississippi. The account of the poor might well be charged also with some fair proportion of the highway systems over which they migrate.

Rhetorical absurdities aside, the real policies have not changed much. The Nixon administration is continuing the old programs much as before, but in less pretentious style. There is some shift in emphasis, reflecting a desire to dispense a little less sociology and a little more hard cash. There remains a fixed conviction that a great many other priorities come first.

Some broader approaches have been put forward in very tentative fashion by both Republicans and Democrats. The Nixon administration suggested two schemes, and congressional Democrats countered with two others. The plans incorporate diverse theoretical merits and share one common defect: all are proposed at fiscal levels way below what it would take to do the job.

President Nixon advanced the Family Assistance Plan. It was in theory the most sweeping welfare reform in forty years. It would have wiped out the long-standing "man-in-the-house" rule which makes many dependent children ineligible for aid if the father is present. It established a national floor for welfare payments to families. It provided a sliding-scale system in which low-wage earners could still receive apportioned benefits. The practical shortcoming was that it set the assistance level at a miserly $2,400 a year for a family of four. It offered no help to cities which had already established higher levels. It didn't reach great numbers of the poor, and those it was designed to reach would in most cases have still remained below the poverty line.

The Democrats responded with a larger national welfare plan. It was more expansive in reach, more generous in payments, but it, too, fell short of raising all the prospective recipients to the level which the government itself defines as minimum subsistence. Both the Democratic and Republican plans, moreover, incorporated a curious oversight: it was assumed that such living costs as rent are the same in a rural village as in New York City.

President Nixon's next major proposal was revenue sharing, in which the federal government was to return tax monies to the cities to spend as they saw fit. It roused briefly a flurry of debate on the philosophical merits. Proponents saw it as strengthening

grass roots democracy, providing mayors with the means to exercise their mandates, and leaving local voters to judge the results.
Opponents wanted safeguards to prevent cities from simply
accepting the bonus and cutting back on their own expenditures
for vital services. Blacks were skeptical about any benefits to
their people in cities where they lacked political clout. The theoretical debate lost most of its interest when mayors examined the
proposed gift and found that nearly all of it was simply a repack-
aging of money they were already receiving under old programs.
There was about $1 billion in new funds, but that is small change
by standards of the urban crisis. If it were allocated entirely to
poverty problems, it would provide the mayors with about 25
cents per person per day for the millions of poor huddled on
their doorsteps.

The counter-proposal of the Democrats was a public works
program, put forward as a special measure to counter recession.
It was again more extensive than the Republican plan, but again
not by much: the sum was $2.5 billion a year.

At this writing a temporary urban relief program has been
adopted and the other measures are log jammed in the political
stream. All of these approaches are grossly inadequate: the proposed or anticipated expenditure levels range from about one-
tenth to one-half the minimum estimates of what is needed to
relieve the bottom level of rank poverty. They do not begin to
extend to the other urgent urban problems. Even so, the mere
discussion of such plans represents something new in national
attitudes. For the first time the two parties are groping their way
toward the idea that a national crisis requires national measures.
It is progress of a sort.

Some of the proposed reforms have been dressed up politically
with the suggestion that welfare clients will be put to work. A
work program for the able-bodied would indeed have merits, but
the notion of a sweeping welfare reduction is largely a political
chimera. Great numbers of the destitute are in that condition

because they are either unemployable, or because the jobs they hold do not provide a decent living. A report of the Social Security Administration offers a clear view of where that matter stands. The agency listed 25.9 million poor in 1967 and tabulated their status as follows:

5.9 million (23 percent) lived in households headed by persons aged sixty-five or older.

1.6 million (6 percent) lived in households headed by disabled persons.

8.2 million (32 percent) lived in households headed by persons who worked the full year. More than 1.5 million of these people were in households headed by women.

6.5 million (25 percent) lived in households headed by persons who worked only part of the year. Of these, 2.4 million were in households headed by women.

3.7 million (14 percent) lived in households headed by persons who did not work during the year. These included 3 million in households headed by women.

When the tabulation is re-examined by working status, the poverty roll included 9.5 million among whom the household heads were unemployed or semi-employed. Of these, 5.4 million were female heads, 4.1 million male heads.

Given the fact that most of the poor are ill-educated and unskilled, and considering the prevailing wage for female labor, the self-help prospects of these female-headed families are slim indeed. A woman abandoned in the ghetto with three or four children is not going to scrub her way into any affluent society. If such women were retrained for industry, and if industry were prepared to absorb them at good wages, and if society is willing to furnish day-care centers to attend to the children, then some could break the poverty cycle. As it stands now most of them will remain in need of public aid, and the only realistic question is whether the poverty cycle can be broken for the next generation.

For the unemployed or semi-employed males the prospects are

better, but not good. This group includes all the displaced farmers who became displaced laborers and now in middle years or later are scuffling around, looking for something to do. Some are not even looking, because they have become utterly demoralized. The unemployed and semi-employed include also all the high school dropouts, all the reformatory graduates, all the social casualties who are not displaced but rather, have never been placed. Employment programs to absorb these people would have to be much more extensive than anything attempted so far. Moreover, if all these men became fully employed at wages sufficient to sustain families, it would reduce the poverty rolls by only one-sixth.

As for those now fully employed at a poverty level, they would be helped most by an increase in the minimum wage, provided that did not result in the wholesale elimination of already marginal jobs. Here again massive retraining and employment programs offer the only real prospect for much improvement.

In short, the need for public welfare will not soon fade away. There have been proposals for such alternate solutions as negative income tax and guaranteed annual income but these are merely public aid by a new set of rules and under different names. The rules are always worth serious attention, for they determine the program's quality. The labels do not matter that much.

For urban governments the big question is, who pays? The latest proposal might offer some additional help, by increasing the present federal contribution, but all the higher payment urban areas would still have to pick up a large bill.

What urban leaders have been pressing for is not piecemeal assistance with this problem or that but rather cash, in large amounts, in some form of tax-sharing arrangement. One study estimated that between 1967 and 1977 the cities would need at least $260 billion over and above their own revenues if they were to maintain necessary urban functions. With the period in question already well advanced, there is no such aid in sight and mayors devote much of their time and energy to importuning state and federal alms. Some observers have held that the single most important attribute of a mayor today is not his administrative talents, or his social philosophy, but rather his skill at wringing money from other public agencies.

In his recent political memoir *The City*, Mayor John V. Lindsay gives an ironical account of his annual hat-in-hand trek to seek help from the state:

"In New York, the Mayor and the Governor have a special tradition of commemorating the major religious holidays in the Judaeo-Christian tradition. Each December, sometime around Christmas and Chanukah, the Mayor writes the Governor a letter outlining the fiscal needs of the city for the coming year and describing the severe consequences that will result if the city does not receive a fair share of the taxes collected from the city and state. The Governor then acknowledges the needs of the city and describes the financial pressures on the state that will make such help unlikely.

"In April, at about the time of Easter and Passover celebrations, the Mayor makes a pilgrimage to Albany, the state capital, to present the case for additional city money. The legislature leaders greet this request with a level of enthusiasm traditionally reserved for the bearer of such tidings. Then, at the last minute, the ritual ends with a sudden burst of intensive negotiations, and stop-gap measures are applied to carry over the crisis to the next year. Looking back at this custom, I think I understand why it is that, when I prepare for the Albany journey, I think of Henry Hudson, who began his own journey as captain of the stately *Half Moon* and ended it in a rowboat somewhere off the coast of Canada."

Mayor Lindsay and Governor Nelson Rockefeller always play out a political pageant in the final days of the negotiation. The mayor strides from meeting rooms looking tight-lipped and drawn and he addresses the waiting TV cameras with the air of a man who cannot much longer preserve the appearances of political civility. He will, if he must, let the people know who is strangling their city. The governor for his part always assumes the attitude of one who is trying hard to remain calm and fair, while being put upon. It is a political poker game for big chips and the mayor does not hold very good cards. The governor can, if he must, endure the mayor's political attack. The mayor cannot write off the governor's money.

Federal solicitation follows a different script, being conducted generally behind closed doors as urban representatives maneuver for special grants. There are political legends as to how it is done.

"I'll tell you how it really works," said Donald Malafronte, at the time a top aide to Newark's mayor. "It's a hustle. There's money in Washington, but you have to know how to find it.

"There are hundreds of programs," Malafronte said. "The mere description of them would fill a bookcase the length of my office wall. As you can see, I don't have those books. I wouldn't have time to read them. And anyway, that's not how you get the money. You have to know the people who hand it out. You have to know what kind of programs they like, what kind of application. Dick Lee (former Mayor Richard Lee of New Haven) really established the pattern for the whole operation. He went down to Washington and hired himself some bright young men who had held jobs in the right places. They knew who was running what. After that New Haven was always at the head of the line when the money was passed out. Dick set the quota, and the rest of us have been shooting at it ever since."

Lee has described his techniques more sedately, saying that his staff came up with highly creative ideas, often establishing new approaches which other cities then imitated. In any case, he was regarded as the pace setter, the builder of the model city. Former

Mayor Jerome Cavanagh of Detroit was another of the standouts and he took frank delight in combining social planning with a slick political hustle. In an interview published in *Harper's* Magazine Cavanagh told reporter Fred Powledge how he pulled off one coup. It happened during the Kennedy administration. Cavanagh was invited to Washington to witness the Presidential signing of a public works bill and he found that the administrator of the new act was somewhat perplexed about drawing up specific guidelines. Cavanagh offered to lend a hand. That was on a Friday. He rushed home, gathered his staff, and worked feverishly all weekend.

"On Monday morning," Cavanagh told Powledge, "I went to Washington with the rules and regulations—the *suggested* rules and regulations—and, at the same time, a big batch of applications. All the work was done for the people in Washington, so they adopted practically all the rules, and at the same time they started to hand out money. They wanted the act to get moving; they had to spend the money in a year; they wanted to show some progress in these cities. And where else to do it but in Detroit, which was all geared up and ready to go? We got forty million under that act, and I think there was only one hundred fifty million or two hundred million for the whole country. The Kennedy administration recognized not only the socially redemptive value of the programs but also the obvious political value."

Such are the devices by which mayors have sought to keep their cities intact. In the end none of them have been able to hustle enough. New Haven, Newark and Detroit were all out front in various kinds of urban programs. When the riots came, they all blew up.

"If we're the model city," Lee said, "God help the others."

Chapter 8

PROFILE OF A GHETTO

Wherever our cities are going, Newark will get there first.
                                    —Mayor Kenneth A. Gibson

"NEWARK," says Malafronte, "is the purely distilled form of the problem. Without disguises. In a size you can see what the conflicting forces are all about."

It is all of that. Within its twenty-three square miles and among its 378,000 people, it embodies in intense form nearly everything that is happening in urban America. It might almost be called the city that became a ghetto.

It is the pure form of the problem partly because of geography. Newark is almost all core city, all downtown and slum and factory district. There is no significant area of middle-class housing for almost as soon as that appears the residents adopt a suburban identity and declare their divorce.

It provides a classic case study, too, because of its history. Just about every element of the urban crisis happened here first. Or most.

Nearly all central cities have been losing population in recent times. Newark reached its population peak in the 1930 census, when it was home to 442,000 people.

It's a city which has changed color over the last generation. In the 1930s about 9 percent of the population was black. That rose to 17 percent in 1950, 34 percent in 1960, 52 percent in 1969. Another 9.5 percent are Puerto Rican. It is the first major city after Washington, D.C., to attain a black majority.

In another sense, Newark continues to change color twice a day. Commuters, shoppers and others use the city in such numbers that its human density is almost doubled in daytime. Every weekday morning it turns white, and every night black again.

Within such framework Newark has experienced acutely every aspect of urban crisis. It is a city all but devoured by slums. In unemployment it has ranked for years as one of the most chronically afflicted urban centers. Its general demoralization is attested by a staggering incidence of crime, alcoholism and drug addiction. Still other signs of social collapse are the high rates of illegitimate birth, family breakup and school dropout, all warning of a generation of disaster yet to come.

Newark's general problems are hugely magnified in its inner ghetto. In the course of a Model Cities application the city surveyed a core area that comprised about one-sixth of the city. Here in concentrated form was found a fourth of the poverty, and nearly a third of the housing ruin. Every other index of disaster was multiplied by two or three times in the shattered neighborhood.

Newark has tried all the supposed solutions. On a per capita basis it ranks second among major cities in the receipt of federal aid. Its programs of public housing, urban renewal and job training are as extensive as any in the nation. Its local services are supported by one of the highest urban tax rates in the country. But none of the programs have really worked.

It has had its riot. In July, 1967, white policemen roughed up a black taxi driver and riot erupted. When it was over, twenty-three were dead, twenty-one of them blacks, and about $10 million worth of property was reduced to smoking ruins. The then-governor, Richard Hughes, declared it "a criminal insurrection." Some blacks, with quite a different meaning, called it "the insurrection."

Three years after the riot Newark's blacks seized political control, electing as mayor one of their own. It was, among other things, an event confounding those who take at full face value all the rhetoric of racial politics. The ghetto's choice was Kenneth A. Gibson; he is no fist-clenching radical but rather a cool, tough, highly practical political man. He's also a man who might have stepped straight out of the storybook of the American legend. Gibson was brought to the city by migrant parents, grew up poor on the ghetto streets, and worked his way through night school to win for himself a place in the world. He was a successful engineer before he turned to politics. He became the first big city black major to preside over a predominantly black community.*

For Gibson as individual, the American legend has worked: by dint of intelligence, hard work and steady purpose he bootstrapped himself. The question is, can Mayor Gibson bootstrap his city? The answer is important, not just to Newark but to the country, for every urban problem is represented here in the rawest, most naked form. To walk the streets of this battered, tenacious city is to see those problems take on a recognizable human dimension.

"Beautiful, isn't it? Just beautiful." The mocking observation was delivered by a young black man named Tyrone Roe. He's a

---

* Technically, Washington, D.C., was the first large city to acquire both a black majority and a black mayor. Washington, however, is not a true political entity since the mayor there is an appointed official who serves at the President's pleasure.

member of a Newark street group called HOPERS, and he was conducting the reporter through the inner ghetto.*

The place looked as though it had been bombed, as of course it had been. Roe indicated a fire-blackened hulk with a wave of the hand, saying: "This one is from the big riot. That other one over there is from the little riot, when Dr. King was killed."

"And this one?" The question indicated a third shattered building within a bomb's throw of the other two.

Roe shook his head at the implication. "This one," he said, "just fell down. This one is the way things are in Newark."

On closer inspection the derelict structure could be distinguished by the fact that it had merely collapsed in on itself. Roe predicted, however, that eventually it, too, would probably burn. It would happen when some hazy-minded junkie built a fire in the ruins to keep warm, or when a wino fell asleep with a cigarette in his hand. Or when a child tossed a firecracker into the heap of rotting debris.

"Fire," said Roe, "is Newark's urban renewal."

One fire did lead to renewal. A new school now stands on a site where several tenements burned to the ground during the riot. There is, however, a cruel twist to the story. The school playground occupies a spot where two small children died in a blazing building.

Most of the wreckage is not a legacy of riot. It has occurred

* HOPERS is a Newark street group born out of the city's turmoil. The name is an acronym, standing for Help Other People Ease Racial Situations. It was formed after the 1967 riot. The founder of HOPERS is Frank Grant, a man who has been variously a boxer, a street hustler, an extortionist and a convict. He recalls that the first time he ever saw city hall he was brought there in handcuffs. He's also a natural leader. The riot politicized him and he gathered together some twenty young men, most of them with backgrounds almost as harsh as his own. Their purpose was to serve as emissaries between the ghetto street people and city hall. One of their several accomplishments was the founding of a youth center on a street of despair where no such facility had existed before. They located the center in the kind of place that street most readily afforded—an abandoned bar. This reporter owes and here gratefully acknowledges numerous personal debts to the HOPERS. They were honest guides to a white stranger in their town.

rather through brutal day-to-day attrition. Newark's ghetto has been shattered not by assault, but by grinding siege.

On a walking tour of the Central Ward, at the core of the ghetto, this reporter observed one or two abandoned buildings along almost every block. In one instance an entire block-long row of old wooden frame buildings stood empty. The condition of most such structures was either beyond repair, or rapidly approaching that point.

Some of the abandoned buildings were boarded up, but most were not. The distinction is important, for boarding up constitutes a form of maintenance in such neighborhoods as this. The empty house that is not boarded quickly becomes a lair for drifters and a dangerous enticement for children. The boarded places are not safe, of course; they can be broken into and often are, but it presents a difference of degree in terms of general hazard and public nuisance.

An inspection of one unboarded site revealed a heavy transient traffic, most of it presumably by night. The ground floor was profusely littered with old wine and whiskey bottles. Much of the glass was broken. The debris was such that any future squatters will have to clear a space for themselves before settling down for the night.

With practice, an observer learns to spot the buildings that probably will be abandoned next. Thus the place where the winos gathered was adjacent to a sagging two-story house which bore an important mark of decay. The wooden front door was pierced by a jagged hole large enough to admit a hand to force entry. It looked like a job that had taken some little time, probably accompanied by considerable sounds of hacking and scraping, but the police evidently had not intervened. The hole was completed.

The ground floor of that building was not occupied. Ghetto people avoid when possible any easily accessible ground floor in a rough neighborhood. Some tenants were holding out on the second floor; the stairway might seem a small additional barrier, but again safety in the ghetto is a matter of degree.

The street tour turned up one isolated family living in an otherwise vacant apartment house. It was a big brick building, half a block long and six stories high, and the general abandonment was signaled by row on row of empty windows. On an upper tier, however, one window was still framed by a pair of curtains. Presently a head appeared between the curtains and a young woman looked out to survey the street. A request for an interview was conducted through shouts and gesticulation and she nodded assent, granting us permission to come up for a talk.

The young woman turned out to be Mrs. Thelma Williams and on the face of it, her circumstances were ordinary enough. The apartment house had been condemned a month earlier, to make way for urban renewal, and the Williams family was simply the last one out. They had made all the preparations for moving, stacking their possessions in cardboard boxes, but they were still looking for a place they were willing to live in and able to afford. In a different context the problem might have presented a mere difficulty. This was happening in the Central Ward, however, and it had therefore assumed the dimensions of crisis.

Mrs. Williams had recently given birth to her first child, and the abandoned building afforded no water with which to attend the infant. She had to walk down six flights of stairs, obtain the water from a neighboring house, carry it back up the stairs, and heat it over a stove. She was trying to maintain the baby's daily bath, but she had just about given up on keeping the bedding clean.

The reporter assumed that the water problem stemmed from bureaucratic mistake or malfeasance, and suggested a strong complaint to city hall. Mrs. Williams said that wasn't it at all. The water had been left on until a night two weeks earlier when vandals came and ripped the plumbing from the walls to sell for junk.

Mrs. Williams' husband works as an industrial night watchman, and she was alone in the apartment house when the vandals
came. She had no phone with which to summon aid. She did
have a dog, a big, fierce looking animal that earns its keep by
killing rats. She sat up that night shushing her baby, and keeping
the dog by her side, while the house wreckers roamed through
the building tearing out the plumbing. They were drunk and
made a raucous affair of it. They never bothered her, probably
never knew or cared that a frightened woman was huddled in
one of the apartments, but she endured it as a night of siege.

Ironically, the Williams family could have settled for an apartment available in one of the city's public housing projects. Mrs.
Williams turned it down because that particular project has a
terrible reputation. Its halls are strewn with garbage, she said,
and muggers waylay people in the elevators. She was holding out
for some of the better-class slum housing, something about equivalent to the condemned building from which she was being
evicted. She complained that in the Central Ward a month's
notice did not allow time enough for such a search.

The dilemma of the Williams family is by no means unique.
Ghetto housing which meets minimum standards has always been
hard to find, and over the last decade the situation has worsened.
In Newark during the 1960s the abandonment of ruined or condemned tenements has outpaced one of the nation's most active
attempts at urban rebuilding.

The proliferation of empty buildings seems at first glance a
remarkable paradox, one which refutes all the supposed economic laws. Thus Newark has one of the highest population
densities in the country and the competition for living space is
intense. In theory, and up to a point in practice, the crowded
slum tenements yield large profits. Even the vacant sites have a
theoretical value of about $30,000 an acre. And yet the inner
core is becoming a wasteland. House after house is abandoned
first by tenants and then by landlords as though the place were

infected by a plague. The infection spreads from street to street, until whole neighborhoods display the signs of massive desertion. One fourteen-block slice of the Newark ghetto lost 38 percent of its population between 1960 and 1968.

In a Model Cities application filed in 1967 Newark cited this wholesale abandonment and flight as a special and unusual problem. It has since become apparent that there is nothing odd about such event; it is merely a final stage of deterioration. And Newark was merely one of the first to spot it. One city after another is now reporting the same phenomenon as old slums and ghettos begin to collapse.*

The cycle of decay has been studied in depth by Dr. George Sternlieb, a professor at Rutgers University, who used Newark as his urban laboratory. In his book *The Tenement Landlord* he traced the pattern of erosion over a twenty-year span, demonstrating how the blight fed on itself as it spread through the heart of the city. In the process he disposed of some familiar shibboleths on slum housing and showed the problem to be more complex than is commonly supposed.**

* The disintegration of slum and ghetto neighborhoods is signaled by both population exodus and building abandonment. It is most marked in the big industrial cities of the East and Midwest.

A preliminary census report in January, 1970, estimated that the poverty areas of major cities experienced a net population decline of about 15 percent or some 800,000 people in the years 1960-68. Whites were leaving such areas at proportionate rates about twice as fast as blacks, but the black departures still amounted to some 160,000.

The exodus indicates of course that some are escaping from poverty. Some others are only escaping the poverty area, taking their problems somewhere else. The cities in either case are left with the dilemma of deserted ruins. This phenomenon was surveyed by *The New York Times* in an article published Feb. 9, 1970. The newspaper estimated that New York City alone lost 114,000 apartment units to abandonment in the years 1965-69. Other large-scale abandonments were reported by housing officials interviewed in Boston, Philadelphia, Washington, D.C., Detroit, Chicago, St. Louis, Houston and New Orleans. In New Orleans, for instance, one five-block ghost town area was simply sealed off and declared uninhabitable.

** From *The Tenement Landlord*, by George Sternlieb, Rutgers University Press, New Brunswick, New Jersey, 1969. Dr. Sternlieb is professor of the Rutgers Graduate School of Business and Director of the Rutgers Center for Urban Social Science Research.

Reports of this kind tend too often to assume certain causes or conditions. Sternlieb didn't assume anything. He tracked through Newark's slums district by district to measure changing housing conditions as revealed in 1940 and 1960 census tract reports. He then cross-checked each district for changes in such other factors as income, education and race balance of the population. The careful search yielded some quite predictable findings: the poor housing was inhabited by poor people, the hard-used old tenements crumbled progressively with age, and the inevitable effects appeared in both white and black neighborhoods. But there were also some unexpected findings which suggest that there is much more to a neighborhood than the factors usually ascribed to a socio-economic profile. The report is instructive for both what it did and didn't show.

Surprisingly, one of the things it didn't show was a direct correlation between the degree of poverty and the extent of blight. Poverty is a basic pressure, of course, but it is only one of several, and in terms of housing decay it is not always the most decisive. Another thing not found was a decay index based on racial factors. Reams have been written about the effects of supposed attitudes and cultural patterns both white and black, but the simple fact is that predictable black and white patterns did not emerge on the streets. These non-findings are important in clearing the air, and they are amply documented in a block-by-block examination of exactly where and how the disintegration occurred in Newark.

Sternlieb found the most rampant blight in a district labeled "Area 1." It consists of seven census tracts and it corresponds roughly to the political subdivision of the Central Ward. It's a classic slum, a battered ugly old neighborhood which has absorbed wave on wave of Newark's newcomers; one report described it as the city's "traditional barracks and training camp for the poor." The last immigrant groups to pass through were the Italians and Jews, mostly Italians, and they left the barracks in pretty bad shape. The 1940 census found that almost a third of the housing units were in need of major repairs.

When the black migrants began arriving *en masse*, Area 1 became a principal reception point. Black population in the neighborhood jumped from about 29 percent to 75 percent between 1940 and 1960. Meantime the original bad housing was reduced almost to total ruin. The 1960 census revealed that 91 percent of the dwelling units were deteriorated or dilapidated. In one census tract only 2 percent of the housing was still rated as sound.*

At first glance one might write off Area 1 as a district that was always a slum, and still is. On closer inspection, however, that does not quite explain the housing shambles that took place over twenty years. In 1940 this neighborhood was a catch basin for the poorest, most deprived people in Newark. Twenty years later it still held that status but the relative conditions had actually improved. The unemployment was considerably less, the average income had risen, the education level was creeping up. In general, 1960 was a better year to be poor than was 1940. And yet in Area 1, the housing conditions had grown a great deal worse. (For details of neighborhood change, see TABLE 20.)

If these standard socio-economic explanations do not suffice, then what? Slum conditions have been attributed also to race attitudes, the assigned reasons ranging from supposed cultural deprivation of blacks to repression and exploitation by whites. The housing collapse in Area 1 coincided with a dramatic shift in the race balance, and so it might seem logical to seek the causes along some such lines. The race factor dissolves, however, when one turns to "Area 2," a district where blacks and whites were subjected to similar pressures.

* Exact comparisons between 1940 and 1960 are not possible, as during that period the Census Bureau changed both its terms and standards. In 1940 the criterion was "needing major repairs" and in 1960 "deteriorating and dilapidated." In practical terms the federal standards have been upgraded, but not sufficiently to account for Area 1's threefold increase in units rated substandard.

TABLE 20
Profile of Area 1, Newark, N.J.
1940-60

	1940	*1960*
Population	29,743	25,283
Racial Mix	70.3% White	75.5% Non-white
Unemployment Rate	20.7%	12.8%
Median Income, Families and Unrelated Individuals	$2,231	$4,274
Median School Years Completed by Persons 25 or Older	7.1	8.1
Housing Rated Substandard	32.3%	91%

Adapted from tables in *The Tenement Landlord*, by George Sternlieb, Urban Studies Center, Rutgers, The State University, New Brunswick, N.J., The Quinn & Boden Co., Rahway, N.J., 1969. Data from the U.S. Census, 1940 and 1960.

Area 2 forms a loosely defined ring around Area 1. Its neighborhoods are variously predominantly black (labeled 2A) and predominantly white (2B). Its people, whether black or white, are in the middle range of slum poverty, a step or two above the residents of Area 1. The housing is of similar construction but it was originally in somewhat better shape. In 1940 about a fourth of the Area 2 dwelling units were in need of major repairs. Over the next twenty years Area 2 suffered severe deterioration while retaining its relative position as Newark's second-worst slum. By 1960 nearly two-thirds of the dwelling units were rated substandard. As to race comparisons, the black and white neighborhoods were sliding downhill on parallel slopes, with the white sectors declining a bit faster (TABLE 21).

Some still more interesting comparisons emerge when we turn to a district which Sternlieb labeled "Area 3." It embraces Newark's best-kept slum neighborhoods. Geographically it lies generally along the rim of the slum complex but the pattern is irregular, weaving in and out of the middle zone. There are again 3A segments that became predominantly black, and 3B segments

TABLE 21
Housing Conditions by Predominant Race
Newark Areas, 1940-60

	AREA 2A (Becoming Predominantly Black)		AREA 2B (Remaining Predominantly White)	
Race Mix				
1940	21.7%	Non-white	80.5%	White
1960	74.7%	Non-white	64.5%	White
Substandard Housing				
1940	23.3%		24.4%	
1960	62.6%		67.3%	
Other Characteristics				
Population				
1940	39,644		14,503	
1960	35,743		12,496	
Unemployment Rate				
1940	18.7%		19.9%	
1960	9.9%		7.4%	
Median Income, Families and Unrelated Individuals*				
1940	$2,414		$2,533	
1960	4,843		4,546	
Median Schooling, Persons 25 and Older				
1940	7.9		7.7	
1960	8.6		8.6	

* Explanatory Note: The higher 1960 income of blacks suggests incorrectly that they held better jobs. The actual circumstance is that husband-wife wage-earner combinations are more common in the black families.
Adapted from *The Tenement Landlord*, derived from U.S. Census.

that remained predominantly white. In other terms it presents a decidedly mixed picture.

The whites in Area 3 began and ended the period with the highest income levels among all the slum neighborhoods involved. The blacks in this district began as nearly the city's poorest, and ended as the absolute poorest.

The whites began with the best housing of the slum lot. The blacks wedged into decaying pockets where the state of the housing very nearly rivaled the worst.

The white Area 3 neighborhoods were the most stable in terms of population change. The black neighborhoods underwent a drastic out-movement of the old residents and in-movement of new. The black sectors moreover lay generally closer to the hardcore slums where the most severe blight was taking place.

When one compares housing deterioration in the black and white sectors of Area 3 one expects to find a major difference. There was indeed a difference, but it defied all formulas. The more favored white neighborhoods were decaying almost twice as fast as the black.

The white neighborhoods started the period with 20.6 percent of the housing in need of major repairs. Twenty years later the substandard index had exactly doubled, 41.2 percent of the housing being rated deteriorating or dilapidated.

The comparable substandard ratings in the black neighborhoods went from 30.6 to 43.1 percent. Considering the fact that rating systems had been changed and upgraded, the black sector may have come fairly close to holding the line against further decay. In any case it suffered the least additional damage of any area (TABLE 22).

Let us glance back now at devastated Area 1 and compare it to the black sector of Area 3. The two districts lie within a few blocks of each other and along one border they adjoin. Both are in the heart of the ghetto. They are so closely matched in migration history, in income, and in general socio-economic profile that they seem almost identical twins. And yet over twenty years one of these neighborhoods was deteriorating almost five times as fast as the other. (For detailed comparison, see TABLE 23.)

What happened in Area 1? Why did this one black neighborhood fall apart? Why was the other black neighborhood the most decay-resistant of all the city's festering slums? Why did the best

TABLE 22
More Stable Neighborhoods
Newark Areas, 1940-60

	AREA 3A (Becoming Predominantly Black)		AREA 3B (Remaining Predominantly White)	
Race Mix				
1940	31.5%	Non-white	93.8%	White
1960	74.8%	Non-white	76.2%	White
Substandard Housing				
1940	30.6%		20.6%	
1960	43.1%		41.2%	
Other Characteristics				
Population				
1940	52,818		44,651	
1960	48,284		44,589	
Unemployment Rate				
1940	18.9%		17.9%	
1960	12.9%		9.5%	
Median Income, Families and Unrelated Individuals				
1940	$2,442		$2,889	
1960	4,202		5,059	
Median Schooling, Persons 25 and Older				
1940	7.2 years		7.9 years	
1960	8.6 years		8.7 years	

Adapted from *The Tenement Landlord*, data from U.S. Census.

performance come from the poorest neighborhood? What kind of sense can one make of the decay pattern, and what does it reveal about the mechanisms at work? These questions do not yield to simple answers. The ecology of an urban neighborhood can be compared to that of a river; in both cases the processes which sustain and nourish life derive from a complex interplay of dynamic and often subtly balanced forces. And in the neighborhood, as with the river, maintaining a balance is often far easier than trying to restore it once severe erosion begins.

TABLE 23
Profile of Two Newark Areas
FACTORS IN 20-YEAR CHANGE

Race Mix	Area 1 .....from 29.7% nonwhite to 75.5%
	Area 3A.....from 31.5% nonwhite to 74.8%
Median Incomes	Area 1 .....from $2,231 to $4,274
	Area 3A.....from $2,442 to $4,202
Education	Area 1 .....from 7.1 to 8.1 years
	Area 3A.....from 7.2 to 8.6 years
Housing Index	Area 1 .....from 32.3% substandard to 91%
	(Rate of change, −58.7)
	Area 3A.....from 30.6% substandard to 43.1%
	(Rate of change, −12.5)

Adapted from *The Tenement Landlord.*

One of several erosion factors in Area 1 is industrial litter. The problem is common to other parts of Newark's inner city, but this is the worst neighborhood. Nearly a third of the tenements are in close proximity to factories or junkyards. The district has insufficient industry to be economically viable, but too much and of the wrong kind to hold any residential attraction. That, of course, is why it became one of the chief reception points for black migrants. It's also why the present black inhabitants escape when they can.

Another kind of erosion has just been stated by implication. Sternlieb cites numerous factors in urban decay and then offers the "gross oversimplification" that "the problem of the slums is one both of plumbing and morale." The morale influences the plumbing in many ways.

Morale or the lack of it can be seen and felt in the streets. It's a compound of many things but it boils down to the fact that people view a neighborhood in relative terms of hope or despair. Either judgment tends to reinforce itself. If it tips the wrong way, if an area seems to be falling apart, then those who can, get out. Their departure stimulates the flight of others, until the place is left to the most hopeless and trapped. In particular, such neighborhoods lose the more stable family elements while collecting the transients and drifters.

Mass flight from a decaying area is sometimes piously deplored as reflecting "white middle-class standards." Such view is a myth; it patronizes the black poor while romanticizing the bleak conditions of their lives. Ghetto people do not differ from others in preferring the better neighborhood to the worse. They differ only in the range of choices.

In slum-strewn Newark, Area 1 is nearly everybody's last choice. Over the twenty-year span the district suffered a net population loss of almost one-sixth. The decline was much sharper than that of any other neighborhood irrespective of poverty level or race mix.

Such aura of decay has profound effects on tenants and landlords, on bankers and realtors, on all who play either personal or economic roles in a neighborhood's destiny. The ecological analogy is again in order: there are forces which feed on healthy growth, and other forces which feed on rot, and each tends to create and augment its own natural habitat.

Ghetto landlords exercise one of the more potent forces for good or ill, depending on their stake in the property. The question is more involved than might appear, and requires an examination of who buys slum property and why.

Popular image presents the tenement owner as a slumlord, a corporate operator who presides over row on row of squalid flats. Such landlords exist but their significance is overrated. Sternlieb's study found that in Newark only a sixth of the tenements were owned by large-scale professionals, the class being defined as those who possessed twelve parcels or more. Most of these owners were real estate dealers who live in well-to-do suburbs and specialize in slum property. Interestingly, they are not the worst of the ghetto landlords.

Being professionals, the big operators know how to do the

most necessary things at minimum cost. Their holdings are sizable enough that they can retain full time repairmen to make the rounds. In a typical case the maintenance outlay may run around 18 percent of the rental income; the figure, of course, varies greatly from one landlord to another. The profit usually runs around 10 percent. These landlords could afford better maintenance, but not on a scale sufficient to rehabilitate the slums. In any case, they are not interested in rehabilitation. They are interested in making money, and they strive for the most profitable balance between income, expense and preserving the property. How well they preserve it depends in part on their coldly realistic estimates of the neighborhood's future.

A second class of landlord is similar to the first, but less competent. These are the small operators who dabble in the market. The typical representative is a roofer, a plumber, a small contractor. He does a job in the neighborhood, hears of a place for sale, and learns that he can pick it up for a modest down payment. He begins to deal in such properties and before long he is a minor slum realtor, owning perhaps half a dozen parcels.

The small operator may purchase his first house with reasonably good intentions. He thinks he can maintain the place in his spare time. When he acquires a string of properties he finds that it requires constant attention; he hasn't the time or interest and his holdings do not justify hiring a manager. He neglects the maintenance, and with old tenements that leads to very rapid deterioration. The Newark study found that owners of seven to twelve parcels had much the higher percentage of poorly kept houses.

If there is a worse landlord than the semi-professional it is his heirs. In Newark the first heir is typically a widow of the old Italian cultural pattern. Her husband ran the business, and she the home, and she takes over with almost no experience at property management. Aging and alone, clinging to her resources, she views the rent income as something to see her through the last years. She will not prorate the cost of a plumbing or wiring job over the ten- or twenty-year period that such maintenance might serve. She settles for as bare a patch-up as she is forced to make.

Eventually the property passes to her children. They are long gone from the old neighborhood, moved out to suburbia. They may be embarrassed by the property, or merely indifferent, but in any event they usually want to sell and be rid of it. By now, however, there may be precious little left to sell. If it's a ruined house in a ruined neighborhood they may let it settle into the last stages of vacancy and abandonment. If they find a buyer he will be a slum-housing hustler who specializes in picking the bones of a tenement carcass.

Finally, the slum landlords include the resident owners. In Newark in 1960 more than a third of the tenements fell into that classification. The black owners predominated over white by a margin of nearly two to one, and they were a younger age group by nearly a decade. Their emergence represented clearly a changing of the ethnic guard.

Typically, Newark's black resident landlords are men turning fifty, usually employed as craftsmen or factory workers. Quite often they have large families and have bought tenements in part to satisfy their own housing needs. They are attracted also, of course, by rent income and property acquisition. They are a striving lower-middle class, and they mortgage themselves to the hilt to acquire worn old two or three-story buildings housing five or six families.

This type of landlord suffers from many grave disabilities. He is often just a step or two above poverty, and his handhold on the next rung of the ladder may be very slippery indeed. He's buying a beat-up house, in a run-down neighborhood, within the framework of a ghetto economy that is sunk in permanent depression.

He finds it almost impossible to get orthodox financing and so he goes to the financial gray market, paying the heavy penalties which that entails. He may buy in for $1,000, accepting short term, high interest loans and mortgages for $10,000 or more. Frequently he is financed by the previous owner, and is required to pay several thousand dollars more than the property is worth as a kind of premium on his note. In effect, he gives odds that he can make it. He may or may not know how deep he is getting in, and he may not have any reserves for major repairs. For all these reasons his struggle to maintain the place is liable to be extremely precarious, particularly in the early years when his debt burden is heavy. Nonetheless, his motivations and advantages outweigh his disabilities, and he is far and away the best of the ghetto landlords.

Psychologically, the resident owner has a huge stake in the venture. It is more often than not his first house, a major step up in the world, and success or failure is intimately involved with his pride. Economically, it's the biggest and most important investment he has ever made. It represents his best hope of acquiring some small security for himself and his family. He has struggled to gain this, and he will struggle to hold it.

Beyond that, it's his home. He lives there, too. If the furnace doesn't work his family is cold, and if rats overrun the place they will not distinguish between owners and renters.

Finally, and not least, he is regularly on the premises. He can get on his tenants if they abuse the place, and they can get on him if maintenance flags. His wife may well be his most demanding tenant. His availability is important also in terms of the stitch-in-time repairs which are most critical to the upkeep of old houses. He spots the small, spreading stain on the ceiling and fixes the pipe before the plaster is soaked and the wiring shorted. He sees the staircase shudder under the impact of a hurtling child, and he shores it up while a few well placed four-by-fours will still do the job. The owner of an old, heavily used tenement acquires a lot of sweat equity if he attends diligently to such matters week by week.

In sum, from the housing standpoint, the resident landlord provides literally and figuratively the glue of the neighborhood. The Newark study found that such landlords outdid big operators by more than five to one in the proportion of well kept premises. On a three-level rating scale—well kept, reasonably kept and poorly kept—the resident landlords out-performed all others in both achieving the best and avoiding the worst (TABLE 24).

TABLE 24
Newark Tenement Maintenance
By Type of Owner, According to Performance

	Well Kept	Poorly Kept	Reasonably Kept	Positive Rating (Well or Reasonably Kept)
Resident Landlords	38.1%	8.6%	53.3%	91.4%
Owners of 12 or More Parcels	6.6%	21.3%	72.1%	78.7%
Owners of 4 to 6 Parcels	14%	23.3%	62.8%	76.8%
Owners of 7 to 12 Parcels	6.7%	30%	63.3%	70%

Adapted from tables presented in *The Tenement Landlord*. Ratings are those assigned in spot surveys conducted by George Sternlieb and research associates.

There are some definite limitations to the role of the resident landlord. Operating in a slum economy he can offer at best concerned and diligent maintenance of an aging building. He can help to bulwark a sagging neighborhood if there is still something to save. He is not a private enterprise version of urban renewal, however, and he will not invest in disaster. He won't buy the ruined property that the heirs in suburbia would like to unload. He is reluctant to buy even good property in a badly decayed area for he is heavily influenced by the long-term prospects of the neighborhood as a place to live. The commercial operator, on the other hand, has no inherent stake in the future. He can profit from long-term investment or short, providing only that he estimates the prospects correctly. If an entire neighborhood is disintegrating, he picks up cheap property, skimps on repairs, and gambles that the house will hold up long enough to yield a quick return from rent. The result is a kind of Gresham's Law of ghetto housing: as decay progresses the bad management drives out the good and once that process begins it becomes extremely difficult to reverse. Newark's hideously blighted Area 1 had the lowest proportion of resident landlords, about one in four. In the other neighborhoods resident ownership ranged from about one-third to one-half.

Sternlieb concluded that black home buyers have already bypassed the hardcore slums, leaving such areas to the absentee owners. In some other neighborhoods a critical transition is still being made. Thus in most of Newark's tenement districts the remaining white resident owners represent both an age group and an ethnic bloc that is fading from the scene. Almost inevitably they must be replaced either by emerging black residents, or by slum realtors. "The dynamics of the situation are clear-cut," Sternlieb observed. "A deciding role in this decision will be played by government legislation—or its absence."

The present public policies do not help and often hinder the rise of ghetto homeowners. Newark's case is typical. The city is heavily dependent on real estate taxes, and it upgrades its tax base by sharply increasing the levies when properties are improved. This makes sense enough in a stable and prospering neighborhood. In slum districts it would surely make more sense to provide tax incentives, rather than penalties, for those resident owners who will take the risk of improving old tenements. Newark has, in fact, adopted such plan in urban renewal projects, but any large-scale application would require massive federal support to make up the tax loss. As it stands now the city is so squeezed financially that it has little room to maneuver, and it is locked into a tax structure which often penalizes the most reponsible landlords.

Federal loan policies are similarly discouraging to resident owners. In theory the Federal Housing Administration could create private housing capital in the ghetto, just as in suburbia, by the simple expedient of underwriting the loans. On paper there are special programs designed to that end. In practice, it's a token effort. The government is quite as reluctuant as any private bank to accept the risks of this poor man's market. An FHA official put the matter bluntly in a conversation with Malafronte:

"You show me a policy memo that says I get promoted for a high failure rate," the FHA man said, "and I'll be down there writing loans tomorrow."

The particular official was only following his bureau's implicit instructions. As to the policy, it reflects a remarkably short-sighted view of what constitutes high failure rate. By avoiding some loss on individual houses the FHA contributes to the total failure of whole neighborhoods.

Blight can occur also as a by-product of restoration attempts. Part of that is the temporary and inevitable dislocation that results from any attempt at large-scale rebuilding. But much also must be blamed on the creaking, uncertain nature of the restoration machinery. City planners are hugely dependent on federal assistance, and that means that all long range efforts hinge on the year-to-year uncertainties of the policy changes and budget decisions emanating from Washington. Newark provides a classic example of the pitfalls existing in such an approach.

Over a fifteen-year period (1952-67) Newark initiated seventeen urban renewal projects. The total effort came to about $180 million, more than two-thirds of it in federal funds. It involved the complete clearance and rebuilding of 1,045 acres, the general rehabilitation of 1,387 acres more. As of 1967, however, only 45 acres (.018%) of this reconstruction was actually completed. The rest of the projects were scattered all over the lot in stages ranging from final paperwork to the start of construction.

It required an average of three-and-one-half years for the Department of Housing and Urban Development to give final approval to an application. About five years elapsed between a typical application and the first ground-breaking for new construction. One big project was in the works for twelve years, from spring of 1955 to late summer of 1967, with the job still far from complete at the close of that period.

With all this huge backlog still on its hands, Newark applied for a Model Neighborhood program. That project was to have had a scope larger than all the others combined, and the city officials were given some reason to believe that this time Washington was ready to roll. A great swath of blighted area was surveyed and condemned, and the city girded itself for a major rebuilding. Almost immediately, however, the federal government began to back away from the commitment. Four years later, the city is still awaiting the appropriations which would allow it to begin the major work.

There is in this situation much more than mere progress halted and hopes deferred. An urban restoration program that is slowed in mid-stride tends actually to create decay. It occurs when buildings are condemned and boarded up, but not demolished, or demolished but not replaced. The proliferation of empty buildings contributes to the syndrome of vacancy and vandalism. The former residents are scattered to other areas through processes of both eviction and flight. Small shopkeepers lose customers and soon boarded up stores begin appearing, too. The remaining property owners expect the bulldozers to come through in a year or so, and they cut maintenance to the bare minimum. Over the past two decades great areas of Newark's inner-city ghetto have been relegated to this limbo of paralyzing uncertainty.

The resulting demoralization is most acute among the resident owners. Sternlieb found that about three-fourths of the medium- and large-scale commercial realtors expected to receive a fair settlement if their property is condemned. Only half of the one-parcel owners shared that optimism. Those differing views derive, of course, from quite different positions. The professional operator is thoroughly sophisticated in the condemnation process, he can afford appraisers and lawyers, and he makes it his business to know the officials who count. The small property owner has no such array of supports, and he belongs to a class that traditionally views city hall with suspicion. He regards himself as a little man unequally pitted against a big bureaucracy. He sees urban renewal as a steamroller that will flatten his home, he at least half expects that he will be cheated in the process, and he becomes extremely wary of any interim investments in maintaining the place. Thus ironically, perhaps inevitably, the most immediate effect of an urban renewal announcement is a crisis of confidence among those who have the most stake in the neighborhood's future.

Some of the urban renewal side effects might be eased by better contact between city hall and the people on the street. Much of the problem, however, must be accepted as simply inherent. A decision to knock down the block and start over is necessarily upsetting to owners, tenants, small shopkeepers, the whole social and economic fabric of the neighborhood. A recognition of that fact has led urban planners to reappraise the bulldozer approach. It is true also, however, that in the inner ghetto one sees block on block that is simply too far gone to yield to any lesser effort. The obvious solution is a level of financing which would allow the city to get on with it once so drastic a verdict has been reached. It is slow death for a neighborhood to sit and wait year after year for bulldozers that may not even come.

The foregoing quick scan of Newark's housing decay might seem to suggest that government is a prime agent of the disaster. That would be a distortion. Government has failed to meet the problem, and indeed has made serious contributing errors, but the question must be viewed in larger context. The housing collapse in Newark's inner city is a product of the so-called free market economic forces. To the extent that rebuilding exists, Newark's public program is just about the only game in town.

About one Newark citizen out of ten lives in a public housing unit. During the 1960s the public sector accounted for a third of the new housing built throughout the city and all or nearly all of the low income units in the inner city slum. Newark is fifth among the nation's cities in per capita investment in public housing and urban renewal, and first among major cities in funds reserved for future projects. For twenty years it has consistently led the way in developing such programs.

Not all of it has worked well, but then mistakes are a usual penalty for being out front in experimental activity. Thus Newark went through its period of concentrating the poor in massive housing complexes. It seemed the quickest, easiest way to relieve large-scale misery. In Newark as elsewhere, however, such projects have often degenerated into high-rise concrete slums. The besieged woman cited earlier, expressed a quite common ghetto attitude in preferring the hazards of the street to a housing project that has gone sour.

Some Newark housing projects enjoy a good reputation. These are small, cohesive units; some are well-integrated racially and all are integrated economically in that tenants range from poor to middle class. There is no doubt that these places are preferable as social units. However, they cost more, which translates into less housing on a given urban budget, and the acceptance of mixed income tenants means a longer line for the waiting poor. It's a question of quantity versus quality. There is no perfect answer, not when decent housing is in short supply.

Still larger quandaries arise from the priorities assigned to urban renewal. Newark has been charged with shunting the poor aside to make room for industry and to create commercial enclaves which serve the interests of the middle class. Some of those complaints can be substantiated when particular projects are viewed through a single focus. A city, however, is a complex organism and urban planners cannot give sole attention to low-cost housing. Business and industry must be attracted if the poverty cycle is to be broken. The middle class must be retained if the city is to have a tax base sufficient for the ever-rising costs of social services. Moreover, some of the charges against urban renewal have a discordant ring. In the distemper of the times some militants today denounce commercial development and middle-class housing as intrusions on the ghetto neighborhood. Only yesterday the lack of such features was cited as reducing the ghetto to a shabby prison for the poor.

The real difficulty is that urban blight does not yield to one-shot piecemeal approaches, and the development which relieves one stress may exacerbate another. The Model Cities program was to have resolved that, by providing the means for a concerted attack on all the problems. Newark proposed a serious test as to whether that proposition would work or not.

In its application for funds the city described itself as an ideal testing ground, a place "large enough to count and small enough to manage." The laboratory aspect was further enhanced by what was then the Model City formula of intense concentration on selected neighborhoods. In Newark, the designated area began downtown, ran through the heart of the ghetto, and extended to an adjacent, slum-ridden white district. The project area embraced 10 percent of the city, some 40,000 people, and it contained in concentrated form every aspect of urban decay.

The program was to be achieved by marshaling the full resources of federal, state and local government, plus private enterprise, universities, and quasi-public institutions of various sorts.

The effort was to range over the entire spectrum of jobs, housing, education, health problems, crime control; the goal was to explore new techniques and consolidate old ones while creating tangible, visible improvements in every aspect of neighborhood life. As a scale model experiment it was as ambitious as anything ever proposed by an American city. To so characterize it, however, is in itself a commentary on our urban past. The grand design in Newark was no utopian scheme, but merely a serious, earnest effort to bring up to standard one small core area of a stricken city. Newark officials decided that a realistic schedule required a year or two to sct things up, and, after that, five years of hard work. The target date for a finished job was 1974.

In housing the plan called for 5,000 new and 5,000 rehabilitated units. As a perspective, that total nearly equals all the public housing built throughout the city in the two previous decades.

The housing approach included both public and private restoration. Resident landlords were to receive help through tax abatement and revolving credit funds. Tenant cooperatives were to have similar encouragement. One of the major aims was to reduce absentee ownership by 75 percent. Another was to achieve mixed-income neighborhoods with decent housing at all levels. Rent supplements were to assist those who couldn't afford such quarters at a realistic market price.

Other aspects of the package program were designed to bring in business and industry, intensify job training, upgrade the schools, provide an adequate health service available to all. No one feature was particularly new or remarkable; what was new was the proposed intensity and scope. Within five years the unemployment in this Model Neighborhood was to be reduced to the national average. The children were to have the benefit of an average education. The people who suffered from ravaging disease were to have the necessary examination and treatment, with the fees adjusted to ability to pay. The people coming home with their hard-earned paychecks were to have ordinary protection against lead-pipe assault on their persons and pocketbooks. Moreover, the people along the street were to contribute an important part to this renaissance. Neighborhood residents were to take part as paid, trained, paraprofessional aides in agencies ranging from the schools to the police department. That was partly to augment services, partly to establish a better understanding between city hall and the community it is supposed to serve. In short, a social, economic and above all human disaster area was to be transformed into a reasonably healthy part of a functioning city. And if it worked, if even part of it worked, that was to be regarded as a practical model for all other neighborhoods needing similar repair. As the Newark proposal put it, "If the Model Neighborhood area can be turned around, so can the rest of the city."

Some details of the Newark plan aroused objections from radicals. The riot soon followed, leading commentators to suggest that dissatisfaction with the program was one cause of insurrection. The reasoning was logical, but esoteric. When the poor riot it is over some inflammatory street incident which brings forth all the pent-up frustrations of their lives. They do not riot over the fine points of city planning. To put it another way, the riot was a sign of Newark's deep sickness. The political confrontation between officials and radicals was a part of the city's fitful struggle to get well.

At issue was a state medical college to be built in the ghetto; it was intended to serve the health program, bring in new money and form an institutional bulwark against further decay. Leaders of SNCC, CORE and other local groups objected, charging that the community had not been sufficiently consulted. In fact, city officials had talked it over with the old-line black organizations, but this was a new crowd demanding recognition. The community action agency backed the militants and for a time federal funds were cut off. Under such pressure the city had no choice but to negotiate. The week-long public hearings began with a televised session of acrimonious exchanges on white racism, black power, and the like. Then the television cameramen went away, the participants got down to serious in-fighting, and a city official put the politician's question: "What do you want?"

The militants huddled over that and came back with practical and not at all radical demands: cut down the size of the college campus, allocate the extra space to ghetto housing, and guarantee ghetto workers a larger share of the construction jobs. After some hard bargaining, an agreement was reached. The militants got what they wanted, which was partly the principal substance of their demands, and partly the public recognition that they were in there fighting for their people. That, of course, is how leaders build constituencies. It may or may not have been part of the settlement—it's one of those delicate questions which politicians do not discuss—but the city later threw in a little something extra in the interests of harmony. The planners went back to their drawing boards and redesigned the Model Neighborhood to include LeRoi Jones's Street.

All this was in the classic urban tradition of ethnic blocs and pressure groups, of confrontations and negotiations, of give-and-take politics. It's a process which produces some sort of rough balance when the pressures are sufficient, and when there is enough in the pot to provide something for everyone. The hopeful thing in Newark was that a new breed of emerging black spokesmen were getting a piece of real action for the first time. The trouble was, the pot began to melt away while various factions were still arguing over how to divide it up.

The Newark Model Neighborhood package came to about $250 million, almost all of it in federal money. Major work was to have begun in 1969, but didn't, because the big appropriations were not forthcoming. Early in 1970 the city was awaiting word from Washington, the bulk of the project was a year and a half behind schedule, and the only serious question was how much could be salvaged. It was by that time absolutely apparent that America would not soon build a Model Neighborhood, in Newark or anywhere else.*

Meantime, the blight spreads. In 1967 Sternlieb conducted a follow-up spot survey in Newark in collaboration with Rutgers professors Jack Chernick and Bernard P. Indix. They found that during the 1960s the vacant housing units in the core area had nearly doubled, from 2,681 to an estimated 4,707. There was other alarming evidence of continuing deterioration. In 1960 about one-fourth of the vacant units had been rated unusable. By 1967 an estimated half of the vacant units were beyond repair, and two-thirds of the remainder were in poor condition.

The vacancy rate in the core area had risen to an estimated 14 percent. Thus about one dwelling in seven stood empty, and one in fourteen was an abandoned ruin. The increase in ruined buildings negated all the public housing constructed in the inner city throughout the period. The progressive deterioration gave warning that large areas were sliding past the point of no return.

Newark has sought also to arrest such decay by attracting private developers. A successful program would require huge subsidies, however, for private enterprise is in flight from this disaster area. Malafronte was musing on that aspect one day and he remarked that whatever the method employed it all comes down to dollars. "People talk about the complexity of urban renewal," he observed sardonically. "There is no complexity. I know how to get the job done in a hurry."

"You do?"

"Sure. You show me how businessmen can make good money building good housing in the slums, and I'll find people who want to get started on it right away. No trouble at all. We could rebuild this city in two or three years."

---

* If the Newark plan were extended to all inner-city slums the price tag would be at least $80 billion. The combined federal expenditures for Model Cities, urban renewal and public housing amounts currently to about $1.5 billion a year.

Money, or rather the lack of it, is the root of the evil. At last report about one-fourth of those in Newark's inner ghetto were subsisting on family incomes of less than $3,000 a year. About half were under $5,000. The typical rent is $70 to $80 a month for a shabby three- or four-room tenement apartment. That's far more than many can afford and yet not nearly enough to secure good housing at the going urban price.

No amount of outcry can alter the economic facts, and piece-meal reforms can only alleviate the worst consequences. In Newark, and in all the stricken cities, the basic situation can be resolved in only one of three ways. There must be created in the slums and ghettos a viable economy, one which generates a flourishing private market in substantial housing. Either that, or the necessary cost must be met from the public purse. Or else the blighted urban cores must continue to rot.

The ghetto's economic problem is sharply focused in Newark. Historically, it's an old factory town and half its people used to derive their livelihood from that source. In the last twenty years, however, it has not added an important new plant, and it has lost about a fifth of the manufacturing jobs it formerly had. The industrial decline, like the housing decay, is visible in the form of empty space in the heart of the city. More than three hundred acres of industrial tract are vacant; there are some 125 acres of floor space in unused, essentially abandoned factories.

Industry's flight from Newark is symbolized for this reporter by a grimy old brick building that one passes on a bus route into town. It used to be a major brewery. Now it's empty. It happened that the reporter visited the brewery about fifteen years ago, on what seemed at the time a minor industrial story. In retrospect the item takes on significance as clue to a slow-moving, powerful force that transformed a city.

The story involved a then fairly new industrial technique called pallet loading. The idea was that merchandise need not be shoved around in the warehouse by manual labor. Instead it was stacked on ricks, or pallets, for easy handling by fork lift tractors. The tractor was equipped with movable steel arms which inserted into a small slot at the base of the pallet, gripping the load securely. At the touch of pushbutton controls the tractor operator could pick up five or six hundred pounds, roll across the floor with it, and deposit it neatly in a waiting truck or railroad freight car.

Generations of immigrants sweated their way through this and other Newark warehouses but now no more: one man with a tractor can outwork a dozen laborers. The tractor, moreover, was just one of many similar innovations. It became possible to set up an operation so that from start to finish a brewery worker need hardly lay hands on a case of beer. The change had ultimate effects which went far beyond the disappearance of particular jobs. The full use of the new technology required a new kind of plant. The old brewery was a vertical plant, its multi-storied building geared to the cramped necessities of urban land use. The new methods called for a horizontal plant, one with large expanses of open floor space to permit the unimpeded flow of mechanized traffic. Tracts large enough for such purpose were most readily available in suburban industrial parks. That's where the brewery went. Left behind in the city were such vexing problems as traffic congestion and high taxes, along with all that surplus labor.

Over two decades the combined forces of automation and exodus cost Newark more than twenty thousand factory jobs. The factory worker is usually a family breadwinner, and so the loss amounted to at least eighty thousand places around the industrial dinner table. Meantime, the migrants and their progeny were swelling Newark's ghetto population by about one hundred and fifty thousand. These people came bearing with them all the unresolved problems of places like Taliaferro

County, they poured into an urban society which has plenty of unresolved problems of its own, and they arrived at a time of major industrial dislocation. That is the heart of Newark's economic crisis.

The city has adjusted to dislocation by shifting its economic base. The general line of change has been from production to services, from blue collar to white collar; the overall result has been a slight net gain in jobs for the twenty-year period. In such balance, however, there is no compensation for the factory worker who is laid off, and no opportunity for an unskilled migrant who is trying to wedge in. Newark consequently has a white unemployment rate half again higher than the national average, and a black rate three times as high.

As for those new jobs, Newark is creating wealth for others while its own people remain poor. The greatest growth areas in the city's economy are architecture, engineering, industrial research. Commuters draw most of these paychecks. The ghetto blacks, and for that matter the slum whites, remain mired in a steadily shrinking blue collar and low-skill job mart.

Escape from such urban underclass has always been a slow and difficult process; that's witnessed in Newark by tens of thousands of third-generation whites who have not made the transition yet. For the blacks, the vast majority of them first or second generation residents, the escape routes are not even in sight. About one-fifth of Newark's adult blacks did not complete grade school. A third of them never entered high school, and another third didn't finish. Less than one in forty has a college diploma.

The migrants have been essentially barred from some occupations at which they might have earned a livelihood. Despite the city's high unemployment there is a shortage of ironworkers, masons, carpenters and other skilled construction men. These occupations are tightly controlled by unions and, in Newark as elsewhere, the blacks have been granted only token admission. A city report took note of an irony: if funds were forthcoming to rebuild the ghetto the task would be seriously hampered by a lack of trained workers.*

Another and even larger barrier has been the de facto segregation which confines most blacks within a ghetto. For employment of almost any kind, the ghetto is where the action isn't.

The blacks have partially resolved the dilemma by becoming reverse commuters. That phenomenon has gone largely unnoticed but it constitutes a human traffic of major proportions; in Newark's case about half the ghetto labor force is employed outside the city. A good many black women commute to domestic jobs. Black men follow the factories to areas where they can work, though not live. Some also go into suburbia to perform essential but generally ill-paid public service. They pick up the garbage, and deliver the mail.

The total circumstances add up to a ghetto state of permanent depression. Unemployment in the city's inner ghetto hovers around 12 percent, and subemployment is estimated at more than 40 percent. The latter category includes the unemployed, the partially employed and those who work full time at wages too low to permit escape from poverty.

Bad as it is, the situation could well grow worse. The ghetto population is heavily weighted toward young people, and they are entering the employment market at a rate far faster than the city's economy is creating jobs. A recent Rutgers University study found that by 1975 Newark would acquire 16,000 new job seekers, while adding only 2,000 to 5,000 new jobs. Moreover, to gain a fair share of even that employment, the emerging black generation will have to break through the numerous fences which confined their elders.

As a final bleak perspective the chronic unemployment and the now-widening job gap have been the ghetto lot during a long

---

* On a national basis, blacks would gain an estimated 350,000 jobs if they could gain proportionate entry to all construction trades.

period of general prosperity. On the desolate streets of Newark's Central Ward, and in all the other places like it, the affluent years have yielded only marginal existence. If a major recession should occur, the already crippled ghetto economy would suffer a massive blow.

In job programs as in housing, Newark has been the scene of one of the nation's more intensive efforts. And as in housing, the city's experience only illustrates how huge is the gap between problems and solutions.

A walk through the ghetto streets suggests a lot of action, one store front office after another offering job help to the poor. In Newark the principal agencies bear such labels as TEAM, NAB and BIIC.* There are others; so many others, in fact, that agencies have been created to coordinate the agencies.

Most of the programs have evolved since the mid-60s and in the early phases particularly there was a lot of fumbling. A 1968 report commissioned by the city found that training courses had been set up helter-skelter, with little or no regard for matching the courses to available jobs. At least a third of the job applicants were hastily processed and then shoved back into the kind of dead end employment from which they were trying to escape. Some agencies were so swamped in confusion that they could give no real account of what they were doing. The city report observed that "It is exceedingly difficult to ascertain the exact number of active programs and projects available, the number of [training and placement] slots handy, and the number of per-

---

* TEAM is Total Employment and Manpower, a joint federal-local agency which has the primary responsibility for job training and placement. NAB (National Alliance of Businessmen) is a quasi-public organization which works closely with official agencies. NAB seeks to promote more open hiring policies on the part of business, and serves as a conduit for on-the-job training grants given to firms which employ the ill-educated and unskilled.

TEAM and NAB are, of course, national programs. BIIC (Business and Industry Coordinating Council) is unique to Newark and is co-sponsored by local firms and the Urban League. BIIC maintains a job clearing house and the Urban League processes the applicants.

sons trained and/or placed. It is not possible to evaluate these programs systematically."*

It will not do, however, to blame all the failures on incompetent bureaucrats. The agencies are attempting to solve major problems on minor budgets, and they can offer, at best, remedial aid to a fraction of those in need. The training programs have their occasional triumphs—the high school dropout who becomes a data processor—but mostly it doesn't go that way. Mostly success consists of helping a handicapped man run a little better on a very muddy economic track.

The limitations are sharply illustrated by a look at one of the best projects, an O.E.O. operation called the Work Experience Program. It's federally financed, locally administered, and was run in Newark by knowledgeable black representatives at city hall. The approach included basic education, vocational training and personal counseling. It was aimed primarily at men who headed needy families and family support was provided during an often extensive training course. Over an experimental three-year period the agency's Newark center trained two thousand men, and placed twelve hundred of them. When it issued a progress report, the agency cited success stories like that of Artis Hearns.

Hearns was a middle-aged migrant who worked at odd jobs. He was trying to get by on a sixth-grade education, and a bad one at that—his reading level was first grade. In many important ways his illiteracy made him functionally blind. He couldn't fill out the simplest application forms, and so was automatically barred from large areas of employment. Street signs, bus sched-

---

* Such confusion has been the general rule. In a national study of job training, Garth L. Magnum found that "No Federal Manpower Program currently has a reporting system capable of producing data of the kind and quality needed for evaluation." Manpower Development and Training was given the best marks for coherent reports but "such praise is based on comparing the inadequate to the abysmal." (From *Contributions and Costs of Manpower Development and Training*, Garth L. Magnum, The Institute of Labor and Industrial Relations, University of Michigan, 1967.)

ules and printed instructions of any kind presented complexities which further narrowed the range of his job hunting. His arithmetic was at a higher level—about fifth grade—but still not good enough for many commonplace and workaday needs. He had to start over with the kind of basic schooling he should have had as a child. It took seventeen months to bring his education up to a low level adequacy. A vocational course stretched his total training period to nearly two years. He graduated as an apprentice baker and obtained a job at $2 an hour. He took his $80-a-week paycheck home to a wife and ten children.

Roosevelt Robinson had a very similar history. He was a migrant who arrived in the city with a fifth-grade education. He became an off-and-on construction laborer, an in-and-out welfare case. After auto shop training he obtained a job as a garage attendant and apprentice mechanic. The pay was $100 a week. He has nine children.

For others in the program the circumstances were only a little less severe. The typical enrollee had six to seven children, an incomplete grade school education, and a history of erratic employment. Frequently he had health problems as well, and more often than not he was a man emotionally hobbled by a lifetime of frustration, humiliation and chronic failure. "The trainee," said the project report, "has a distrust of his environment and low self-esteem. He often has an unrealistic way of attacking his problem." A vocational course and a job as garage attendant does not strike away all that at a blow. For that matter it doesn't get a man to the place where his problems will yield to a "realistic" attack. It does help him escape welfare dependency while struggling up to the middle rung of ghetto poverty. The average project graduate came out earning about $5,000 a year, or about par for the ghetto course.

A complete audit of the training programs in Newark would yield several thousand "success stories" of that sort. There remain some 30,000 failure stories—the unemployed and subemployed who have not been helped at all. With a candor unusual for civic boosters, the Greater Newark Chamber of Commerce summed up the city's job programs as the "development of techniques which have kept the unemployment rate from climbing drastically higher."

The inner city economic crisis is mirrored in a collapse of social services. It could hardly be otherwise. All the greatest needs are concentrated at the point of least resources.

One of the massive problems is health. That's reflected in Newark by a death rate a third higher than the national average. There is an even larger toll in half life, in debilitated energy and wasted human potential. One major employer in the Newark metropolitan area estimated that a third to a fourth of all rejected job applicants are turned down for health reasons. A welfare department study assigned one-third of the city's case load to the same factor.

Some of the ills represent the migrant heritage. Thus Newark is consistently one of the leading cities in reporting so-called new cases of tuberculosis. Actually, many of these are old cases newly discovered. Migrants arrive with the infection, having harbored it for years, and it becomes a matter of public record when it turns up at some clinic check or industrial examination.

The ghetto itself breeds other afflictions. Ghetto illness, in fact, begins in the womb. The chances that a child will be born to an anemic mother are three times as high in Newark as in the surrounding suburbs. In a recent year the city registered the nation's highest maternal mortality, and the second highest infant mortality. The infant mortality has climbed to a point almost exactly equal to that of thirty years ago. In effect, three decades of medical progress has been canceled out by social failures.

The wretched housing is responsible for many ills. Pneumonia, for instance, is a condition that modern medicine is supposed to have under reasonable control. In Newark's drafty old tenements it is the fifth leading cause of death.

There are special hazards for youngsters. Small children are prone to put things in their mouths—all the more so, of course, if prompted by hunger—and in the ghetto tenements they often eat paint which they peel from the flaking walls. It can cause brain damage. Newark has recorded up to one hundred such poisonings a year, and an intensive study of one neighborhood suggests that half the cases may go undetected.

It is not difficult to envision the unrecorded tragedies in such environment as this. A child gets sick, he is nursed through the crisis without benefit of medical examination or treatment, and he seems to recover. After that he is never quite right, and no one knows why.

Still other ills result from general demoralization. By conservative estimate Newark harbors at least four thousand drug addicts, and in the more stricken neighborhoods one can find four or five along almost any block. Their condition is socially infectious in the largest sense. Addicts peddle drugs in order to buy them, and teenagers are their natural prey.

Alcoholism is less spectacular but even more prevalent. The Newark ghetto probably contains three alocholics for every addict.

For these and a host of other afflictions the city has few remedies. The Newark hospital which serves most of the ghetto patients is called by local blacks "the butcher shop." It is not that, but neither is it a facility in any way adequate for the overwhelming problems that are brought to its door. As for private medicine, there is an acute shortage of physicians; in the ghetto neighborhoods nearly half of the former resident doctors have closed their offices and moved out.

The social ills are at least equally grievous. The brutal strains of ghetto life create such interlocking circles of disaster as family disintegration, school failure, crime and welfare dependency, and the spiraling problems all magnify each other. In Newark the sociologic fever chart reads like this:

One-fourth of the children in the inner ghetto are born to unmarried mothers. Nearly half the ghetto youngsters grow up in broken homes. Often enough these children of poverty and despair are propagated by parents themselves just out of childhood; the city's high schools record some 300 pregnancies a year.

The school system is barely able to maintain a semblance of order, and fails miserably at its primary task of education. By the sixth grade about half the children have fallen eighteen months below national average in reading skills. By the twelfth grade a third of them have dropped out.

Teen-age dropouts roam the streets, rootless and wild, contributing heavily to a crime rate that is one of the nation's highest. This rather small-sized city reports annually about 90 murders, more than 200 rapes, and some 4,500 assaults. There are on the average 4,000 robberies, 7,000 auto thefts and 24,000 larcenies and burglaries. About 80 percent of the crimes occur within a two-mile radius of the city's core. In specific terms the besieged enclave produces about one crime a week on almost every block.

The ghetto is of course the source as well as the scene for most of these crimes. What is often overlooked is that a ghetto minority commits the acts, while the ghetto majority provides most of the victims. In Newark's inner ghetto about one person in three is attacked or robbed every year.

Amidst such general chaos the city's social services have all but collapsed. The per capita expenditure for municipal functions is twice that of surrounding suburbs, and yet falls far short of the need.

In the welfare department ill-paid, often ill-trained caseworkers are assigned to handle a hundred clients apiece. In theory caseworkers are supposed to consult closely with applicants, determining their needs and helping them work out individual problems. In practice about all they can manage is to process papers and hand out a subsistence dole.

The schools are similarly swamped. Most are crowded well above the rated capacity, in the worst instances by as much as 50 percent, and some 20,000 youngsters go to school on double shifts. Even so, the education bill in 1970 was about $20 million over budget and for a time there was talk that the schools might not open for the fall term.

The city has threatened publicly to close its public library and museum. That apparently was something of a bluff, designed to draw attention to its woes, but the use of such tactic is itself an index to the extent of disaster.

The municipal breakdown extends to such matters as parking meters that don't function. In Newark the meters are nearly all broken, a consequence mostly of vandalism and crime. Meter revenue to the city should be about $400,000 a year, but the actual income is only $11,000.

Street maintenance at one point was all but abandoned. Junk and garbage were piled everywhere, derelict autos sat rusting at the curbs, and broken glass littered the sidewalks. An inspection of one block yielded more than forty broken windows pock-marking a row of empty buildings. If you asked a resident how long a particular eyesore has existed the usual response is a shrug. Who knew? What was the point of keeping count?

The general disarray is symbolized in one small detail. On a visit to the Central Ward this reporter stopped at an intersection to check bearings and realized suddenly that there was no street sign. The sign post was there, but the sign had been ripped away. There was no sign at the next corner either, or the next. The placards may have been torn down in some angry, defiant gesture, or then again perhaps they were merely looted by some youthful vandal intent on collecting a few pennies worth of scrap metal. In any case the streets without names seemed oddly appropriate, for in this neighborhood all directions led to the same scenes of general ruin.

All this occurred in a city that has strained its resources to the limit. The property tax has doubled over the last fifteen years. The current level is such that a man who owns a $20,000 home in Newark pays taxes equivalent to a $50,000 home in sheltered suburbia. Newark's middle class inveighs against such extortion, the poor demand services which cannot be provided, and all parties turn for redress to a beleaguered city hall.

Clearly much of Newark's crisis is rooted in economic rather than racial factors. The immense influx of the poor and dispossessed was bound to create great strains, whatever the origin of the newcomers. Indeed, this archetypical city has not yet resolved all the difficulties generated by the earlier waves of white immigrants, as witnessed by the comparisons of white and black slums.*

In the Model Cities application Newark officials stressed this point, saying of the black migrants: "Their impact has not caused an urban crisis, but revealed it, for if the dimensions of the problem are new, the patterns are old. Poor housing, limited and inadequate public facilities, the myriad other social and economic problems began not with the newest wave of in-migrants, but at the turn of the century, when the city first confronted a sizable wave of the culturally different. Newark was then as it is now, a basic training camp for the poor. . . . The training was never efficient but its worst flaws were overlooked in boom times, noticed only during the Great Depression and covered again by World War II."

This truth is important, but it cannot obscure the fact that the

* The continued existence of white slums is a factor too often overlooked in discussions of the urban crisis.

Federal reports do not employ the term "slum," but they enumerate so-called metropolitan poverty areas. These are neighborhoods with a heavy concentration of the poor and they contain generally all the concomitant social problems.

In 1969 about 4 million American families were living in metropolitan poverty areas. The total included about 2.5 million white families, 1.5 million black families.

On a percentage basis, of course, blacks are far more likely to be trapped in such circumstances. About one family in ten lives in a poverty area among urban whites, as compared to about half for the blacks.

experience of black migrants has been especially painful. Thus the harsh question remains: how much has racism contributed to ghetto misery? The answer is necessarily speculative but the Newark experience offers some insight.

The Sternlieb report found that slum rents for blacks averaged almost $10 a month higher than those paid by whites. Many white landlords admitted openly to such surcharge, justifying it by the supposed deleterious effects of black occupancy. The attitude has its considerable irony in view of the findings that the city's poor black neighborhoods often held up better than their white counterparts. A crueler irony was that some black landlords agreed on the undesirability of black tenants.

"Negroes have ruined the property," a black landlord told one of Sternlieb's interviewers. "My people are just not ready! My family were the first Negroes on this block; there were nice lawns and the property was well kept. Now those who try to keep yards nice are fighting a losing battle." In fact, his property was located in a district where the objective ratings showed black and white housing performance to be closely parallel. The entire area was deteriorating, however, and he blamed the blacks, because white society had taught him to despise his own kind.

Other ghetto dwellers ascribed the ruin of black neighborhoods to the contempt and indifference of white authorities. One black homeowner who had been a longtime resident of Newark put it this way: "You know the neighborhood has really changed terribly since we moved in here. At first it was mostly German and Jewish and the police in the city took care of things. No trucks parked overnight in the streets and no noise or anything like that. Now there is mostly Negroes and they don't seem to care any more. If you complain they want to put you in jail." Said another: "When I went to complain to the police department about overnight truck parking and teenage hoodlums on the block, the cops made me feel like a criminal. I was glad to go home and kind of hide myself behind the door."

The effect of race bias on housing thus adds up to a good deal more than an overcharge of $10 a month. The ghetto dwellers are herded into mean quarters, they develop crippling self-doubts about their own ability to establish a viable community, and they come to believe that every hand is turned against them. Out of rage and frustration some of them wreak wanton destruction on the places where they live.

A profound distrust of society pervades every other aspect of ghetto life. Suspicion, resentment, defiance and fear act as corrosive agents at all the points of contact between the street people and the civic institutions. State and federal inquiries both noted the big role that played in Newark's 1967 riot.

The President's Riot Commission surveyed black attitudes in the city, sampling both those who said they took part in the action and those who said they stood aside. Among the self-identified rioters less than one in twenty expressed general trust in the good intentions of the local government, while more than two out of five revealed almost total distrust. The answers of the non-rioters were in a way even more ominous. They represented much the larger group, they had chosen to remain passive, and yet their bitterness and alienation ran almost as deep. About one in eight of these people said they usually trusted the local agencies, while one in three said almost never. In sum, there was clustered in the heart of the city at least 70,000 people who felt that they had no reason to expect compassion or even simple fairness and justice from the schools, the hospitals, the job agencies, the welfare department, the police or courts.*

---

* In a larger survey, taken in 20 riot-torn communities, the commission found that main grievances of the ghetto were expressed in the following order: (1) police practices; (2) unemployment; (3) inadequate housing; (4) inadequate education; (5) poor recreational facilities and programs; (6) ineffectiveness of the political structure and grievance mechanisms; (7) disrespectful white attitudes; (8) discriminatory administration of justice; (9) inadequacy of federal programs; (10) inadequacy of municipal services; (11) discriminatory consumer and credit practices; (12) inadequate welfare programs. The complaints on police practices, unemployment and housing were much the most intense.

In this atmosphere every grievance is magnified, every circumstance is seen as a conspiracy to oppress the victim. "Segregation and poverty," said the National Advisory Commission on Civil Disorders, "have created in the racial ghetto a destructive environment totally unknown to most white Americans."

Much earlier the novelist James Baldwin had described one of the environment's most destructive effects: "To be a Negro in this country and to be relatively conscious is to be in a rage almost all the time."

During the violent summer of 1967 the rage erupted into more than forty black uprisings in cities across the nation. The Newark riot, like much else in the city, was merely an extreme case of the general sickness.

In Newark, two police incidents contributed to rising tensions which preceded the riot, and a third police affair provided the trigger. That was pretty typical of the general experience in ghetto riots. The riot commission found that eruptions usually followed a series of abrasive events, each one adding to a slow-building anger; police actions were frequently involved and served as a final spark in about half the cases.

Ghetto hostility toward police is double-edged. They are accused both of failing to protect the community and of employing harsh and repressive enforcement practices. The charges are not necessarily contradictory. Police may treat minor offenders in an offensive or brutal manner while allowing crime syndicates to flourish. It is an article of ghetto faith that criminals shake down the neighborhood, while police shake down the criminals.

The other side of the coin is that the ghetto is an anarchic society. Many of its inhabitants regard the law simply as a system to beat, and many others are highly ambivalent on the question. It is an attitude rooted in both class and race. The poor generally tend to regard the law as a device rigged for the rich, and the ghetto brings to that view a special edge: the sight of gun and club in the white hand is not a symbol to inspire confidence in black eyes. Add finally the human element—the things that can happen when tough cop collides with tough young street fighter —and the police issue becomes explosive.*

Newark's police were aware of the danger, at least at the top levels of the department, and had made some efforts to establish contact with the ghetto. All officers were required to take courses in human relations, youth programs had been established in every precinct, and precinct captains met monthly to talk over problems with community leaders. The police had also instituted a Citizens' Observer Program in which black representatives were invited to ride patrol cars and pay inspection visits to the station houses. On paper it was a good program, but it never really reached the streets. A lot of blacks continued to see the cops as their natural enemy. The police force—90 percent of it white—contained a lot of cops who reciprocated the feeling. On the night of July 12, at about 9:00 P.M., the human relations program came unglued as officers Vito Pontrelli and John De-Simone confronted citizen John Smith.

Smith was a forty-year-old black migrant, up from North Carolina. He was atypical in that he had a partial college education.

* The general emotional atmosphere of police and ghetto confrontation was etched sharply in a vignette by Piri Thomas, the Puerto Rican author of *Down These Mean Streets*.

In the summer of 1967 a policeman shot and killed a resident of New York's Spanish Harlem, while attempting to break up a knife fight, and for two days the barrio seethed with incipient riot. Thomas walked the streets, trying to cool it, and recorded this conversation with a young man named Chino:

"Fill me in baby. What happened and how did it happen?"

"It's on, like the word is out. Un policia shot and really wasted one of us Puerto Ricans."

"Yeah, baby, but I heard the cat had a blade and was trying to mess up that cop."

"Whatever it is, like we don't like it. Maybe the cat had it coming to him, and maybe not. But a whole lot of us have been thinking of all the *inocentes* that didn't deserve it and got it anyway."

Such attitudes are grounded partly in police practices, and partly in a general anger for which police become a handy target. Said Thomas of the young men he met on his Harlem peace walk: (They) "would not or could not differentiate between *un policia bueno* and *un policia malo*. In their minds, anyone with a blue uniform, a badge and a helmet was *el enemigo*."

He was apparently a man of some creative and intellectual bent as witnessed by his avocations: musician and chess player. He was stuck in a dead-end economic street as evidenced by his vocation: cab driver. He was a bad driver, quite possibly an angry one; his license had been revoked after eight or nine violations and accidents. He was driving without a license when the police stopped him for a minor infraction.

What happened next can never really be known except to the participants. Smith said he was beaten without provocation. The police said he resisted arrest. There is no question that he was beaten; much later on that turbulent night he was taken to a hospital for treatment.

Initially he was booked at a precinct station that stands just opposite a ghetto housing project. He was dragged from the patrol car, being either unable or unwilling to walk, and people saw it from the project windows. Within minutes a woman was summoning civil rights leaders by phone. Black cab drivers heard of it, passed the word on their radios, and organized a motorcade protest. People began to assemble, pouring out of the project and flocking from the tenements that were close-packed around. Shortly there was a crowd of several hundred. For three hours they held the station in siege, hooting and jeering. Some black leaders appeared with bullhorns and tried to divert the outbreak into a peaceful mass march. It didn't work. About midnight someone in the crowd threw a homemade fire bomb. A fifty-foot stream of fire curled down the stone wall of the station house, flared briefly, and died. When the police formed a defense line in front of the station they were barraged with rocks and bottles. The police charged then, dispersing the crowd, but that only spread the disorder. For the next four or five hours small groups roamed the streets, smashing windows and looting stores.

The next morning brought a brief lull. The city made gestures of conciliation: a blue ribbon investigation was promised in the case of John Smith, and a police reorganization plan was hastily prepared for the purpose of appointing the first black captain.

Otherwise Mayor Hugh Addonizio tried to play down the eruption, calling it an "isolated incident." Police Director Dominick Spina thought otherwise. This was his day for the regular monthly session with ghetto representatives, but no one showed up. It was not a good sign. The ghetto was boiling over a confrontation with police, and there was not a black leader in town who was still willing to talk with the police director. Spina mobilized all available men, extended the shifts, and prepared for trouble.

The ghetto was mobilizing in its own fashion. One segment, led by community organizers, was still trying for a peaceful resolution. They wanted to seize the occasion for a dramatic and powerful demonstration, something that would shake the city to its depths, but they didn't want mass violence. They knew they were walking a very tight line. Another segment was eager for riot. They had no real leadership, no organization at all, but they were drawn together by the urge for action. From the commission report and other inquiries there emerges a convincing profile of this volatile group. They were for the most part young males who had grown up wild and angry on the ghetto streets. Typically they were city born, aged fifteen to twenty-five, past or present high school dropouts, irregularly employed at menial tasks. Mostly they were nonpolitical, not belonging to or believing in any movement or party, but the turmoil of the times had infused them with a fierce race pride. Cop fighting to them was an affirmation of manhood. They were in sum the young lions, restless and prowling; society had provided no outlet for their energies and aspirations and now all their aggressions were elevated to an act of race patriotism. They had been out front in the rock throwing and looting the night before, they had seen the enemy recoil in fear, and for a few hours the streets had belonged to them. The next day they gathered in bars and pool rooms, reliving their exploits, and passing the word one to another: "You ain't seen nothing yet." By mid-afternoon that prediction had come true.

The second day's action began as a political demonstration, a police brutality protest rally in front of the precinct station. In minutes it became a melee. The director of the city's Human Rights Commission, a black official, was stoned when he tried to calm the crowd. A black detective tried next, attempting to half bully and half jolly the people into going home. He, too, was stoned. The police broke it up with a club-swinging charge but again the effect was like scattering fire. As the crowd surged through the streets mass looting broke out on a scale far heavier than before.

The liquor stores were hit hardest. Next came clothing stores, furniture stores, grocery shops. The proprietor of one large furniture store was in an urban renewal area and had told city officials it would take him two months to move. He was cleaned out in four hours. People formed block-long human chains in front of liquor stores, passing bottles hand to hand as looters treated the crowd. There were innumerable small, vivid scenes caught by reporters or spectators. A woman walked into a store carrying her baby and walked out wheeling the infant in a shiny new carriage. Another woman escorted four youngsters into a shop and emerged with each of them riding a tricycle. A small boy was seen struggling manfully to take home a lamp bigger than he was. No one really knows how many took part but by any estimate they numbered many thousands.*

---

* In a study of the combined Newark and Detroit uprisings the riot commission attempted a survey on participation. Interviews were anonymous, and respondents were assured of immunity in an effort to elicit honest answers. The results: among ghetto residents aged fifteen or over about one in ten said they were active rioters while one in six said they were counter-rioters who tried to cool it. The rest identified themselves as bystanders or said they stayed home to avoid trouble.

The estimate as to active rioters seems not unreasonable. Among Newark adult and teen-aged ghetto dwellers it would have come to a small army of 10,000. As to counter-rioters their numbers on the street were few, and the subsequent responses may well have been loaded by some skepticism as to who was asking the questions and why. However, even the counter-rioter estimate becomes credible if one includes all the mothers who tried to restrain their children from what soon became bullet-ridden streets.

Ghetto attitudes, of course, are not all of a piece, anymore than in any other community, and so the outbreak of looting brought mixed responses on the streets. There were some, mostly middle-aged or older, who were shocked. They saw it as hoodlumism, nothing more or less. There were others, mostly young, to whom it was a glorious uprising. At levels in between the fear of consequences mingled with feelings of pride, defiance, acquisition and revenge. The overriding attitude was that the ghetto had been taken by society time and again, and now it was taking a little back. "Man," said one street hustler, "they were getting a taste." A concurring view came from a black intellectual, a man who played a prominent part in the city's anti-poverty program. He was out on the street when it all began, he tried hard to break it up because he didn't want to see anyone hurt, and when mass looting broke out despite his efforts he could not resist a sardonic thrust. Turning to a companion he observed that here at last was the thing so long promised: an anti-poverty street program that offered maximum feasible participation of the poor.

The violence was directed almost entirely against property. Roving arsonists began setting fires—"hitting and moving," as they called it—to keep the police occupied. The police for their part were under tight rein in the early stages. They shot into the air and if that had no effect they often just stood by and let matters proceed. When Molotov cocktails splattered around one police car an urgent call crackled over the radio: "We're getting bombed here. What should we do?" The police dispatcher's laconic reply was, "Leave."

Mayor Addonizio tried to calm things, issuing periodic reports that the worst was over, while making day-long efforts to reach a truce. Negotiation proved hopeless—there was no one who could speak for the rioters—and after each seeming lull the outbreak would flare again. At about midnight the police were given orders to use any force necessary, and some two and a half hours later the state police and national guard were summoned as reinforcements. Addonizio by then was apparently in a state of shock. When asked to brief a state police official, the mayor reportedly just sat there shaking his head, mumbling "It's all gone. The whole town is gone." A city hall aide added that tears were streaming down Addonizio's face when he put in the call for the national guard. "He couldn't believe it was happening in Newark," the aide said. "Right up to the last hour he thought he had good relations with the black community." If in retrospect that seems naive, it was a mistake shared by a lot of urban liberals.

By dawn the first contingent of national guardsmen was clattering through the streets. Close behind came Governor Richard Hughes who toured the riot area with an armed escort. The governor was shocked and repelled to discover a "holiday atmosphere" in the embattled enclave. People were milling around in high good humor, as though the looting and sacking were some boisterous form of street carnival. That, in fact, is a stage commonly observed in urban riots.* To Hughes it seemed like "laughing at a funeral." He took charge, issuing a stern statement that "The line between the jungle and the law might as well be drawn here as any place in America."

When Governor Hughes assumed command, the riot had run about half its course, with a death toll of two persons. At the next stage the streets were strewn with casualties. Twenty-one persons were killed after the guard marched in, and hundreds were wounded or injured.

One kind of jungle law was, in fact, replaced by another. Previously the rioters had launched wholesale attacks on property. Now police and guardsmen struck back with indiscriminate attacks on people.

Hughes was a liberal, a man with a good record in civil rights, and there is no reason to believe that he intended such result. He, too, lost control. Newark that bloody week was a case study in a society out of control: it had failed to maintain the prerequisites for order, and when the breakdown came it lacked even a measured and disciplined means for containing disorder.

Some of the killing that followed can be ascribed to panic and accident. Scared, ill-trained, trigger-happy guardsmen fired at shadows, and at each other, and the bullets ricocheted through the crowded ghetto with disastrous effect.

Much of the killing was wanton. Fusillades were pumped into apartment houses and street crowds on little or no provocation. Once the police and guardsmen were turned loose riot control degenerated into a punitive expedition against the entire ghetto.

Major General James F. Cantwell, chief of staff of the New Jersey National Guard, made a revealing statement in subsequent testimony before the Armed Services Sub-committee of Congress. "There was too much initial firing against snipers," General Cantwell said, because of "confusion when we were finally called in for help and *our thinking of it as a military operation* (italics added)." The danger from snipers was grossly exaggerated, as will be evident a little later in this report. As for the guard's response there was indeed disastrous confusion but the heart of the tragedy was that they conducted themselves as though engaged in a war.

One of the standard tactics in house-to-house fighting is to post riflemen to cover the windows. Guardsmen were told to watch the windows for snipers, and some of them interpreted that as an instruction to shoot at any movement they saw. One victim of that policy was Mrs. Rebecca Brown. She was in her apartment when a flurry of shots rang out on the street below. Starting up, she saw her two-year-old child standing at a window and she rushed to pull the youngster away. She was framed in the window for only a moment and had turned away when a guardsman got off a snap shot. Mrs. Brown fell dead with a bullet in the back.

Another fatal shooting occurred at a roadblock. A man was driving his family home from an evening out at a restaurant when he saw soldiers blockading the street ahead. He panicked, swerved sharply to turn around and flee, and a soldier fired. The shot plowed into the car and killed a six-year-old boy.

One ghetto mother thought that things on her block had quieted down and so, late in the evening, after carefully checking the street from a window, she sent her eleven-year-old son out to empty the garbage. When the boy stepped under the arc of a street lamp he was shot dead. Presumably some policeman or soldier was enforcing curfew.

On occasion, enraged blacks would rain down bottles from their apartment windows. When a bottle cracked against the pavement guardsmen would whirl and fire at the window, or some window nearby. Sometimes such a shot would set off a barrage as other soldiers and police joined in.

Two columns of guardsmen and state troopers poured mass fire into one housing project which they believed harbored snipers. People were watching from tenement windows across the street and the troopers whirled and fired on them, too. The senseless fusillade killed one woman in the project and another in the tenement.

Judged even as a military operation, it was a bloody fiasco. Casualties would have been minimal if the affair had been conducted efficiently, securing and occupying each block in turn. There wasn't manpower enough for that, however, and so the ordeal went on and on, the action swirling unpredictably through the streets. Looters would scatter at the approach of soldiers and then return as soon as the troops had swept through. Bystanders would huddle in their apartments for awhile and then, drawn by curiosity and lulled by apparent safety, would drift back to the streets. Sooner or later the police or soldiers would reappear, sometimes firing wildly as they roared up in patrol cars or jeeps. Numerous bystanders were cut down in that fashion.

Some of those killed were, of course, looters. A *Life* reporter-photographer team of Dale Wittner and Bud Lee recorded one such event. The drama began casually on a street corner where the rioters were in temporary control. A Black Muslim was lecturing Wittner, telling him that the riot would continue "until every white man's building in Newark is burned." A young black man named Billy Furr broke into the conversation to say that wasn't the way of it at all.

"We ain't riotin' agains' all you whites," Furr told the reporter. "We're riotin' agains' police brutality, like that cab driver they beat up the other night. That stuff goes on all the time. When the police treat us like people 'stead of treatin' us like animals, then the riots will stop."

The parties went their separate ways but a little later Furr and Wittner met again a block down the street. Furr and several friends were helping themselves to some beer they had found in a store already well ransacked by earlier raiders. "Have a beer on me," Furr said, extending a can. "But if the cops show up get rid of it and run like hell."

Wittner took the beer and continued about his reportorial duties. Some minutes later he emerged from a nearby tenement to see a police car screeching to a halt at the curb. A policeman blasted a shotgun warning, firing into the air, then cops were jumping from the car with guns at the ready. The looters inside the store were caught by surprise and they froze, hands up. Furr was on the sidewalk, holding a six-pack. He acted on the advice he had given Wittner, the advice that all his life had conditioned him to follow. He dropped the six-pack and ran like hell.

Wittner was in the line of fire as the policeman leveled his shotgun. "Get down," screamed the policeman. The reporter flung himself to the pavement as a blast exploded above his head. The shot was high, accompanied by a shout to halt. Furr kept running. "From the ground," Wittner wrote, "I looked up into the sweating face of the policeman as he squinted down the long barrel. I prayed he wouldn't shoot. He pulled the trigger."

Furr spun to the pavement, riddled with shotgun slugs. People watching from the windows shouted obscenities and bottles came flying from rooftops. A girl knelt sobbing over the fallen young man, ignoring police commands to "get the hell out of here."

"I'm his girl friend," she cried. "Help him. Please do something. God, don't let him die." Within minutes he died.

About a hundred feet or so up the street lay another casualty. He was Joe Bass, Jr., aged twelve, struck in the neck and thigh with random pellets meant for Furr. The Bass child lived, though severely wounded.*

What of the snipers? Was there a revolutionary element in the urpising, and how much did that contribute to the bloodshed?

Early in the riot looters broke into a gun shop and seized a quantity of arms and ammunition. As the insurrection spread there were innumerable reports of snipers. Much of the white community believed itself to be in imminent danger.

The reports that crackled over police radios at the time gave every evidence of a running battle. Later those estimates were scaled far down. Youngsters caught up in the excitement were throwing firecrackers, and such explosions were mistaken for shots. The shots actually fired were often reported from four or five positions, magnifying the impression of combat. Above all there was so much wild firing by police and guards, especially the guards, that they often mistook each other for snipers.

"In my opinion," police director Spina said afterwards, "guardsmen were firing on policemen and policemen were firing back at them. . . . I really don't believe there was as much sniping as we thought."

At one point a hundred or more police and guardsmen were in battle positions around a housing project, crouching behind cars or lamp posts in preparation for a shoot-out with supposed snipers. A shot was heard and a young guardsman ran out from behind the corner of a building. Spina collared him and asked if

---

* Paraphrased from "The Killing of Billy Furr," by Dale Wittner, *Life* Magazine, July 28, 1967, © 1967 Time, Inc.

he had fired the shot. Yes, said the soldier, he had fired a warning shot to frighten a man away from a window.

"Do you know what you just did?" demanded Spina. "You have now created a state of hysteria. Every guardsman up and down this street and every state policeman and every city policeman that is present thinks that somebody just fired a shot and that it is probably a sniper."

Malafronte has an earthy recollection of the fear and confusion that prevailed on the streets. There was a moment when he was down on his stomach, trying to crawl under a car, while bullets whined close around him. "A guardsman was standing over me, returning the fire," he says. "I was shouting to him, 'Get the bastard.' I thought then that a sniper was trying to kill me. Now I don't know. I was probably caught in a crossfire between a couple of amateur soldiers."

Amidst such chaos a small band of snipers was at work, pursuing their own version of a military operation. While the riot still raged, *Life* reporters conducted an anonymous interview with a group of rifle-toting young men who identified themselves as guerrilla warriors. They claimed a membership of about twenty-five persons in Newark, and said they were reinforced by about twenty-five more from other cities after the action began. They engaged in harassing fire, they said, as a form of para-military demonstration. Their proclaimed purpose was largely symbolic, and did not involve a serious attempt at large-scale killing. One of them put it this way:

"Why kill for no purpose? Five or six shots in the air are enough to draw cops thick as fleas on a dog and still give time to get away. We had other things on our mind than killing. The important thing is that our people know we're there."

The guerrillas saw themselves as ideologic Robin Hoods, assisting in an informal redistribution of property while building a base of mass support among the people. Asked if ghetto dwellers would follow their lead one of the young warriors replied,

"Damned right, they'll follow. They're getting what they want, aren't they? While the police are busy tearing buildings apart looking to kill snipers, our people are getting color television sets, refrigerators, clothes—whatever they couldn't afford, they got it."

The guerrilla statement is consistent with events in one important respect. The rabbit warren of tenements offered endless possibilities for deadly ambush, especially at night, but most of the sniping was apparently not conducted with lethal intent. There were two white fatalities, a policeman and a fireman, out of more than five thousand police, firemen and soldiers engaged. A National Guard report concluded that most of the sniping seemed to be "deliberately or otherwise inaccurate."

The evidence suggests also that the guerrillas greatly exaggerated both their numbers and their general activity. The final police report credited only 79 instances of sniping spread over a five-day outbreak. Half a dozen determined gunmen could have accounted for all of that at a daily rate of two or three attacks apiece.

As a military force, then, the snipers were insignificant. On a political level, however, they were at least partially successful. They established a ghetto presence, which was their prime objective, and despite the danger they invited, they were not repudiated. A black activist in Newark, a man not identified with the guerrillas, offered this assessment:

"Baby, look, if you accept the idea that the snipers exist, which they do, you see what's going to come next? Whose apartment windows were they shooting from? Why didn't anyone turn them in? Think about that. Once a riot is on, this community isn't about to turn in *any* black man."*

In fact, no looter, arsonist or sniper was turned in by the black

* The guerrilla account is paraphrased from "In a Grim City, A Secret Meeting with Snipers," by Russell Sackett, *Life* Magazine, July 28, 1967, © 1967 Time, Inc.

community. In Newark's trial by fire, race polarization had come down to exactly that.

Three years after the riot Newark elected a black mayor. Recent years have produced more than fifty other black mayors but the Newark election marked nonetheless an historic moment in the American experience. The candidate, Kenneth A. Gibson, was nominated and sponsored by an all-black-and-Puerto Rican convention in a clear demonstration of ghetto power. It was the first time that a big city black majority asserted itself in such fashion, and it appears a sign of things to come. Up to now blacks have played largely the minority role of lesser partners in urban coalition politics. During the decade ahead they seem destined to take over physically, and presumably politically as the predominant group in numerous cities.*

Emerging blocs of urban blacks are thus beginning to re-enact a traditional American drama, one in which politics is employed as both sounding board and stepping stone for the aspirations of the group. The Newark story offers some insight into both the opportunities and limitations involved in that process. It provides also a view of a city reacting to fears and pressures as white power gives way to black. And finally it sheds some light on a more subtle point, namely the difference between rhetoric and

---

* The 1970 census found black majorities of the indicated percentages in the following cities: Washington (71.1), Newark (54.2), Gary (52.8) and Atlanta (51.3). Of that group only Atlanta still had a white mayor.

Major cities with large and fast growing black minorities include Baltimore (46.4), New Orleans (45), Detroit (43.6), St. Louis (40) and Oakland (34.5). All appear headed toward a black majority in the 1970s if present population trends continue. Baltimore, for example, lost 131,000 whites and gained 95,000 blacks during the last decade. If the next ten years produce similar change the city will have a 67 percent black majority. Comparable projections indicate decade-end black majorities of Detroit 60 percent, St. Louis 60 percent, New Orleans 56 percent, Oakland 51 percent. In Chicago, Cleveland and Philadelphia the balance is shifting at slightly lower rates; all now have black minorities of a third or more and appear headed toward 1980 proportions of 40 to 45 percent.

reality when the genuine tensions become entangled in the exaggerated rituals of American politics.

A political leader mirrors his constituents in many ways. Newark's Mayor Addonizio personified much of the city's past and seemed a figure almost typecast out of the old melting pot. He was born in the Central Ward to immigrant parents in 1914, a time when Newark's population was 3 percent black and 60 percent foreign born. The Germans were then the predominant group, but the Italians and Irish were making their presence felt. Addonizio represented a striving second generation on the way up. He went to Fordham University on a football scholarship, rose from private to much-decorated captain in World War II, and came home to launch a political career. He became that typical product of urban politics, an ethnic-based pragmatic liberal with back-room machine connections. For two decades the combination served him well.

He served in Congress for fourteen years, sponsored some of the major housing legislation of the era, and supported actively such causes as civil rights and higher minimum wages. In 1962 he was elected mayor, coming to office at the head of a newly forged Italian-black coalition, and sweeping out of city hall a long-entrenched Irish crowd that had overstayed its time.

Addonizio's administration brought in numerous blacks in positions up to department head and deputy mayor. Later, it became something of a fashion to characterize those people as "toms," "city hall blacks," and "oreo cookies (black on the outside, white on the inside)." In fact, they were merely emerging black politicians who ranged across the usual human spectrum in degrees of ability, integrity and concern. Their problem was that they arrived just before the nick of time. They came to power as the lesser members in a political alliance, and by the time a black majority had formed they were too closely associated with the old regime to change sides. Some, indeed, didn't want to switch.

Addonizio's strengths included that traditional political virtue, the ability to inspire strong personal loyalty. Some black loyalists chose to go down with him, and wept when he lost.

For five years Addonizio held his city and his coalition together. During that period riots broke out in New York and Watts. Newark stayed calm, at least on the surface, and Addonizio claimed political credit for keeping the peace. Then Newark exploded, and Addonizio had to take the politician's rap. He became a personal symbol of all that had gone wrong.

In the riot's aftermath Governor Hughes appointed a Select Commission on Civil Disorders, and that body came in with a blistering condemnation of the city administration's neglects and failures. The commission charged more than mere incompetence. It quoted anonymous witnesses who said that "There's a price on everything at City Hall." It suggested strongly that corruption was a major cause of the general breakdown, and a chief stimulant to the riotous anger which welled up in the ghetto.

If the commission's finding was simplistic the corruption charge was nonetheless true. It is a flaw deeply imbedded in the general fabric of urban politics, and it presents yet another aspect of the city problem. In Newark, corruption stems from a loose alliance between elements of politics, business and organized crime. It has a particular focus in that poor man's lottery called The Numbers Game.

The numbers game is run in Newark by so-called Mafia families. Actually they are oldtime bootlegging rings that have converted to organized gambling. The racket bears a close resemblance to bootlegging as a social phenomenon. Numbers enjoys among its patrons the same kind of social acceptance the speakeasies once had, and for the same reason: it provides a service which a lot of people want. On what might be termed the consummer end it's a small-change affair, an investment of dimes and quarters in the rich dreams engendered by payoffs up to 600 to one. On the producer end it's a big business. In a city the size of Newark the gross handled adds up to many millions a year.*

Any attempt to close down the numbers game would meet with strong ghetto opposition. At the same time it constitutes a drain on the ghetto economy, and it is a corrupting influence in city politics. To protect the racket, the mobs extend their tentacles in many directions. Mob-owned business firms in Newark specialize in rigging public contracts, not so much for the incidental graft as for the purpose of putting politicians in their pockets. They have other persuasions which extend far beyond such coarse exercise as passing out money in sealed envelopes or brown paper bags. Their approach to a politician frequently begins with a campaign contribution channeled through a seemingly respectable front. After that comes the offer of a lucrative fee or private business deal—again behind a legitimate facade. The progression from contribution to fee to loan to gift to outright bribe is often a slow, insidious entrapment. All this, of course, is a classic pattern that can be found to greater or lesser degree in many cities. In Newark, it was greater. When Gibson took office as a reform mayor he poked through the books and estimated that city contracts embodied a "corruption tax" of 10 percent. It was not the root of the city's ills but obviously it constituted a surcharge the bankrupt community could not afford.

The public focus on corruption brought down on the city squads of federal, state and local investigators. Amidst a general head rolling, Addonizio was convicted on wide-ranging charges

* The numbers game is endemic in every ghetto, and the impulse that supports it is presumably as ineradicable as the middle-class desire to hit it big on the stock market. In Harlem, Congressman Charles Rangel has suggested that if the city authorities can't stop the game they ought to join it, by sponsoring comparable municipal lotteries. New York, in fact, already has a state lottery. The difference between the lottery and the numbers game is essentially one of class: lottery players invest folding money while numbers handles a lot of action in denominations that clink.

of graft and conspiracy. He has appealed the verdict. Actually, on the basis of the trial evidence it appears that he profited personally in rather minor and peripheral ways. He had, however, presided over a political machine that was well-lubricated with graft. Like many another politician, he had paid the going price for position and power. Unlike most, he had been caught, and his indictment and trial coincided with the 1970 mayoral election. Against that background he waged a last embittered campaign, seeking vindication at the polls.

In a seven-man free-for-all contest he was able to garner only 25 percent of the vote. That was enough to squeeze him into a runoff against Gibson. During the final stretch run he was confined by day to the courtroom, listening to the drone of evidence which spelled the ruin of reputation and career. Far into the night he was out on the hustings, conducting a stubborn, weary rendition of the last hurrah. He had only one thing left, and he used it. Capitalizing on the black power slogans, he tried to rally a final display of Italian power.

"Huey," said an admiring aide, "is going down like a wounded bull."

White extremists were represented by Anthony Imperiale. He's an immigrant's son with a high school equivalency diploma. He's also an ex-marine and has been variously a private detective, a karate instructor, a small-time contractor. After the riot he organized the North Ward Citizens' Committee, a group that verges on the thin edge of a para-military vigilante band.

Imperiale is a squat, powerful man; his five-and-a-half-foot frame carries 230 muscular pounds. Tattooed on one of his brawny arms is a dagger-pierced inscription reading, "Death Before Dishonor." He comes across as Tough Tony, a two-fisted primitive, but the bully-boy air conceals a measure of shrewd calculation. He works at his image.

He knows how to pluck the nerve-end responses of hate and fear. Especially fear. His appeal is addressed to people only recently escaped from poverty, and still living on the edge of it both physically and emotionally. His North Ward bailiwick is a once-solid but now somewhat frayed and decaying neighborhood. To the blacks who are moving in in increasing numbers it's a step up from much worse surroundings. To the whites who remain, it's where they're stuck. Imperiale focuses on their most elemental fears, and the appeal is strong because many of the fears are in themselves valid enough. The streets do grow increasingly dangerous. The schools aren't working. The modest homes acquired through years of work and sacrifice are deteriorating in value. The paychecks are everlastingly squeezed by the mounting spirals of inflation and taxes. Beyond that, the people involved feel ignored and put upon by a society they deem indifferent to their problems and needs. Imperiale tells it like they think it is:

"We're all just Americans, concerned for our people and for our lives. . . . Just plain folks, just frightened Americans."

He appeals also to the strong physical attachment the Italians have for the old neighborhoods. "I was born here," he tells his followers. "I live here. I intend to die here. With my shoes off." The lofty liberals, he suggests, look down with scorn from privileged sanctuaries far removed. But what do they know, what would they care, about the struggles of a plain man to defend his home?

He is not, he insists, anti-black—just anti-mugger, anti-rapist, anti-welfare chiseler, anti-dirty bum. And then he drops in a usually veiled, insidious suggestion that most blacks are such. "We're poor, too," he says, "but soap and water are cheap."

Sometimes he switches to a kind of street populist vein, presenting himself as a defender of all the common, ordinary, working people, both white and black. The trouble with Newark, he says, is that it's being bled to death by big business, by commuters, by swindling politicians. When he's in that mood he claims that a lot of blacks support him, and he likes to drop in a story illustrating how well he gets on with his black neighbors. But then he switches again. The trouble with Negroes is they are controlled by extremists, and the extremists are controlled by the Communists. And there's only one answer for that:

"We oughta register the Communists—not the guns."

He has observed that the country's problems might be solved by "about forty more Joe McCarthys" and he was a vociferous supporter of presidential candidate George Wallace. When Governor Lurleen Wallace died he used the occasion to step up his race rhetoric: "I didn't see any flags in the city of Newark lowered to half mast. Why not, when they could do it for that Martin Luther Coon?"

Imperiale has a considerable platform talent. There is, however, a diminishing return in the emotions aroused by endless repetitions of the same harangue. Imperiale offers his supporters something more: a taste of action, with a prospect that there may be more to come. From the cinder-block building which serves as headquarters, he nightly dispatches street patrols in radio-equipped cars. "Jungle Buggies," he calls the patrol cars. For a time his men dressed for patrol duty in army fatigues. They do not go armed—the police enforce that through occasional frisks —but if the occasion arose they could presumably muster arms in a hurry. Imperiale has boasted that he keeps in reserve a rude version of an armored car and a helicopter available for gunship duty. Whether that's true or not he commands something dangerously close to a small private army.

He claims, of course, that his men are merely protecting the neighborhood. As with the commanders of larger armies, however, he draws a thin line between defense and reprisal. A bomb exploded once outside his headquarters and he announced that if it happened again he could not be responsible for what his people might do.

Imperiale probably enlists at most a couple of thousand hard-core followers, but his general support is much broader than that. A year after forming his organization he won a city-wide election as councilman-at-large in a vote split sharply on racial lines. By this time he was apparently carrying a gun. He was clowning one day in a corridor of city hall when a revolver fell to the floor and went off. The affair was passed over, the witnesses developing a lapse of memory as to what had transpired.

In 1970 Imperiale ran for mayor, offering himself as an alternative to "black extremists" and the "quisling" Addonizio. This time he fell far short, getting only one-sixth of the total vote. A good many who had endorsed him for councilman apparently couldn't quite make it to the idea of Mayor Imperiale. Even so, his vote translated to about one-third of the white community. It can be viewed as an index of hardcore white racism, or as a sobering reminder that when things go badly a lot of frustrated and frightened people become easy prey to demagogues. In any case, the large bloc of Newark blacks who didn't trust any agency of government was matched by about an equal number of whites who thought government's main function was to wield a club.

There were numerous spokesmen for the black militants but none more angry or eloquent than Imamu Amiri Baraka, born Everett LeRoi Jones, Jr. He, too, is a son of Newark, a product of the city's small black upper strata. He grew up in a moderately well-to-do home, and earned a master's degree in comparative literature by way of Rutgers, Howard and Columbia universities. He has rejected his middle-class background, and has gone back to the ghetto in search of his blackness.

Jones, as he was known then, was the poet and playwright of black rage before that became a common literary form. For a time he headed a Black Art movement in Harlem, and aligned himself in a fitful, chaotic way with the political left. Eventually he disavowed the left, because it was contaminated by whites. Even his art became suspect to him if whites read his poetry and came to see his plays. He seemed to fear that he would become like a circus lion, snarling and pacing as a spectacle to bemuse his captors. In 1966, at age thirty-two, he turned his back on the New York literary world and went home to Newark to start over. He founded there the prosaically named Black Community Development as nucleus for a cultural revolution. He installed his headquarters in a shabby old three-story ghetto building and to that he gave a name which came much closer to expressing what he was about. He called it Spirit House.

The spirit he invoked was African heritage. He sloughed off LeRoi Jones and became Imamu Amiri Baraka; the Imamu is Swahili for "spiritual leader." His followers likewise discarded western names, and spoke Swahili whenever possible. They dressed in African costume, celebrated African music and dance, worshipped in the African Kawaida (Muslim) faith. The movement was not introduced as a mere retreat to a separate way of life. Baraka taught that blacks must forge their own nation if they were to throw off the white nation that oppressed them. To imitate or accept any part of the enemy's culture was to risk a soul-sickening weakness that might destroy the will to fight. Presently, Spirit House, too, acquired a para-military organization, a corps of hard-eyed, tightly disciplined young men called Simbas.

During the riot police arrested Baraka for possession of weapons; when he was brought to the station he had a bloodied head which required several stitches. There were, as is often the case, two versions of what happened. Police said they stopped a car Baraka was driving, and found in the glove compartment two loaded revolvers. The head wounds they attributed to a random bottle thrown during a general melee which attended the arrest. Baraka said they dragged him from the car, beat him up, and planted the weapons. It would seem highly probable that they did beat him, but the truth of the weapons charge is anyone's guess. It requires no conspiratorial theory of history to imagine a frame-up. The police were under attack, they blamed it on the incitements of men like Baraka, and when they spotted him in the midst of the riot they might have seized on the chance opportunity to even scores. Or then again he might have had the guns. Bearing arms at a time of black insurrection was entirely consistent with his expressed philosophy. At the subsequent trial Judge Leon Kapp read to the jury a poem Baraka had published in Evergreen Review; the work was an impassioned tribute to riot which can be briefly summarized as: kill whitey.

Baraka stood trial attired in his dashiki symbol of black revolt. When found guilty and sentenced he engaged the court in a defiant dialogue:

JUDGE KAPP: It is my considered opinion that you are sick and require medical attention.

BARAKA: Not as sick as you are.

JUDGE KAPP: Your talents have been misdirected. You have the ability to make a wholesome contribution . . . . Instead we find you in the vanguard of extreme radicals who advocate the destruction of—

BARAKA: The destruction of the unrighteous.

JUDGE KAPP: —of our democratic way of life. On the basis of your conviction for unlawful possession of two revolvers—

BARAKA: And one poem!

JUDGE KAPP: —judgment that you be confined to the New Jersey State Prison to serve a term of not less than two years and six months and not more than three years, and that you pay a fine of one thousand dollars.

BARAKA: The black people will judge me. History will absolve me.

As events transpired, he didn't have to wait for history. He appealed the court decision and won acquital in the second trial. Meantime, he was shifting to a far less violent stance. He was still an intransigent black nationalist, but he talked less and less about street insurrection, and more and more about gaining power through orthodox political channels. In his new mood he reserved some of his harshest attacks for the "murder mouthings" of white revolutionists who would use black bodies as cannon fodder.

He even worked out with Imperiale a *modus vivendi*, the two installing a hotline between their respective headquarters. Like much larger powers they agreed that if bloodshed came it should be by intent and for cause, and not as a flash response to some misunderstanding or accident. Reportedly the Newark hotline was used several times to avert prospective clashes.

"I won't say I love LeRoi," observed Imperiale at this period, "but I respect him."

"At least," said Baraka, "Tony Imperiale is an authentic spokesman for his people."

The two had, in fact, more in common than their hotline. Both despised the moderate center, and both underestimated it. Baraka discovered that when he sought election to the Model City project's board of directors. Running in a ghetto district he got only a third of the vote. The blacks, like the whites, were wary of too sharp a confrontation. The observation, however, must be qualified. A shrewd black street politician who worked for Addonizio's city hall analyzed Baraka's defeat this way:

"That vote doesn't mean that most ghetto people are against him. It means that most are for him only part of the way." There were, it seemed, a good many in the black community who applauded Baraka's sentiments while rejecting his views.*

Baraka responded by again shifting ground. His overriding passion was an affirmation of black pride and power, and for that he was prepared to sacrifice nearly anything else. He began to talk coalition, urging that blacks should put aside all factional and ideological differences and get together behind a political leader who could unite the ghetto. He had by now no illusions that it would be him.

---

* A ghetto slate backed by a toned-down Baraka has since won an election of a community action board.

In November, 1969, a community convention assembled in Newark with some three hundred delegates attending. The participants ranged across many shades of the political spectrum but the skin color shades were restricted to just two: black and brown. The ghetto and barrio dwellers had gathered to do their political thing.

At stake was control of the city. The election for mayor and city council was then seven months away, the incumbent white administration was in deep trouble on every front, and the blacks were on the edge of acquiring their political majority. The blacks, however, faced some serious obstacles. They had to overcome the mixed distrust and indifference which the ghetto traditionally exhibits toward the political process, and they had to bridge huge chasms in their own ranks. The convention delegates included ardent black separatists and men who had worked all their lives for integration. They ranged also all the way from left-wing intellectuals to essentially conservative small shopkeepers. They were united in only one thing, a conviction that blacks had to control the institutions which determined their lives. In Newark, that meant running their town.

The man they turned to was Kenneth A. Gibson. He is in the broad sense a moderate. Politically, he has described himself as endorsing the general positions represented by the late Robert Kennedy. In personal approach he is quiet-spoken, even-tempered, realistic and practical. His style reflects his former occupation as an engineer. He discusses political and economic questions with the coolly analytic air of a man estimating how much stress a particular structure can be expected to bear.

During the sometimes frenetic campaign Gibson observed: "People say I'm the coolest man in the race. I agree. I've been keeping cool all my life. My mother says that when all the other kids were running around breaking their arms and legs I was sitting still, thinking. I've never broken anything in my body."

In mingled affection and exasperation his aides have applied to him such other adjectives as "square" and "corney." His life in fact presents the square, old-fashioned saga of a man who pulled himself up from the bottom by determination and hard work. He was born in the bleak depression year of 1932 in the little town of Enterprise, Alabama. At age eight he was brought by his parents to a burgeoning Newark ghetto. His father was a butcher, his mother a seamstress, and the family's first home in Newark was a one-room apartment. He has recalled his childhood as poor but not blighted or mean. He and a brother Harold grew up in a neighborhood where the streets were still safe, a place where youngsters formed sidewalk athletic clubs and identified their teams by sewing on letters cut from old felt hats.

Harold became a Newark policeman. Kenneth went to work in a factory after graduating from high school. Presently he enrolled in night school. Army service, marriage, and the birth of two children intervened, but he kept plugging away at the night classes, and after twelve years earned his engineering degree. He became active in such groups as the NAACP, the Urban League and the YMCA, and helped to found one of the city's job aid agencies to assist the poor.

One is tempted to speculate on how and why a man like Gibson emerged as the ghetto's chosen spokesman. His quiet solidity may appeal to a people who are weary of fragmentation and despair. Or perhaps he just worked harder at the political tasks than anyone else. He made his first bid in 1966, when he entered the mayoral contest as a last minute surprise candidate. He ran quite well in the ghetto, but polled only 20 percent of the total city vote. The experience taught him that a successful campaign can't be put together in a few hasty weeks. He has said that he began his second race the day after he lost the first. By 1970 he was ready. He won the black and Puerto Rican endorsement and then proved his mandate on the street, out-polling by more than five to one two black rump candidates who had defied the call for a united ghetto front.

The runoff election between Gibson and Addonizio brought
the city to a confrontation of black and white. The blacks were
the larger group, and the Puerto Rican alliance swelled their
ranks to more than 60 percent of more of the city's total. The
ghetto populace is heavily weighted with children, however, and
many ghetto adults have not acquired the voting habit. Despite a
vigorous black registration drive the whites went into the election
with a thin edge in voters. One advertisement for Addonizio said
simply, "If we vote, we win."

The New York Times characterized the Addonizio campaign
as "stridently racial." It was not quite that simple. Both candidates were playing the ancient game of bloc politics, but Gibson
was doing so from a better position. He represented the legitimate aspirations of a people long suppressed and denied, and he
could with equanimity accept a nomination overtly labeled as a
demonstration of racial power. At the same time he announced
that he intended to be mayor of all the people. His strategy was
to hold his group solid with race appeal while cutting into Addonizio's support on the corruption issue.

Gibson was able to put together at least a semblance of a
bi-racial campaign. He was endorsed by one of the lesser white
candidates who had been eliminated in the previous round. He
got help from such other disparate forces as college students
practicing the new politics, and corporations accommodating to
change. It was clear, however, that he could count on only a
small fraction of the white vote, and he had to stand or fall on
his ability to bring out a massive black vote. For that he had help
from a stream of black celebrities from the worlds of politics,
civil rights and the arts. Julian Bond, Fannie Lou Hammer, the
Rev. Ralph Abernathy, the Rev. Jesse Jackson, Harry Belafonte
and Dick Gregory all came to walk the streets of Newark and
rally the brothers. Black organizations from all over the state
contributed campaign workers.

Addonizio was trying to hold his bloc on ethnic loyalty, but he could not call quite so openly for a show of Italian power. He went in the back door of the question, professing surprise and shock that Gibson had sullied the election by introducing so un-American an issue as race. In the process he took care to remind whites that the blacks were ganging up.

"I want to make it clear," he said, "that I haven't brought [race] into the campaign. My opponent has, though. I wasn't selected by a white convention. But he was selected by a black convention."

The tough talking in the Addonizio camp was handled by Malafronte, a man who enjoys shocking liberals. "I think we're entitled to at least a percentage of the black vote," he said. "I don't know as Gibson is entitled to any white votes."

In private Malafronte was philosophical. He found it entirely natural that the blacks should take over city hall at their first opportunity. As they increasingly became the chief residents of the city, they would of course insist on dominating its politics. To Malafronte, however, that didn't mean that they could expect to have power handed to them as a benign gift from the previous holders of the franchise. If the blacks wanted city hall they would have to take it away from the Italians, as the Italians had taken it away from the Irish. He predicted with cheerful fatalism that the 1970 election would mark a watershed, "the last time for the white mayor, or the first time for the black."

He judged that the transfer of power would have consequences less drastic and far-reaching than blacks hoped or whites feared. "When the blacks take over," Malafronte said, "the man who sits at my desk will think pretty much the way I do. He'll have to. He'll be up against all the same damned problems, and he'll discover the same limitations wherever he turns."

As a matter of fact, when the blacks did win one member of the new regime thought exactly like Malafronte, because the man behind the desk was still Malafronte. Gibson took campaign rhetoric at a generous discount, and he retained such of the previous functionaries as he thought would serve him well. Mala-fronte, of course, had to step down from his former position of Number One aide, the man-to-see around city hall. He stayed on for awhile as special consultant in his preeminent field, which is hustling project money from the federal government.

In the view from the top the campaign was thus far less polarized than appeared on the surface. It was nonetheless a rough election. In black-white confrontations fear is an issue, and both sides used it. Addonizio's people played on it by exaggerating Baraka's role in the black front. Baraka's more bloodthirsty odes were given wide circulation in white sections of the city. The tactics can be viewed on one level as a cheap but common political trick, it being standard procedure to embarrass any candidate with irrelevant acts and statements of his supporters. On another level the city was undergoing too tense a transition to afford that kind of politics-as-usual. Statesmanship comes hard to losers, however, and Addonizio was a cornered, embittered man; he felt that he had been made a scapegoat for all the city's ills and he was going down swinging. In the last weeks he invoked fear by denouncing it, campaigning against "the leaders of race hate," and urging Gibson to "renounce the extremist."

Gibson adroitly declined the invitation to split his ranks. Coolly, smilingly, he identified Baraka as one of his many friends and supporters, one of the many people he talked to and listened to. He suggested pointedly that in Newark the ability to talk with angry blacks was a definite mayoral asset. "No one," he warned, "can rule a divided city." Some of his supporters went further, suggesting that black victory was almost the only alternative to riot.

All this was sound and fury signifying a political campaign. On June 16, 1970, Newark went to the polls and elected Gibson by a comfortable margin. The morning after the defeated faction blandly disowned all its alarmist rhetoric. A newspaperman bustled around city hall trying to work up some final confrontation copy, and Malafronte cut him short with "The hostilities are over." Addonizio and Gibson appeared jointly on television to urge a united city, and Addonizio called on his former supporters to cooperate in every way possible with the new regime. "They are going to need," he said somberly, "all the help they can get." This too, of course, was part of the established political ritual. After slugging it out like prizefighters the contestants dutifully shook hands at the bell.

The election spectacle had fallen far short of the textbook description of democracy at work. To this observer it seemed, nonetheless, a basically healthy event. It laid open the deep racial division, but that was already known, and the schism was perhaps not as severe as sometimes appeared under the magnifying lenses of politics and journalism. The contest had all along been conducted in the knowledge that it would have to end in accommodation. Beyond that, the political system seemed to be almost the only thing in town that was really functioning. However crude the process, it had produced what it was supposed to produce: peaceful change.

The thing not changed at all was the economic system, and no one was more aware of that than the mayor-elect. On election night Gibson's victory party was a study in the contrasting moods of the candidate and his constituents. A big music hall had been rented for the occasion and ghetto people came in such numbers that the gates had to be locked to prevent a dangerous press of humanity. Those on the outside remained half the night, standing shoulder to shoulder to share the victory in a communion of flesh. Inside the hall was packed with jubilant campaign workers. The Rev. Jesse Jackson of Chicago evoked a tumultuous response with a poetic recital of the long hard road the race had traveled on the way to this moment. "We are," he cried, "a great people! Our time is now! What time is it? Our time!" The crowd joined in, chanting the lines in choral response, as the triumphant litany boomed through the hall.

Then Gibson came on. Another man might have taken the night off to bask in victory, but Gibson is too serious for that. He spent only a minute or two talking about what a great night it was for black people. He hurried on through the necessary acknowledgments and thanks. Within five minutes he was speaking earnestly of the larger national changes that would have to come if Newark was to have rebirth. His theme was the neglect of the cities, the disordered priorities, the national failure to attend to the basic necessities of public housekeeping. It might have been Mayor Lindsay talking; or, for that matter, Mayor Addonizio. Only this was a black mayor, chosen by the most neglected of the city's people, and now he had to demonstrate how much difference that would make.

"You've put a good man in a bad job," this reporter suggested to one of the celebrating campaign workers. "What can he do?"

"He can pick up the garbage," was the reply. "He can crack down on the hoodlums."

A man nearby nodded his assent at those limited objectives but added that there was more to it than that. "He's a symbol," he explained. "Our people will look at him and know that we can achieve this. That's important. It will help us in all the other things we have to do."

Three months after Gibson took office, the National Guard returned to Newark's ghetto. Gibson called them in, to help with a cleanup drive which removed hundreds of derelict auotmobiles from the streets. It was an imaginative exercise in picking up the garbage but more than that it demonstrated the importance Gibson placed on his symbolic role. The guard was the subject of still fresh and bitter ghetto memories. The riot dead had left behind hundreds of friends and relatives, and there were thousands who had endured or witnessed the murderous fire poured into apartment houses. If a white mayor had brought the guard back for any purpose it would have been a grossly insensitive act, quite possibly an incitement to new violence. For a black mayor it was different; he could summon guardsmen to serve the ghetto, and employ it as a healing gesture.

In another revealing incident Gibson adroitly defused a confrontation between the police and a Puerto Rican group called the Young Lords. The two parties clashed during a Puerto Rican Day parade. There was some pushing and shoving between police and paraders, a couple of cops received minor injuries from thrown bottles, and half a dozen Young Lords were arrested. Afterwards the Young Lords smashed some windows as protest. It didn't really amount to much, but riots have begun with less. Gibson cooled it by bringing in a mediator. Other mayors have tried that, too, but Gibson's trump card was a mediator the Young Lords could not scornfully reject. Appointed as peacemaker was none other than Imamu Baraka.

Kill Whitey? What was Baraka doing trying to head off a battle between police and ghetto rebels? Obviously he was trying to help the new mayor. He was also trying to rebuild a city, and that was no sudden conversion. It had gone almost unnoticed during strident campaigning, but he had confessed then to a growing change in his outlook and mood. About two weeks before the election he discussed it with a *New York Times* reporter:

"When people don't have an object to put their energy into you get that free-flying rhetoric. But rhetoric has to have the responsibility for turning into programs. You have to take the responsibility for doing something besides being mad. When you start making changes, then you have to make adjustments with what is possible."

One of Gibson's great assets—perhaps the greatest asset of any black mayor—is the ability to bring angry and alienated ghetto dwellers into that process. It takes some of the inflamed heat out of the running sores which afflict the cities. It does not, however, cure the sores. The accumulated social problems will not yield to anything so intangible as rapport with ghetto victims, or understanding of their needs. Indeed, some of the urban ills are so severe that even the easing of race friction leaves the sores almost as inflamed as before. The Newark experience demonstrates that aspect, too.

One of the most difficult and sensitive ghetto problems involves education. When Gibson took office he gave top priority to improving the miserable level of Newark's schools. As events turned out he had to struggle hard to keep the schools open at all. Twice in his first six months he was plunged deep into a school crisis.

The first-round crisis was a relatively simple matter of not being able to pay the school bill. The Addonizio administration had averted a teacher strike the year before by accepting a union package which included large pay raises. The city council, however, refused to appropriate the additional funds. The council was not about to raise taxes with election coming up and there was no reserve on which to draw. In "buy now, pay later" fashion, the city thus signed an installment contract it had not the means to meet. Gibson inherited the situation at a time when there was a quite serious question as to whether the school system could flounder through the rest of the year. He got over that hurdle by some draconian fiscal measures and then he had to cope with a school strike anyway. It dragged on into a ruinous affair, the longest school strike in the nation's history.

The basic strike issue was control of school procedure. On the surface it was a dispute between the teachers' union and the school board over grievance machinery and the right to determine certain classroom conditions. At a deeper level it was an event as significant as the riot. It posed fundamental questions of both educational and political philosophy, and it involved a direct clash between black power assertions and the prerogatives claimed by a well-entrenched public service bureaucracy. Newark was a natural cockpit for such struggle, but the same essential battle has been fought also in New York City, and it may well prove one of the most volatile urban issues of the years ahead. Gingerly efforts to avert the travail have already been launched or projected in Chicago, Detroit, Philadelphia, Boston and Washington, D.C. In order to see the Newark school strike in perspective, it is thus necessary to enlarge the focus, considering first the broad issue.

In most big cities teachers have banded together in increasingly well-organized and assertive associations or unions. They are primarily concerned with exercising control, or at least an effective veto, over such procedures as hiring, firing, promotion and transfer. That, of course, is a standard union approach to protecting the membership. The teachers defend it also on the larger grounds that theirs is a professional service which should not be subject to every caprice and passion of the body politic. The middle-aged citizen need only recall the late Senator Joseph McCarthy to recognize the serious implications in that question.

The other side of the coin is that schools cannot be set aside as neutral ground if the society itself is deeply divided over the goals and values which education is supposed to serve. As historic case in point, Catholic immigrants founded a parochial system because they felt that Protestant-dominated public schools were inimical to their heritage. Today many blacks, though by no means all, advocate some measure of educational separatism for ghetto schools. The more extreme proponents would mobilize such schools as bastions of black resistance to the "slave culture" imposed by whites. The moderate and much more sizable faction argues simply that the educational system was constructed by and for the white middle class, and is not responsive to the ghetto's problems and needs.

At base, the separatists ascribe ghetto school failures to the dereliction of teachers. White teachers are charged with being at best insensitive, at worst, racist. Black teachers fare hardly better; if they defend the school system and try to work within it they are often accused of having sold their heritage for a mess of middle-class pottage. Most teachers react as one would expect: angrily. They feel that they are being made scapegoats for the ills of society, and they fear that the attacks will destroy such tenuous authority as they now maintain in the often turbulent and dangerous classrooms. Under such circumstances the questions of pedagogical procedure become highly inflammable. In both Newark and New York City the mixture ignited. A comparison of the two episodes offers some insight into the problems involved and the forces at work.

New York presents the problem in that community's customary gigantic dimensions. The city employs some 57,000 teachers, enrolls more than one million students, and has constructed a sprawling, cumbersome educational bureaucracy with a headquarters staff of more than 3,000 people. It is a remote, inaccessible system in its decision-making process, and yet it deals daily and intimately with one of the most important human concerns. The barriers between the school and the neighborhood are raised still higher by race: more than 90 percent of New York's teachers are white while more than 50 percent of the public school children are black or Puerto Rican. It must be added that no evidence supports the proposition that black children do better under black teachers, and New York's ghetto school performance is actually slightly better than the national average. That, however, is not saying much, for the record everywhere is one of massive failure. Thus in the view from the ghetto, the New York schools can be described simply as aloof, autocratic, white-operated institutions which do not serve the needs of black children.

In response to that and other problems, the city decided to break up the system into numerous small, semi-autonomous districts, each operating under its own community school board. The United Federation of Teachers (UFT) took immediate alarm. The UFT attitude partly reflected mere labor politics. A monopolistic union much prefers to deal with a monopolistic employer, thus insuring standard conditions across the board. Partly, also, the union feared being plunged into a maelstrom of ghetto confrontations. The objections might or might not have been resolved through a careful, considered approach. In the actual event the city tried to paper over the conflict. Three experimental local districts were set up as demonstration projects, each with its own community board, under directives so loosely worded that no one knew precisely what powers were being conferred. The approximate effect was that of a peace treaty which neglects to define the borders. The UFT and a community board clashed fiercely as each sought to occupy the ill-defined disputed ground.

Battle was joined at a Brooklyn ghetto school district called Ocean Hill-Brownsville. The *cause celebre* was a minor incident, the transfer of nineteen teachers and assistant principals whom the community board wished to exclude from the project. The action itself was quite commonplace. Superintendents in the New York system regularly employ transfers to palm off people they want to get rid of. It involves a tedious process, however, and the community board brushed aside the amenities. The persons involved were summarily removed amidst public charges that they had "sabotaged" the experiment or were "unacceptable" to the black community. The union demanded adjudication through the established grievance machinery. The board refused. Thereafter the dispute became hideously tangled but the real issue was simple enough, a test of strength over whether or not the experimental district had to hew to a strict union line on personnel matters.

Through the spring of 1968 the UFT harassed Ocean Hill-Brownsville with a series of mini-strikes. Over the summer the embattled district recruited a sufficient non-union staff, so that it was prepared to reopen whether the UFT acquiesced or not. The union hauled up its big guns then, striking New York's entire school system to force the surrender of Ocean Hill-Brownsville. It lasted, with brief intermissions, for more than two months.

Twice it seemed settled and then flared up again over some provocative act. On one occasion a thousand policemen were marshaled to usher the UFT teachers back into the disputed classrooms. There were small scale riots in and around the schools, death threats were made to teachers, and furious confrontation became almost a daily event.

About three-fourths of New York's teachers are Jews, and the conflict split wide open a traditional alliance between the city's black and Jewish blocs. It provided, also, an ironic commentary on how race issues have shifted over recent years. The union president, Albert Shanker, had marched with Martin Luther King at Selma. The community board was headed by the Rev. C. Herbert Oliver, formerly of Alabama, who had been active there with the Southern Christian Leadership Conference. During the course of the turmoil the city's Board of Education devolved on John Doar, a former Justice Department official, who had once escorted James Meredith into riot-torn University of Mississippi. He was to encounter almost as much trouble getting New York teachers back into their schools.

Despite such leadership the contest swiftly degenerated into public harangues between the combatants. The blacks assailed the teachers as racists who were deliberately bent on inflicting "cultural genocide" on the pupils. The UFT replied by calling its opponents "vigilantes," "gangsters" and "fascists."

Some anti-Semitism surfaced in a fringe element of the blacks, and the union seized on it to turn the race question around. Union handbills gave wide circulation to an anonymous piece of random scurrility that was stuffed in the teachers' mailboxes at two of the schools. The text:

"If African-American History and Culture is to be taught to our Black Children it Must be Done By African Americans who Identify With And Who Understand The Problem. It Is Impossible For The Middle East Murderers of Colored People to Possibly Bring To This Important Task The Insight, The Concern,

The Exposing of The Truth That is a *Must* If The Years of Brainwashing And Self-Hatred That Has Been Taught To Our Black Children By Those Bloodsucking Exploiters and Murderers Is To Be OverCome. The Idea Behind This Program Is Beautiful, But When The Money Changers Heard About It, They Took Over, As Is Their Custom In The Black Community. If African-American History And Culture Is Important To Our Children To Raise Their Esteem Of Themselves, They Are The Only Persons Who Can Do The Job Are African-American Brothers And Sisters, And Not the So-Called Liberal Jewish Friend. We Know From His Tricky, Deceitful Manuevers That He is Really Our Enemy and *He* is Responsible For The Serious Educational Retardation Of Our Black Children. . . ."

The proclamation was interesting not for the addled mind that produced it, but for the sophisticated minds that were willing to use it. There was, in fact, no reason to ascribe anti-Semitism to the community board. The anti-union staff which the board assembled was about half Jewish, and three-fourths white. Nonetheless, the community board became such a prisoner of its own confrontation rhetoric that it would not disown the wildest, most irresponsible attack made on the union. UFT, for its part, played up every lurid item as though it were a statement faithfully representing the community board. The union handbills broadcast the anti-Semitic diatribe with a provocative summing up:

IS THIS WHAT YOU WANT
FOR YOUR CHILDREN?
THE U.F.T. SAYS NO!

When the fight began the union was prepared for some measure of compromise settlement. By the end it had raised its demands to unconditional surrender. It was able to achieve that through a climactic five-week strike which brought to their respective knees Mayor John Lindsay, the New York Board of

Education and the State Department of Education. The terms of settlement: all the controversial teachers who so wished were returned to the district, the community board was suspended, and Ocean Hill-Brownsville was placed under a state trustee with stern warnings that its schools would be closed if there was further trouble. Meantime, the state legislature had taken alarm and at strong union urging it had thoroughly emasculated the city's plan for independent school districts. The affair thus ended in a total but perhaps Pyrrhic victory for union power. When it was all over it was the teachers who had to go back in and try to pick up the pieces, and they returned to schools more strife-ridden and chaotic than before. As one small index of that problem, the New York schools were the scenes of 231 physical assaults on teachers in 1967, the year before the strike. Three years after, the rate had risen to around 300 a year and the level of violence was steadily increasing. The level of ghetto school performance remained where it had been: abysmal.

For militants, the battle was an object lesson in the fact that ersatz power can only be pushed so far. The community board had in fact never exercised any real power in its own right. Its status had been conferred as a gift by the city hierarchy, and when that got too expensive the gift was withdrawn with a stroke of the pen. After scornfully rejecting various compromises, the community board was reduced at the end to a pitiable concession. The settlement imposed by UFT barred the suspended community board members from setting foot in any of the schools involved, except in places where a board member's own children were enrolled. The concession, obtained after some pleading by mediators, was that the final humiliation would be stipulated privately, rather than spelled out in the public agreement.

Newark lives almost literally in New York's shadow, and the Newark Teachers Union drew its own conclusions from the Ocean Hill struggle. A year later they held a strike threat over the faltering Addonizio administration and extracted a big settlement; it included not only the pay raises the city couldn't afford but also contract stipulations tightening teacher control of the schools. In 1971 a new, black-dominated school board rescinded the control concessions and the teachers struck. The issues were essentially the same as in New York, but the circumstances were quite different, and the events reflected that fact.

In Newark about 40 percent of the teachers are black. That is well below the general black proportion in the city's adult population, but even so it represents a rather swift ascension among a group whose members have mostly arrived in Newark over the last generation. The president of the union is a black woman, Mrs. Carole Graves. When she was jailed in the course of the strike, the leadership was taken over by Mrs. Clara Dasher, who is also black.

The Board of Education president is a black man, Jesse Jacob. He's a Gibson appointee, and one of a five-man black and Puerto Rican majority on the board. The roster of official participants is completed by Gustav Heningburg, executive director of the Greater Newark Urban Coalition, who was named a strike mediator by agreement of the school board and union. Heningburg is black.

With such line-up it is difficult to reduce the Newark strike to black and white issues. Union critics ranging from Spirit House to the local NAACP nevertheless accused the union president, Mrs. Graves, of being a tool of white teachers. She replied: "This is just a labor-management fight. (They) interject this racial business because it's a good way to break the union and get control of the schools."

They were all over-simplifying, as people tend to do in such pronouncements. It was certainly not just a labor-management fight—not when it involved something so fundamental as school policy in a time of educational crisis. By the same token it was not just a racial clash. It also involved another element often overlooked in the racial clamor, the factor of class. The Newark teachers are variously black, Italian and Jewish in roughly equal divisions. What they have in common is that they are all members of a professional elite. They are being challenged by a ghetto underclass which seeks a larger voice in public affairs. Whether that will produce any improvement in school performance remains to be seen. The expectation exists, and that is a gathering force that must be reckoned with.*

The blurring of race lines did help to make the struggle less absolute, or so it seemed. The schools remained about half open as many teachers crossed the picket lines, black teachers particularly, and the opposing spokesmen restrained from a drumfire of public statements designed to crank up the tension. It was still, however, a bitter contest marked by violent incidents. The union leader's car was fire-bombed, and numerous teachers had their

---

* Any broad statement about popular attitudes is obviously in need of qualification. Many ghetto parents support the school system and wish only for their children to receive the same kind and quality of education available to whites. Many others in the ghetto are disturbed and troubled at the constant turmoil; they would settle for almost any kind of school system that functions peacefully and seems to work.

The range of attitudes is suggested by a Louis Harris poll of 212 Ocean Hill-Brownsville parents during the first round of the disturbances there. In regard to the specific issues the community board was supported against the teachers by a slim margin of 29 percent to 24 percent, with 47 percent undecided. Negative reactions outweighed positive in regard to the city Board of Education (69 percent to 24 percent), the community board (47 percent to 38 percent) and the project administrator (44 percent to 29 percent). Nearly two-thirds of the people queried thought the immediate effects of the entire experiment had been to make the schools worse, about one-third expected things to deteriorate further, while only one-fifth looked forward to improvement.

In Newark, too, there were black dissenters, along with a good many who blamed both sides. One high school youth said, "The teachers don't care about us, the school board doesn't really care about us; all they want is power for themselves."

The samplings available are too slim to offer conclusive judgment but those in the ghetto who are deeply committed to a black power school thrust may well be a minority. They are however, well organized and assertive, and like any determined bloc they exert a major pressure.

242 THE CRISIS YEARS

auto windows smashed. A band of black youths beat up some fifteen black and white teachers. A shot was fired into a board member's home after a warning to change his position.

At one predominantly white school, white parents joined white teachers in blockading the entrance. The door had previously been nailed shut, and the door handle doused with acid. A strike-breaking black teacher, a slight but resolute little woman, tried to get through. The pickets pushed and shoved her, while singing lustily, "God Bless America." A white school child was caught in the melee, frightened and confused, and turned to the black teacher for comfort. It angered the crowd. What the school child thought is not recorded.

All this passion and anger was expended on complex questions that most in the city had scarcely thought about until the struggle began. There were doubtless a good number who participated in the combat without ever knowing what the particular questions were. The details had become, in fact, irrelevant, a mere stand-in for symbolic barricades marked "our side" and "their side." Such battles, of course, are the worst kind. All the pride and prejudice, all the hate and fear, come spilling out.

Gibson worked quietly behind the scenes, apparently trying to ease both sides into some kind of workable settlement. After ten weeks he thought he had it. The teachers were willing to accept binding arbitration of grievances, plus a clause relieving them of responsibility for policing the corridors. The board agreed by a bare majority, though Gibson's own presidential appointee was still holding out for a tough stand. Then the defeated faction asked for public hearings, the meetings turned into tumultuous demonstrations, and the agreement was reversed. The first of the two hearings broke up into fist fights. A white reporter for *The New York Times* was beaten by blacks in an incidental display of rage. The second hearing was orderly but tense: fifty policemen standing by. Speakers rose one after another to make impassioned pleas that the black community must assert its complete control of the school system. Many opened and closed their remarks in Swahili. One woman devoted her allotted ten minutes to repeating with rhythmic variations the phrase, "Do not pass this contract." The crowd picked it up and it became a swelling chant, reverberating through the hall. It was, by chance, the same hall that had echoed a few months earlier to the victory chant of Gibson's campaign workers.

The demonstration turned around one critical Board of Education vote. The official involved was in every way a man in the middle: a black, a Gibson ally, and a trade union official who was devoted to the labor movement. Earlier he had voted to accept the contract. Now he switched. Afterward he told reporters his reasons:

"Last week I voted for the survival of the school system. Today I voted for the survival of the city."

Board President Jacob triumphantly cast the deciding vote, rejecting the contract, and crying out: "In the words of the Old Negro spiritual, 'I'm free at last, free at last, thank God Almighty, we are free at last.' " Then he went into the crowd and embraced the woman who had inspired the mass chanting.

A week later, when emotions had cooled, Gibson pushed through a modified version of his original compromise. The Union had wanted to shuck off on some other agency the often trying and dangerous job of keeping order on the school premises, but they agreed to resume that obligation on a "volunteer" basis. Thus in Newark it was the union that overreached, and had to back down. The terms did not represent an unconditional surrender by either side, but it demonstrated clearly that union power can not ride roughshod over real black power. The larger point went beyond any particular settlement in this city or that. What was revealed at Ocean Hill and confirmed in Newark was a new element in the already entangled factors of the race and urban crisis. The same conflict is surfacing in other cities, and the urban school system generally is probably faced with a deeply troubled period in the years ahead.*

The school strikes in New York and Newark illustrate only one aspect of a larger question in urban affairs. Not only the teachers but the police, firemen, sanitation men, building inspectors, welfare staff and transport workers are increasingly organized into semi-independent fiefs, all of them dug in behind moats of union and/or civil service regulations. That, of course, has done much to improve the salaries and working conditions, and in some cases the standards, of public employees. It also raises problems in that great areas of service have become somewhat removed from accountability to the public. A mayor's mandate for change can be negated by a stubborn bureaucracy that clings to old ways while answering only to its own members. It is a

* In cities which become black-dominated, the school policy will inevitably reflect that fact, as it has reflected white dominance in the past. For most cities, however, the situation in the 1970s will continue to be white majority, ghetto minority, with one faction of the ghetto making a strong push for educational separatism. A sensible compromise solution has been put forward by Christopher Jencks, executive director of the Center for Educational Policy Research at Harvard. He suggests the creation, wherever needed, of parallel school systems. Black separatists would, in effect, be endowed with their own private school system, along lines analogous to the parochial approach. Ghetto public schools would continue to be available for those who preferred them.

The idea has many merits, the most obvious of which is restoring peace to the classrooms. Moreover, it would not require massive new financing even if the separatists were wholly supported from public funds. Separatist schools could simply be assigned that share of the school budget proportionate to their enrollment. As for the educational merits, it will probably not prove a panacea, but there should be no objection to putting it to the test. The separatists may be able to infuse something often grievously lacking, a sense of pride and community involvement in the ghetto schools. Finally, and not least, it would confer responsibility, and that often has a sobering effect. If funding were on a basis of enrollment the separatists could be held strictly accountable in the largest and most democratic sense. They would have to meet parental expectations, or else wither away for lack of public support.

The case for black responsibility in ghetto schools has been put sardonically by Rhody McCoy, the unit administrator of the Ocean Hill-Brownsville experiment. "Everybody else has failed," he said. "Why shouldn't we have the right to fail, too?"

particular irony of black history that they are gaining toeholds on city hall at a time when much of the power and influence have been fragmented in that fashion.

One of Gibson's graver problems when he became mayor was the mutual hostility between the ghetto and the police department. Whether rightly or wrongly, Police Director Spina had become to the city's blacks a personal symbol of repression. Gibson removed him as director but he couldn't fire him, because of civil service regulations. Thus the old chief remains, restlessly exiled to a make-work desk, while retaining the loyalty of much of the force. The mayor and the new chief must tred warily, cajoling the department, if new policies are to have any real effect with the man on the beat.

This reporter asked Gibson what he thought was his greatest mayoral difficulty: the lack of money or the lack of power. He pondered it for a moment, then broke into a broad grin. "If I could have just one," he said, "I'd take the power. You see, I have this tremendous confidence in myself." His hands moved in expansive gesture as he considered what he might attempt if he presided over all the multitudinous boards and authorities which administer a city. Then the hands dropped and he dismissed the subject. He is a practical man. He is not going to get that kind of power, and so he works at using what power he has.

Such are the political problems as a ghetto mayor seeks to give real meaning to his mandate. He must cope also with the financial problem of municipal bankruptcy. That aspect has been cited repeatedly in this report, but it cannot be overemphasized. In Newark's case Gibson knew he was inheriting an empty till but even he was surprised at the extent of the debacle. For decades the city had regularly been plunged into fiscal crisis, each time resolved by another tax raise, but the last time around the Addonizio administration had lacked the will or nerve to face the harsh facts yet once again. They made up an election budget, estimating revenues high and expenses low, and when Gibson took office he found the city $70 million short of operating revenue. The sum represented an addition of some 30 percent to the regular budget, it had to be raised within the year, and it was needed merely to keep things going at the floundering level where they were.

The city was reduced to considering such desperation ideas as asking corporations to pay their taxes in advance. That, however, would merely put off disaster a few months. As for long-range borrowing, the city had long since reached a debt limit fixed by the state.

The main source of revenue was real estate taxes, but another raise in that area seemed out of the question. Extracting the $70 million from the homeowners would have raised property taxes to nearly three times the suburban level. One of the things Gibson and Addonizio had agreed on during the campaign was that property taxes were already confiscatory.

Any new type of taxes required legislative approval, the cities being regarded as negligent wards by states that treat them negligently. Gibson dutifully trekked to the state capitol at Trenton to offer proposals. His first choice was an earnings tax on commuters. He didn't get it, because state legislators naturally protect their own constituents. Gibson had to settle for a hodgepodge of local taxes which will squeeze the city dwellers still more while making it more difficult to attract industry.

Gibson planned to institute the taxes as a two-year emergency measure, but many thought he was being trapped into a disastrous long-term policy. The taxes would become permanent, the critics predicted, because the state and federal governments would wash their hands of the problem as soon as the immediate crisis passed. Heningburg of the Urban Coalition expressed the opinion thus: "What the state gave Newark was a pistol to blow out its brains."

The alternate approach was to hold the crisis over the heads of Trenton and Washington, threatening to let the debacle run its course, and presenting the nation with the spectacle of a major city closing down its public services. Had he chosen that course he could reasonably have been charged with playing Russian roulette.*

As it was, he needed to drum up some new federal money to supplement his tax package. He joined what is for mayors an obligatory pilgrimage, a journey to Washington. He got an audience with Vice President Agnew, a respectful hearing from the Joint Economic Committee of Congress, and numerous assurances of official sympathy. He'll get, of course, some money, too —enough to keep going in the hand-to-mouth fashion that has become the city's lot.

Given such circumstances, what can any mayor accomplish? Gibson's performance bears out his supporters' election-night prediction that he would pick up the garbage, and raise the morale.

About a year after the election this reporter returned to Newark for a final visit, to see what changes, if any, had transpired. One difference was immediately apparent. A swing through the Central Ward revealed that block on block of abandoned buildings had been leveled and cleared away. There were great empty spaces large enough to accommodate a football field. Most of the clean-up seemed newly accomplished, for the earth was still scarred and raw.

On one square block there remained only one structure, a last crumbling vestige which the wrecking crew had not yet reached. It was by chance a familiar place, a building already abandoned when first seen three years before. It was described earlier in this report as the glass-littered ruin where the winos gathered. Next to it was a newly cleared lot which had once held the battered tenement with the fist-sized hole in the door.

---

* In New York City Mayor Lindsay chose the other course, laying off thousands of police, firemen and teachers when the state rejected his fiscal entreaties. Protests soon escalated into a strike of municipal employes, and Lindsay was accused of creating turmoil in order to dramatize the city's problems.

The Central Ward shopping district seemed to have more abandoned buildings than before but that could have been just an impression; the empty places were more noticeable now because they were almost all neatly boarded. The street had presented earlier an impression of general shambles. Now a tidied-up ruin made it starkly evident how extensive the scar tissue was.

At city hall Gibson seemed cheerful, confident, very much the man in charge. He was also coldly realistic about what he had and hadn't done.

He was asked to cite the tangible gains from his first year in office. He repeated the question, accenting the "tangible" as though measuring its precise import. "When I was elected," he said, "my priorities were education, housing and health. You ask for tangible results. I would have to say that in education I have accomplished nothing. In housing, the same. In health, the same."

He added that there were intangible gains which he considered worthwhile. "I believe I am changing the image of Newark. We are trying to change the way people look at our city—both the people who live here and the people outside. That's important to the city's future."

He insists that Newark has a future, and he dismisses impatiently the general proposition that the cities are dying. The cities are still necessary, he says, still serving vital functions, and therefore they will not die. He sees it as a question of how sick the cities will become before the country rouses itself to apply the necessary remedies. He regards his own city as merely a preeminent example of what has to be done, and what might be achieved. "Wherever the cities are going," he likes to say, "Newark will get there first."

The man is a practicing optimist, a trait essential to his trade, and so he makes the prediction hopefully. A pessimist might be justified in concluding that wherever the cities are going, Newark already is.

Chapter 9

BLACK POWER

They want rain without thunder and lightning.
—Frederick Douglass reproves
those who seek change without
agitation and conflict.

THE last thirty years, the span of a generation, have been for black Americans a time of stress and challenge accompanied by painful struggle and sweeping change.

In 1940 when the era began, about half of all blacks were still bound to the serfdom of the rural past. By 1970 the blacks had become the most urbanized of any American racial bloc.

Almost all accounts have emphasized the hardship of the urban experience, and rightly so, for it has been a cruel trial. That, however, should not obscure the tremendous upward thrust which the blacks are beginning to achieve.

The generation of change has been a time of political awakening, from right-to-vote marches in Alabama to the ghetto caucus which chose a Newark mayor. The last decade has probably produced more elected black officials than all the rest of the century-long span since Reconstruction. In the last two years alone the number of such officials has doubled, reaching 1,200. The years ahead will almost surely bring a further quickening of the pace, for blacks are only beginning to realize their full potential at the polls.*

The era has seen also the beginnings of economic movement. That at first was glacial paced, but lately there has been a perceptible lurch in the icepack. In 1950 the black median family income was 54 percent of white; over the next fifteen years it rose one point, to 55 percent. In the following five years, however, it rose to 61 percent, and in northern cities to 69 percent. In real dollars (adjusted for inflation change) black income is now running $10 billion a year above the level of 1965. During the 1960s the proportion of blacks below the poverty threshold dropped from more than half to less than a third. Most important of all, perhaps, is a figure already cited which is here repeated for emphasis. In 1970 there appeared for the first time a black group that has drawn even with whites on the economic scale. In the northern cities the stable black families headed by young parents were achieving par for the economic course. This is still a small group, about one black family out of nine, but hopefully it represents the leading edge of an oncoming second generation of change.

Despite the great limitations, these things represent more progress in a shorter time than black Americans have ever known before. And yet, over the same period, the prevailing note in the black mood appeared to shift steadily from hope to discontent to growing rage.

A decade and a half ago almost all blacks rejoiced at the

* In November, 1970, the Census Bureau reported 6,971,000 registered black voters, 60.8 percent of potential, compared to 68.1 percent registration among eligible whites. Blacks also lag somewhat behind whites in the actual voting by those registered. If these political participation gaps are closed, the blacks will pick up about 1.5 million additional votes.

An equally important element is the growing political sophistication of the ghetto. Heretofore blacks have tended to vote most heavily for such offices as President and mayor. As they develop political leadership they can be expected to give increasing attention to such down-the-ballot choices as congressman and city councilman. At present there are twelve black congressmen. On a population basis the potential is about fifty.

Supreme Court decision desegregating schools. Today a considerable body of blacks demand a new kind of segregation, a black separatism aimed at removing all taint of white influence.

The clasped hands of the civil rights demonstrators have been followed by the clenched fists of black revolutionaries. After "We shall overcome" there came "Burn, baby, burn." One need not accept at face value every militant manifesto in order to recognize that there has been a profound change.

The new mood has angered many whites, and shocked or frightened a sizable number of those who considered themselves sympathetic to black goals. In fact, however, the phenomenon presents no cause for surprise. It is probably an inevitable and necessary stage in the black emergence.

It appears a general fact of human history that rebellion often surfaces not when oppression is worst, but when it is easing. The Hungarians endured Stalin's rigid tyranny, and rose up under Khrushchev's relative relaxations. The British and French were booted out of their African colonies while the more repressive Portuguese were still hanging on. Blacks in South Africa are far more cruelly exploited than South American peons, but it is South America that seethes most openly. The lifting of repression compares closely, in fact, with lifting the lid on a pot which has built up a dangerous head of steam. It is a necessary exercise, but it can cause burns. Americans might do well to simply accept the fact that we are in for a time of some tumult and conflict.

One reason for the turbulence of change is that expectations almost always outrun the immediate improvements. The $10 billion a year black income gain cited earlier impresses many ghetto dwellers the way last year's small raise impresses a factory worker who finds himself still below scale. For all the improvement, the black median family income in 1969 was still only $5,999, compared to $9,795 for whites, and it would take $18 billion more to close the gap. If blacks continue to gain on the white position at the recently accelerated rate of one percent a year they can expect to reach equal status about the year 2010, or a generation hence. It is an interim which many are not prepared to pass patiently.

Another element of turbulence is that progress is not spread evenly. Statistical averages as we have seen can conceal great disparities within the group. There are young men and young women in the ghetto today for whom the changing times mean a real chance to escape the heritage of poverty and despair. If they are not burdened with drug addiction, or criminal records, or the consequences of teenage parentage, if they have somehow extracted a usable education, then they have a future, a life to build. One can find their like on almost any ghetto block. But one can find also the teen-aged girl who has a seventh-grade education, two children, no husband, no job, no skill, and no reasonable hope that anything is going to change for her. And then there are the others, the middle-aged ones, who have lived long enough to see change, but too long to experience it; their prospects are defined and limited by all the deprivations which long since have shaped their lives.

"If you're black, stay back," says an old ghetto adage. The saying contained a measure of bleak comfort for an oppressed people. It provided a blanket explanation for all failures, and offered an excuse for ceasing to struggle when the effort became too painful and difficult. Now the general excuse is being stripped away, but the struggle remains for many as desperate and unavailing as before. They rage against a society which offers the illusion of hope.

There is still another and deeper source of rage. For a long time blacks strove to assimilate into white society on equal terms. Today many question the worth of that goal. They have concluded that assimilation is a fraud, and a poor bargain to boot, and that the only way to deal with whites is on a power basis of race bloc to race bloc.

Consider the case in regard to schools. In 1954, nearly two

centuries after all men were declared to be created equal, almost a century after the Emancipation, the Supreme Court ruled that blacks should be admitted to white schools, albeit with all deliberate speed. It was thought at the time a momentous thing, and men died to fulfill its vision. In 1972 there will issue forth high school graduating classes of young black men and women who were born in the year of the great decision. In the South nearly two-thirds of those students will graduate from predominantly black, essentially segregated schools. In the more ghettoized North the proportion will be nearly three out of four. If this be the fruit of assimilation and integration, so say the separatists, then better to be done with that lie. Let the society recognize its racism, they say, let the division into black and white be open and frank, and leave blacks in peace to establish their own institutions.

A total separatist view would probably not be endorsed by a ghetto majority, but the anger and alienation which it reflects runs as a deep vein through black America. This is not a new problem, merely one of new dimensions in a time of general confrontation. Its roots go back to the very beginnings of American society.

The black experience in America has always been not only separate and unequal, but something far worse. It has been ground deep into the black soul that white America does not fully recognize the blacks as human.

It began with a very special kind of slavery. Blacks were held in bondage not just as enforced laborers but as creatures of a lower, essentially subhuman order. That was an arrangement required by the stern Protestant ethic of our Anglo-American forebears. The Spanish exploited slaves just as ruthlessly, perhaps even more cruelly, but having fewer scruples they did not need to invent a mystique. To the Spanish, slavery was simply the captive's misfortune, a thing that could happen to anyone taken in battle; should some change of circumstances occur, the slave might regain his freedom and rise to a status equal to the former master. The Anglo-American slaveholders could not tolerate so cynical and worldly a view. Had they looked on the slave as a man, their consciences would have cried out to set him free. Since they had no intention of freeing him, they did not look on him as a man. Therein was planted a deadly virus which has sickened American race relations ever since.

Some wise men foresaw where it would lead us. One such man was the French observer Alexis de Tocqueville. He visited America in the 1830s and predicted that race would remain to haunt the nation long after slavery had been abolished.

"We scarcely acknowledge," he wrote, "the common features of humanity in this stranger whom slavery has brought among us. His physiognomy is to our eyes hideous, his understanding weak, his tastes low; and we are almost inclined to look upon him as being intermediate between man and the brutes. The moderns, then, after they have abolished slavery, have three prejudices to contend against . . . the prejudice of the master, the prejudice of the race, and the prejudice of the color."

He observed also that long subjection to slavery had scarred the black soul, producing in slaves behavior and attitudes which reflected a debased view of their own worth. That problem, he predicted, would carry over long after the abolition of slavery. "To induce the whites to abandon the opinion they have conceived of the moral and intellectual inferiority of their former slaves," he wrote, "the Negroes must change, but as long as this opinion persists, they cannot change."

De Tocqueville was proved wrong in the end; a resilent black people is now struggling to throw off the psychologic burden of the past. The forecast was nonetheless deeply insightful as to how difficult that effort would be.

Innumerable blacks have testified to the interior ransom they paid to racism. One witness was W. E. B. DuBois, a giant figure in the early black thrust for civil liberty and equal rights. He was a man who had not been marked by the harsh stigmata of the typical black experience. He was born three years after the Emancipation but he could trace his own freedom back five generations, to a black Revolutionary soldier who was liberated as a reward for valor. He was a product also of Fisk, Harvard and the University of Berlin. He was a man of vigorous intellect, proud, confident and even autocratic, and yet he confessed that the steady, insidious attacks on the black spirit had touched him, too. In *The Souls of Black Folk* he wrote:

"Behind the thought lurks the afterthought: suppose if all the world is right and we are less than men? Suppose this mad impulse (i.e., the demand for freedom and equality) is all wrong, some mock mirage from the untrue . . . a shriek in the night for the freedom of men who themselves are not yet sure of their right to demand it?"

Richard Wright, Ralph Ellison and James Baldwin have all written poignantly about black people caught in incessant strug-gle between the wish to assert their blackness and deny it. The damage to manhood is often stressed, but womanhood has been affected, too, and childhood.

Years ago there was a famous study which showed that black children regularly chose dolls a shade lighter than themselves. Another study found that they tended to draw themselves with-out faces.

Many black women long believed a light mulatto skin color to be the height of beauty in themselves and their children. In *Black Metropolis*, published in 1945, the authors St. Clair Drake and Horace R. Cayton quoted this statement from a Chicago ghetto woman:

"I'm off of love. Some day I hope to get married, but it will be for security. You see, I don't feel there is security in love because love has its limitations. I was very close to, and loved, a boy once, but he decided that because I was dark and he was dark it would be unfair to our children for us to get married and propagate another dark generation. So he went and married a very fair girl and they have a beautiful light-brown child."

Another woman said of her husband, who divorced her for a lighter rival:

"I feel it's my fault in a way. He always wanted children, and I am so black and ugly I just didn't want any children to look like myself. So I wouldn't have any. He is so proud now that he is going to have a child of his own. I am really proud for him. He is a good man and really deserves what he wants. He kissed me good-bye twice. We both cried. Now he is gone."

All this has been an historic part of the black burden. For three centuries the society has hammered it into blacks that they were deformed of body, mind and soul. Some blacks have believed it, and some have railed against it, but almost all have had to define themselves in one way or another in terms of that ugly proposition. Baldwin has described how he finally fled to Paris in order to search out his identity. So long as he remained in the United States, he wrote, "there was not, no matter where one turned, any acceptable image of onself. . . . One had the choice, either of 'acting just like a nigger' or of not acting just like a nigger—and only those who have tried it know how impossible it is to tell the difference."

It is these deep wounds to the spirit that black nationalists would exorcise. They are proclaiming their identity, their color, their history and heritage, everything about them that is black. Sometimes, indeed often, they violently assail everything that is white. Historically speaking it is not a new reaction—Garvey stirred black multitudes with the same message a half century ago—but it is a mood which has gathered new momentum. It is a powerful force which can at times unite almost all segments of the ghetto around an assertion of blackness.

Many of the black nationalists began, as Malcolm X and Baraka did, by urging black withdrawal from the contaminated white civilization. That, however, is clearly self-limiting, leading to a kind of organized political apathy. It was the great weakness of Garveyism that, having urged withdrawal, he had no place to withdraw his multitudes to. Today's nationalists are shifting to a dualistic view of black and white society. They are seeking not withdrawal but regrouping, in order to deal with whites on a new basis. Their thrust is for black control of all essential agencies in black communities. They echo the cry of ex-slave Frederick Douglass who rejected white abolitionist leadership, saying it was right and necessary that "the man who suffered the wrong is the man to demand redress—that the man STRUCK is the man to CRY OUT—and that he who has endured the cruel pangs of Slavery is the man to advocate Liberty."

All through black history the pride struggled against the subjugation. Now the pride is dominant. Malcom X proclaimed it thus:

"If not me, then who? If not now, then when?"

It has its highly practical side. In a guest essay in *The New York Times* Baraka said of black power: "White people tend to call this 'separatism' when black people and Puerto Ricans are involved, but no one is going anywhere. We simply want the power to control the 'space' we are in, not just geographic, but institutional, political and economic."

Some other forms of black power seek to force a new concept of integration on black terms. That is the thrust of SCLC's Operation Breadbasket. The target is business, and the premise is businesslike. Blacks make up more than a tenth of the population and their poverty notwithstanding, they buy annually billions of dollars worth of food, clothing and other essentials. Operation Breadbasket keeps book on corporate hiring policies and threatens black boycott against firms which do not employ sufficient blacks. This again is not new—there were "buy black" movements in the ghetto forty years ago—but it has gained a new momentum.

Unions are feeling the pressure, too. There is, for instance, a Harlem organization called Fight Back, run by a black labor movement veteran named James Haughton. He is trying to open up black employment in the top-dollar construction trades. His weapons are picket lines, the threat of publicity, and patient determination. He makes the rounds of job sites, placing five men here, ten there, and over recent years he has secured jobs for more than a thousand men. He seeks also to engage his followers on broader political issues.

Haughton's associate, Joe Carnegie, operates along another segment of the labor front. He's concerned with public transport workers, and in New York about 85 percent of those jobs are already held by black or Puerto Rican workers. Union leadership, however, is still held by an old Irish hierarchy. Carnegie is trying to set upt a rival union as an instrument of black power.

In every big ghetto there are movements to buy black, hire black, vote black. It is not yet as monolithic as appearances sometimes suggest. The underclass, whether black or any other, contains a lot of beaten, broken men. They are not easy to organize for sustained efforts, and men like Haughton and Carnegie complain that they cannot rouse their followers enough. But they're trying. They represent a gathering force.

The black political surge has already been noted. It is still far from reaching its full potential, but it has already produced an impressive corps of public figures. The direction of the political thrust seems sometimes almost obscured by general clamor. As a poor and deprived people, the blacks might be expected to provide ready tinder for firebrands and nihilists. Instead, black communities have consistently supported such leaders as mayors Gibson, Hatcher, Stokes and Evers, representatives Chisholm and Rangel, and State Assemblyman Bond. Whether the black masses continue in that direction may depend very largely on other choices which the whole nation will have to make. Mayor Gibson was asked how long he could hold his disparate ghetto coalition and he replied with cold realism: "As long as I can produce."

There is, finally, that segment of black power which either advocates or verges on armed violence. It is publicized out of proportion to its true importance. The Black Panthers make good newspaper copy, and attract some sentimental support from whites who like to spice their cocktail parties with talk of revolution. They do not attract many blacks. The best estimate is that the Panthers number about 1,500 members, or less than one black out of a thousand. When a Panther contingent went on trial in New York, a city of more than 1.5 million blacks, the event attracted a relative handful of sympathizers.*

It does not follow that black rage is an invention of journalistic imagination. The Newark ghetto elected Gibson, but Newark blacks also rioted. The balance is frail, and there is a large, angry, mostly apolitical mass that has not yet found a fixed direction. It is an element found especially among the young, and their mood will not necessarily be tempered by time alone. Their general attitude was expressed by a young black man who took part in the Detroit uprising, and afterwards told a riot investigator of his response to the conflict: "I was feeling proud, man, at the fact that I was a Negro. I felt like I was a first-class citizen. I didn't feel ashamed of my race because of what they did."

Thus, there is no one man or movement that can speak for all blacks. There is, however, a prevailing mood. It is more angry and assertive than at any time for half a century. It is a mood which no longer seeks concessions. It makes demands.

It is perhaps roughly comparable to the labor mood of the 1930s. Labor loyalties ranged then across a wide spectrum from AFL to CIO to IWW. The rhetoric and the tactics varied but there was a clear understanding as to whom the workers were organizing against. A large number of black Americans feel that way about whites today.

A struggle of great dimensions always produces a response of

* The Panthers did inspire one big demonstration at New Haven, Connecticut. That, however, was largely a white collegiate affair.

that nature. Indeed, without such response there can be no sustained struggle. Frederick Douglass long ago wrote what could be an epitaph for our time:

"Let me give you a word about the philosophy of reforms. The whole history of the progress of human liberty shows that all concessions, yet made to her august claims, have been born of earnest struggle. The conflict has been exciting, agitating, all-absorbing, and for the time being putting all other conflicts to silence. It must do this or it does nothing. If there is no struggle, there is no progress. Those who profess to favor freedom and yet depreciate agitation, are men who want crops without plowing up the ground. They want the ocean without the awful roar of its many waters. This struggle may be a moral one; or it may be a physical one; or it may be both moral and physical; but it must be a struggle. Power concedes nothing without a demand."

Chapter 10

VIEWPOINT

What are you going to do about it? is the question of today.
—Jacob Riis, in *How the Other Half Lives*

IN the judgment of this reporter the ghetto crisis involves two problems, relating to race and to class. In the national anxiety about race, the class aspect is too often overlooked.

Racism has been, of course, the root of the ghetto evil. The Report of the National Advisory Commission on Civil Disorders put that matter succinctly enough:

"What white Americans have never fully understood—but what the Negro can never forget—is that white society is deeply implicated in the ghetto. White institutions created it, white institutions maintain it, and white society condones it."

The charge is true, the flaw is grievous, and simple justice demands that we strive earnestly to root it out. To this observer, however, it seems true also that the clamor on race has become so all-pervasive that it tends to obscure the equally important question of poverty. The two are not synonymous.

Not all blacks are poor, nor are all the poor black. The point has been made in this report, and is here re-emphasized, that two-thirds of the poverty problem is white. In the urban case the metropolitan poverty areas contain more slum whites than ghetto blacks. Among the rural poor there are far more Appalachian whites than Delta blacks.

Racism has rendered the black escape from poverty far more difficult. That, however, is beginning to change. We are still in the midst of the change, and so perhaps we tend to underestimate it. The fact is that overt obstacles of discrimination are being whittled away, due largely to insistent black pressure. The progress is slow and uneven to be sure, but still, that is the area of gain. Meantime, in some other areas the obstacles are becoming not lower but higher.

The relative gains and losses can be seen in sharp relief by contrasting the prospects of young college-educated black men and women with the situation of displaced tenant farmers, of unskilled high school dropouts, of welfare mothers trapped in the ghetto with four or five children. For the first group the outlook has never been more promising. For the second group, never more bleak.

The elimination of all race bias would not materially alter the fortunes of many blacks now mired in the underclass. Their problems, like those of the white poor, are entwined with social and economic dislocations which go far beyond the questions of race.

It is important to distinguish clearly between those elements. In the view of this writer, the time has come to place a primary emphasis on poverty. The resolution of that problem would take some of the raw edge off of racial confrontations, and help us ease our way toward rapprochement. It would relieve the misery of those who cannot wait for the slow unfolding of social evolution. It would enable us to put aside a national mood of recrimination and handwringing, pouring our energies instead into constructive goals which can be accomplished now.

If we are lucky we may be able to work our way out of our racial tensions over the course of the next generation. We could eliminate rank poverty next year. Cleaning up the social debris of poverty would take longer, but the task could be well advanced in this decade. We need only put our minds to it, and our national resources. Here is one way it might be done.

A serious approach to poverty would begin by distinguishing between those who are capable of playing an economic role, and those who are not. More than half the people on the welfare rolls are too old, too young, too sick or too mangled by life to have any real prospect of self support. These people must be regarded as charges of society. If they are to achieve a decent minimum in living standard, the society must simply make up its mind to pay the bill. About $10 billion a year in additional effort would relieve the gross misery of all the poor, whether black, white, red or brown. It comes to one cent a year on the national income, five cents a year on the federal tax dollar. It is either worth it or not and we should come to a national conclusion on the question. The present policy is to sweep it under city, state and county rugs, with results that should now be evident to all.

A healthy society ought to regard welfare maintenance as the last recourse. It is not difficult to envision programs that would allow many of the present poverty outcasts to become useful and contributing members. The simplest and most sensible solution would be a national work force which would expand and contract as needed, automatically absorbing all the able-bodied unemployed. Nearly every other technologic society has adopted such measure as a necessary adjustment to the complexities of modern economic life. We, in fact, turned to such remedies as WPA when the nation was threatened by the Great Depression. Our inner cities are mired now in a continuing, intractable depression, and the problem simply will not solve itself.

The idea of a national work force seems to stir in us irrational responses. If we adopt it at all it is likely to be through a backdoor approach, as a rider to a welfare bill. The right wing tends to favor putting welfare clients to work if the proposal is put forward in a punitive tone. In Pavlovian response the left-liberal bloc tends to throw sheltering arms around the poor. The view here is that both reactions are wrong. No socially useful work should be regarded as demeaning, and there is no reason why those on welfare should not be expected to perform some service in return. By the same token, however, they should be adequately paid and not pressed into service in exchange for a miserable dole.

There is much useful work that could be done. As one case in point, manual labor has become a highly periodic occupation and at any given time about one ghetto laborer out of four is unemployed. Such men could be mustered to clear out the immense debris of the shattered, abandoned buildings which litter the inner cities. With a little extra effort the vacant sites could be turned into vest pocket parks. They could at least be grassed over and equipped with benches.

This kind of work program would be only a rudimentary first step in reclaiming a slum, and yet it would make a considerable difference in the quality of life. Mothers now cooped up in stinking tenements would have a place to take their children. Neighborhood eyesores could be transformed into neighborhood attractions. In our complex, top-heavy society we have forgotten the value of some simple things. We golf on the moon, but we cannot convert junk-strewn lots into places where children can run and play.

Beyond welfare and public works programs we must enlarge the private economy to make room for the poor. We must also attain a larger perspective on the relationship of rural and urban problems. There are today some 25 million destitute Americans and nearly half of them are tucked away on scrubby little farms or in mostly decaying small towns and villages. They number about 8.3 million whites, 3.3 million blacks and a quarter of a million Indians and others. These victims are not yet clamorous, so we pay them only sporadic attention. We must address their problem both for its own sake, and because the cities cannot recover if required to absorb endless waves of economic refugees.

A continuing rural-to-urban transition is, of course, the inevitable shape of our national future. It should come, however, as a natural and voluntary movement toward greater opportunity, not as a forced exodus from despair. If a balanced farm policy had been adopted thirty or forty years ago it would have immensely eased the travail of the black migration. The correction of that long-standing error would still have major value.*

Farm poverty could be resolved at a stroke. We need only extend to the poor farmer the kind of help already granted to the middle-class operator. Interestingly enough, that would probably cost no more in the long term than the present neglect.

At present the farm poor subsist on as little as $500 a year, more often $1,500 to $2,000, and their condition is such that they cannot utilize even the limited opportunities which their situation presents. Thus this farmer might earn an additional $500 a year from a backyard pig pen. He might, that is, if he could afford good breeding stock, and pay for the feed. He might also increase his truck crop yield if he could afford fertilizer. He would benefit still more if he had the kind of first-rate technical advice and assistance that the Department of Agriculture makes available to middle-class farmers. All that might be, but isn't, and so he is driven from the land to become ultimately a semi-employed urban laborer and a chronic welfare case.

Consider how simply that problem could be solved. Small farmers could be encouraged to take up intensive truck farming,

---

* The original exclusion of the poor from farm program benefits was probably due to political and economic pressures. Southern planters were heavily dependent on sharecropper labor, both black and white, they opposed the creation of an independent peasantry, and they held a strategic position in the New Deal alliance. Ergo, a farm policy which gave to big farmers big subsidies gave to little farmers either very little subsidies or none at all. However exploitive and cynical the policy, one can at least understand the reasons. In a new age of farming we go on excluding the rural poor out of what seems sheer mindlessness or national indifference.

pig raising and the like along the general lines of the SWAFCA operation. Some might choose to do it cooperatively, and others not, but in any case they could be given support enough to make it work. Special agricultural agents could be assigned to serve their needs. Federal farm loans could provide them with the necessary capital. They could probably raise their earnings to realistic levels of $3,000 or so. They could be granted additionally a subsidy of about $4,000 a year. The farmer would now have an income of around $7,000 a year, worth perhaps $8,000 to $9,000 in city wages, and he would be poor no more. He could afford a freezer to store his produce, greatly enhancing his standard of living. Instead of scrounging for food stamps he could enjoy the country man's privilege of setting an ample table. He could afford one of those inexpensive but well-built houses that Blackwell is promoting. The once-poor farmer would still be working hard all his life to make a living, but then that is the general lot. He could be left alone to handle the rest of his problems.

It was stated that such program would cost no more than the policy of national neglect. Some comparisons are in order. The farm bureaucracy to assist such a man would cost no more than the welfare bureaucracy that must otherwise inherit his case. The operating capital he needs can be paid back from his proceeds. The new housing is a benefit he could provide for himself. The only real cost obviously is the $4,000 subsidy. If applied to some 250,000 farm families, or some 1 million persons, it would resolve that segment of poverty for $1 billion a year. The figure is chosen as illustration, because there are on New York City welfare rolls about 1 million persons, and it costs more than $1 billion a year to maintain them in misery.

Would it not be wise to invest the money well, rather than wait awhile and spend it badly?

The principle is quite simple. If a man can make it part way on his own, it is better to help him along than to let him fall and then try to pick him up. That is especially true when the rescue system is something so economically inadequate and humanly destructive as the present welfare system.

The creation of a thriving small farmer class would do much to restore the villages to their natural function as market places. The villages could be buttressed even more by establishing federal subsidies or tax incentives to encourage the development of small factories in stricken rural areas. Again that would require a mere extension of familiar techniques. The government is already heavily involved in managing and sustaining the economy through all kinds of support arrangements for big business. It is time to spread some of the benefits around.

The ghettos also need large infusions of private industry. We could, if we wished, reverse the industrial flight from these areas. An attempt of sorts has been made through the National Alliance of Businessmen but the approach has been largely one of exhortation. There was for a time a good deal of pious talk about inducing industry to set up ghetto branches in a spirit of repentance, and as a service to the country. The results are approximately those one obtains from shaking a tambourine in a bar. We should be more realistic. National service is the function of government, and business is motivated by profit. If the inner city economic disadvantage amounts in a particular operation to $2,000 a worker, then the way to get action is to offer a subsidy of $2,500. It is worth the surcharge if it works. It should be aimed primarily at small industry privately owned.*

Ghetto poverty can be relieved also by pressing more vigorously for equal opportunity, particularly in the fields controlled by unions. The necessary approaches are government coercion and organized black pressure. Again, however, we should be

---

* The nation's direct subsidies to big business now total about $6 billion a year. About $1.5 billion is allocated to steamships and airlines. In bankrupt Newark, one of the big problems is the amount of commercial space taken up by tax-exempt port and airport facilities.

realistic. A union now dominated by whites is not going to throw out a third of its members in order to make room for blacks. Moreover, if such an unlikely response occurred it would only shift the poverty problem around. If we want to make room for more people, we will have to create more opportunities.

We could create new jobs in large numbers if we were to apply ourselves seriously to the task of rebuilding the ravaged neighborhoods. It can be done through either private or public channels. The opinion here is that a large-scale rent supplement program should be tried as an alternate approach to public housing.

Public housing herds the poor together, usually in the least desirable areas. Rent supplements would allow them to make individual choices on where to live. Ghetto dwellers would still confront the obstacles of discrimination but they would at least be in position to challenge such restriction. At present the whole question of open housing is academic for most ghetto dwellers, since they can afford only the poorest places.

A comprehensive rent supplement program would also distribute benefits more fairly than does the present housing program. As things stand now the housing projects accommodate a small percentage of the poor, and the rest receive nothing. Moreover, the income cut-off in many projects discourages incentive, by making people ineligible as soon as they rise just a little from the poverty depths. It can come to a point where a working man can't afford to earn a small raise. A rent supplement program could be applied across the board with the amount of assistance fixed by a sliding scale according to the size of the family, the size of the income and the realistic cost of decent housing in a particular city.

These benefits would be at first theoretical, since there is not nearly enough good housing to accommodate all those who would seek it. But if a huge new housing market were created, and if the price was right, the construction would follow. It is a reasonable estimate that $5 billion in rent supplements would stimulate about $30 billion in building.* That would be more than all the public housing built over the last generation. If the participating builders were held to strict standards of fair employment it would provide a big lever for opening job doors.

A program of such dimensions would change all the circumstances of the housing problem. Under present conditions a mayor who really cracked down on slum and ghetto tenements could reasonably be charged with inciting to riot. He would be evicting into the streets tens of thousands of people who would have no place to go. There would be scant prospect of forcing landlords into major rehabilitation, for they will not put into a place more money than they can get out. Under a rent supplement program, persistent violators could be forced out with impunity, with new investors waiting to take their place.

In his congressional appearance Mayor Gibson suggested that rent supplements be reserved for the houses containing resident landlords. Exclusive application of that principle might stretch out the restoration but there is much to be said for rebuilding more slowly and solidly. Resident landlords should in any case be given first priority in any rebuilding plan, and their emergence should be encouraged by generous extensions of credit backed by federal guarantee. Half of suburbia was created in that fashion a quarter of a century ago when returning GIs were furnished with a broad assurance that their credit was good. Home ownership could be similarly fostered in black urban communities. There has already risen from the poverty morass considerable numbers of blacks who are in position to take this step.

The merits of the resident owner have already been cited. There are other advantages to such approach. In such places as Harlem and Bedford-Stuyvesant there are old brownstones that

---

* There is at present a rent supplement program at a level of about $117 million a year. It has not had appreciable impact on the 25 million poor.

were once lovely and could be again. Their restoration under local ownership would be far better than the erection of cement-walled apartment houses, whether public or private. It would above all be better that the restoration grow out of the community itself.

An attempt to revive shattered communities would require also the provision of some basic services which are now grossly inadequate. Medicine is a particular example. It was noted in Newark that a third of the welfare cases are disabled by medical conditions. There is no reckoning of the toll disease inflicts on all the poor, but the human wastage is immense.

Our medical system, like much else in the country, is out of balance. Technically, there is probably no country in the world that can match our brilliance. We lead all others in open-heart surgery, in organ transplants, in exotic, highly specialized techniques of every kind. But we neglect scandalously many of the simple, essential services that a medical system is supposed to provide.

The number of family doctors in this country has declined seriously, from 95,000 twenty years ago to about 65,000 today. In the inner cities, as in the backwoods villages of Georgia and Mississippi, the general practitioners have all but disappeared.

The total imbalance is illustrated in a reportorial visit this writer paid recently to one of New York City's hospitals. The purpose was to interview a physician who had pioneered the use of laser beams for operations of the eye. He was a brilliant man who was doing important work. The hospital was a great research center and no doubt it contained other men who are fashioning marvelous new medical implements out of ultra-sound and atomic particles. The whole place is a gleaming monument to the top level of American medicine, and as it happens it stands in the midst of a neighborhood which has fallen into ghetto shambles. Within a few hundred yards of the laser beam laboratory there are people wasting away from ills which could be treated quite effectively out of the ordinary doctor's little black bag. They aren't being treated.

A medical school announced recently a special program to train about a hundred black students for future service as ghetto physicians. Such efforts are always worthwhile, but it will be years before the training is completed; when they become physicians the entire group could be dispatched to a single ghetto the size of Newark and they would not be sufficient to bring its medical service up to par.

Medical schools should train many more black physicians, but beyond that it seems to this reporter that we need to rethink the whole problem of medical care. We have become too enamored of professional apparatus. A great deal of a doctor's work consists of quite routine things. It does not really require five or six years of highly expensive advanced study in order to prescribe eyeglasses, give an inoculation, or treat a routine injury. This work could be taken over by skilled, well-trained professional aides, operating where necessary under a physician's guidance. Thousands of such aides could readily be recruited and trained to augment the desperately inadequate clinic services which now prevail. That such a program can be entirely competent is demonstrated by the army's success with medical corpsmen.

Birth control clinics should also be provided in greatly augmented numbers. That is controversial to some on religious grounds, and some blacks see it as an assault on their race. The question is one which individual parents must decide. The fact remains that motherhood imposes dreadful burdens on an unwed teenaged girl, and large families constitute a major economic problem among the poor. The prospective parents should know at least that they have a choice.

The thrust for rebuilding the ghetto should come as much as possible out of the ghetto itself. That was the idea of the Community Action Program, but it took what this reporter regards as a sentimental turn. The poverty bureaucracy went about assembling the poor at endless meetings at which they were invited over and over to express themselves. That is all very well, but they should be invited also to serve themselves. They should be given the opportunity to take over their own communities in the real sense, by taking charge of all the essential tasks. This requires physicians, lawyers, teachers, administrators—skilled people of many kinds.

One of the problems of a poverty area, be it inner city or southern village, is a continual brain drain of the most talented and determined youths. They struggle out of the morass, somehow acquire an education or skill, and shake the dust of disaster from their feet. The impulse is altogether human but it would be in the social interest to offer them an alternate course.

America should recruit tens of thousands of the most promising young men and women from the poverty areas and train them for careers in public or quasi-public service. They might well be offered not just college scholarships but salaries about commensurate with what a noncommissioned officer is paid in army training. In the case where an advanced degree is required, the social investment in such youth might well come to thirty or forty thousand dollars. It should be offered not as a gift but as a loan, with repayment expected not in money but in service. The trainee would be under obligation to go back to his community and live and work there for an appropriate number of years. Skills and talents could thus be channeled back to the communities where they are needed most. The people in such programs would be much more useful than ordinary technicians for they would know their communities, and be known there, and they would provide leadership examples to other young people coming up behind.

Such programs should be extended down to such now poorly regarded positions as policeman. The police task in the ghetto is dangerous, difficult, extraordinarily sensitive. It should be performed by people from the community's own ranks, and they should be thoroughly grounded in both the technical and human aspects of the task.*

The need for such service corps was well put by a young black student whom this reporter encountered at a national conclave of urban sociologists. It was a long session, replete with papers which did not summarize well, and at some point the reporter turned to the young man and said, "What's your answer?"

"I don't have the answer," he said, "but I know this. If the cops and teachers who work in the ghetto lived there, it would make a difference."

It might, indeed, make a considerable difference.

The proposals put forward here are, of course, neither radical nor innovative. They are based on the realistic premise that we live in a corporate state, under a form of managed capitalism, and we ought to manage it both more efficiently and in the larger public interest. Utopians may envision some far grander arrangements for an uncertain future. We would do well, meantime, to work for a livable present.

It is also this observer's belief that radical new approaches are not really required to solve the poverty problem. What is needed is an adequate level of effort. There are any number of anti-poverty programs which would work in theory. None will work in practice unless they are applied across the board, wherever needed, in amounts related to the need.

It would cost money. At a reasonable estimate we could end poverty, restore the urban ruins and accomplish the other necessary things for a social investment of about $50 billion a year. The sum is not as large as might at first appear. It comes to about five cents on the national income dollar, about twenty-five cents on the federal tax dollar. If it is not worth that, then we do not regard it as a crisis.

---

* In Detroit, police work requires only a tenth grade education. During the Detroit riot a local black leader observed to a reporter, "What you've got out there is white drop-outs fighting black drop-outs."

The American public would not greet cheerfully a $50 billion tax increase. Indeed, there would be some reason to scrutinize the bill closely. We already pay to our federal, state and local governments some $300 billion a year. It translates to the fact that the typical American works for his various governments about three and a half months of the year. Few people on earth tax themselves more heavily than we, and none other commits to government so vast a treasure. The problem is we are not getting our money's worth.

A program of national restoration would doubtless require additional taxes. If we were so minded, however, a good deal of it could be financed through some redistribution of the comparative welfare benefits which we now extend to the rich and the poor. Beyond that, any real attempt to address our problems will require some reconsideration of where we sit in the world. We are a world power, and probably we have to act as such, but we do not have to buy up a controlling interest in every disaster that happens anywhere on this planet. After a long, hideously expensive experience we seem now to have nearly discovered that we can not rule effectively in the valley of the Mekong. If we are stubborn about it we shall no doubt have later opportunities to discover that we can not rule effectively in the valleys of the Congo, and the Amazon. We could, if we wished, rule quite well in the valleys of the Mississippi and the Hudson.

The poverty problem, then, comes down to this: we have the means to resolve it. There is no lack of feasible plans, whether along the lines suggested here, or in alternate approaches. What is really lacking is the will. We can get started any time we are willing to pay the bill. Part of the price will be to give up our illusions of grandeur, and settle down to live with ourselves.

There remains the other problem of racism. That is a longstanding ill, and it does not appear so easy to cure. It is deeply ingrained in America's history and culture, and it is bootless to suppose that it can be exorcised in any quick and painless way.

Nonetheless, social attitudes are susceptible to change: viewpoints now are not what they were a generation ago and our children will not be mere carbon copies of ourselves. Societies do sometimes move on to higher ground. Meantime, we have to address our problems where they are at now. If we can not transform attitudes we can regulate behavior. We can deal with racism on an empirical basis, treating the symptoms and counteracting the effects, while we try to sweat it out of our national system.

It may take a long time, and we shall run a continuing social fever so long as the infection persists. The present condition seems clearly a crisis stage. Nonetheless, the general circumstances would appear to offer at least as much cause for hope as despair.

The ghetto crisis does not arise from any worsening of racism. It reflects, rather, a black refusal to go on accepting inequities too long endured. It is in considerable part a measure of newfound pride and strength among a people struggling to rise. In the judgment of this reporter, the prevailing black mood has already moved well beyond the kind of psychologic agonizing which white liberals often invest in the race question. Ghetto dwellers right now are not displaying towards whites much need to be loved. What they want is their share, and they can be expected to seek it through any pressure at their command.

The change is healthy. The blacks would be a long time waiting if they based their expectations on liberal benevolence.

It is well to remember that the society has been down much of this road before. In times past ethnic blocs and economic classes have repeatedly exercised a group muscle in order to assert their claims. Always the process has been accompanied by clamorous struggle. Always before it has reinvigorated the society with the thrust from below. It can go that way again, but the outcome is not guaranteed. We will have to work at change.

A Selective Bibliography

CHAPTER 1

The black experience of emergence from slavery is vividly treated by Lerone Bennett, Jr., in *Before the Mayflower: A History of the Negro in America, 1619-1694*. Chicago: Johnson Publishing Co., 1961, 1962, 1964. The book grew out of a series originally published in *Ebony*. Another good account is *From Plantation to Ghetto*, by August Meier and Elliott M. Rudwick, New York: Hill and Wang, 1966.

There are several collections of documents which cover the period following the Emancipation. Works that were found useful included the following:

Blaustein, Albert P., and Zangrando, Robert L., eds. *Civil Rights and the American Negro, A Documentary History*, New York: Washington Square Press, 1968.

Chambers, Bradford, ed. and compiler. *Chronicles of Black Protest*. New York, Toronto: The New American Library, 1968.

Grant, Joanne, ed. *Black Protest, History, Documents and Analyses, 1619 to the Present*. New York: Fawcett World Library, 1968.

Meltzer, Milton, ed. *In Their Own Words: A History of the American Negro, 1865-1916*. New York: Thomas Y. Crowell Company, 1965.

An authoritative account of how segregation was imposed in the South appears in:

Woodward, C. Vann. *The Strange Career of Jim Crow*. London, Oxford, New York: Oxford University Press, 1966.

Other sources consulted were:

CBS News Series, Of Black America, "The Heritage of Slavery." CBS-TV, Aug. 13, 1968. Narrated by George Foster, produced and written by Peter Davis; executive producer, Perry Wolff.

Duberman, Martin B. *In White America*. New York: The New American Library, 1964.

Lynd, Staughton, ed. *Reconstruction*. New York, Evanston, and London: Harper and Row, 1967.

Meier, August, and Rudwick, Elliott. "The Black Community in Modern America" (*The Making of Black America*, Vol. 2.). New York: Atheneum, 1969.

Nolen, Claude H. *The Negro's Image in the South: The Anatomy of White Supremacy*. Lexington, Kentucky: University of Kentucky Press, 1968.

Quarles, Benjamin. *The Negro in the Making of America*. New York: MacMillan Co., 1964.

Woodward, C. Vann. *Origins of the New South, 1877-1913*. Baton Rouge, La.: Louisiana State University Press and The Littlefield Fund for Southern History, University of Texas Press, 1951.

CHAPTER 2

For a cooly analytical account of the Southern serf system there is still nothing to surpass *An American Dilemma*, Vols. I, II, by Gunnar Myrdal; New York: Harper and Row, 1944. A passionate description of black reaction is found in *Twelve Million Black Voices: A Folk History of the Negro in the United States* by Richard Wright; New York: The Viking Press, 1941.

Anne Moody has written a brilliant memoir of southern rural life as it looked to a black child in recent times. Her book is *Coming of Age in Mississippi, An Autobiography*. New York: Dial Press, Inc., 1965.

Other works:

Baker, Roy Stannard. *Following the Color Line, American Negro Citizenship in the Progressive Era*. New York, Evanston and London: Harper and Row, 1964. (Originally published by Doubleday, Page and Co., 1908.)

Davis, Allison, Burleigh B. and Gardner, Mary R. *Deep South: A Social Anthropological Study of Caste and Class*. Chicago: University of Chicago Press, 1941.

DuBois, W. E. B. *The Souls of Black Folk*. Chicago: A. C. McClung and Co., 1903.

Killens, John Oliver. *Black Man's Burden*. New York: Trident Press, 1965.

Meltzer, Milton, ed. *In Their Own Words, A History of the American Negro, 1916-1966.* New York: Thomas Y. Crowell Co., 1967.

Parsons, Talcott, and Clark, Kenneth B., eds. *The Negro American.* Boston: Beacon Press, 1965.

Raper, Arthur F. *Preface to Peasantry: A Tale of Two Black Belt Counties.* Chapel Hill: University of North Carolina Press, 1936.

Tocqueville, Alexis de. *Democracy in America, Vol. 1.* New York: Alfred A. Knopf, Inc. and Random House, Inc., 1945.

CHAPTER 3

Two "birth of a ghetto" books cover closely the essential circumstances as they occurred in New York and Chicago, providing sharp parallels in the early black experience in northern ghettos. The books:

Osofsky, Gilbert. *Harlem: The Making of a Ghetto, Negro New York, 1890-1930.* New York, Evanston: Harper and Row, 1963.

Spear, Allan H. *Black Chicago: The Making of a Negro Ghetto, 1890-1920.* Chicago and London: University of Chicago Press, 1967.

A detailed statistical study of the long-term southern exodus of blacks is contained incidentally in a Twentieth Century Fund study of the modern South. The reference is:

Maddox, James G., Liebhafsky, E. E., Henderson, Vivian W., and Hamlin, Herbert M. *The Advancing South, Manpower Prospects and Problems.* New York: Twentieth Century Fund, 1967.

Emmett J. Scott, editor of the *Journal of Negro History*, collected migrant letters which caught poignant human glimpses of the first large movement to northern cities. The references:

Scott, Emmett J., ed. "Letters of Negro Migrants of 1916-1918," *Journal of Negro History* (July and October, 1919): pp. 290-340, 412-75.

Scott, Emmett J. *Negro Migration During the War.* New York: Oxford University Press, 1920.

Rich lore on the early migration is contained also in issues of the *Chicago Defender*, a black newspaper which encouraged mass movement during the World War I era.

Other sources are:

Bontemps, Arna, and Conroy, Jack. *They Seek a City.* Garden City, New York: Doubleday, Doran and Co., 1945.

Chicago Commission on Race Relations. *The Negro in Chicago.* Chicago: University of Chicago, 1923.

Drake, St. Clair, and Cayton, Horace R. *Black Metropolis: A Study of*

Negro Life in a Northern City. New York: Harcourt Brace Jovanovich, Inc., 1962.

DuBois, W. E. B. *The Philadelphia Negro, A Social Study.* New York: Shocken Books, 1967. (First published in 1899.)

Garvey, Amy Jacques, ed. *Philosophy and Opinions of Marcus Garvey.* New York: The Universal Publishing House, 1923.

Grant, Joanne, ed. *Black Protest.* (See Chapter 1 Bibliography.)

Jacobson, Julius. *The Negro and the American Labor Movement.* Garden City, New York: Doubleday and Company, 1968.

Kennedy, Louise V. *The Negro Peasant Turns Cityward.* New York: Columbia University Press, 1930.

Meier, August, and Rudwick, Elliott. *From Plantation to Ghetto.* (See Chapter 1 Bibliography.)

Myrdal, Gunnar. *An American Dilemma.* (See Chapter 1 Bibliography.)

Quarles, Benjamin. *The Negro in the Making of America.* (See Chapter 1 Bibliography.)

Spero, Sterling D., and Harris, Abram L. *The Black Worker: Studies in American Negro Life.* New York: Columbia University Press, 1931, 1959.

Woodson, Carter G. *A Century of Negro Migration.* Washington, D.C.: The Association for the Study of Negro Life and History, Inc., 1918.

Woofter, Thomas J. *Negro Problems in Cities.* Garden City, New York: Doubleday, Doran and Co., Inc., 1928.

Woofter, Thomas J., Jr. *Negro Migration.* New York: W. D. Gray, 1920.

CHAPTER 4

The following federal publications contain major data relating to the condition of rural blacks, the decline of small farmers and general economic problems in the South:

Alabama. (*Census of Agriculture*, Vol. 1, Part 32.) Washington, D.C.: U.S. Bureau of the Census, 1964.

Size of Farm. (*Census of Agriculture*, Vol. 2, Chap. 3.) Washington, D.C.: U.S. Bureau of the Census, 1964.

Operators and Persons Living on Farms. (*Census of Agriculture*, Vol. 2, Chap. 5.) Washington, D.C.: U.S. Bureau of the Census, 1946.

Farm Labor. (*Census of Agriculture*, Vol. 3, Part 2.) Washington, D.C.: U.S. Bureau of the Census, 1964.

A *Selective Bibliography* 281

A Socio-Economic Profile of the 1965 Farm Wage Force. (*Agricultural Economic Report* No. 157.) Washington, D.C.: U.S. Bureau of the Census.

U.S. Bureau of the Census. Current Population Reports: *Farm Population in the United States, 1967.* Series Census-ERS, Pg. 27, No. 39, May 23, 1969.

State Payments to Local Governments. (*1967 Census of Governments*, Vol. 6, Topical Studies No. 4), Washington, D.C.: U.S. Bureau of the Census, 1968.

Hathaway, Dale E., Beegle, J. Allen, and Bryant, W. Keith. *People of Rural America.* Washington, D.C.: U.S. Bureau of the Census, 1968.

Hunger and Malnutrition in the United States. Hearings before Subcommittee on Employment, Manpower and Poverty of the Committee on Labor and Public Welfare, U.S. Senate, Washington, D.C. May 29-30, June 12 and 14, 1968.

The People Left Behind. A Report of the President's National Advisory Commission on Rural Poverty, Washington, D.C., Sept. 1967.

Important studies are conducted also by the Southern Regional Council at Atlanta, Georgia. Council reports consulted included *Public Assistance in the South*, Sept., 1966; *Public Assistance To What End?* Sept., 1967; *The Economic Status of Negroes in the Nation and in the South*, by Vivian W. Henderson, (undated); and *Hungry Children*, by Drs. Joseph Brenner, Robert Coles, Alan Mermann, Milton J. E. Senn, Cyril Walwyn and Raymond Wheeler (undated).

Other sources were:

Blackwell, Randolph T., "Out-Migration and Civil Disorders," speech given at the University of North Carolina, Oct. 16, 1967.

Clark, Thomas D. *The Emerging South*, 2nd ed. London, Oxford, New York: Oxford University Press, 1968.

Good, Paul. *The American Serfs, A Report on Poverty in the Rural South.* New York: G. P. Putnam's Sons, 1968.

"Hunger in America." CBS Reports, May 21, 1968. Reporter Charles Kuralt; written by Peter Davis and Martin Carr; produced by Martin Carr; executive producer, Don Hewitt.

Hunger, U.S.A. A Report by the Citizens Board of Inquiry into Hunger and Malnutrition in the United States. Washington, D.C.: New Community Press, 1968.

Franklin, John H., and Starr, Isidore. *The Negro in 20th Century America.* New York: Random House, Inc., 1967.

Friedman, Leon, ed. *Southern Justice.* Cleveland, New York: The World Publishing Company, 1963.

Harrington, Michael. *The Other America: Poverty in the United States.* New York: The MacMillan Company, 1962.

Maddox, James G. *The Advancing South.* (See Chapter 3 Bibliography.)

Mitchell, Glenford E., and Peace, William H. III. *The Angry Black South.* New York: Corinth, 1962.

Watters, Pat, and Cleghorn, Reese. *Climbing Jacob's Ladder, The Arrival of Negroes in Southern Politics.* New York: Harcourt, Brace and World, 1967.

Wakefield, Dan. *Revolt in the South.* New York: Grove Press, 1960.

Magazine and newspaper sources included:

Bagdikian, Ben H. "The Black Migrants," *Saturday Evening Post* (July 15, 1967), pp. 25-29.

"The Southern Roots of the Urban Crisis." *Fortune* (August, 1968), pp. 86-87.

Pritchard, Warren. "The Poor Peoples' Campaign and Other Lobbies," *New South*, periodical of the Southern Regional Council, (April, 1968), pp. 21-27.

"Why Is There Hunger While Funds Go Unused?" *The National Observor* (Feb. 19, 1968).

Bigart, Homer. "Hunger in America." (Five-part series). *The New York Times* (Feb. 16-20, 1969), all articles beginning pg. 1.

"Tobacco Farms Changing." *New York Times* (April 12, 1969), pg. 37.

"South's Relief Aid Sends Many North." *The New York Times* (Oct. 14, 1968).

CHAPTER 5

The material on southern co-ops was drawn primarily from interviews conducted by the author in the summer of 1968.

Interviewed at or near Selma, Alabama, were members of the Southwest Alabama Farmers Cooperative Association, including William Harrison, president, and Freeman Berry, Joe Johnson, and Shirley Mesher.

Albert Turner of Southern Christian Leadership Conference provided helpful information; also I. B. Hopson, a local black leader, and his son-in-law, farmer Tyler Moore, Jr.

Others were L. C. Alsobrook, county extension chairman, Alex Brown, extension farm agent, and Sam O'Hara, office manager of the County Agricultural Stabilization and Conservation Service.

Magazine and newspaper accounts included:

Good, Paul. "The Road to Joe Johnson's Place," *The New South* (Winter, 1968), Published by the Southern Regional Conference.

Miles, Michael. "Black Cooperatives," *The New Republic* (Sept. 21, 1968), pp. 21-23.

"Poverty and Pickles," *Barron's* (April 7, 1969), pg. 9.

Birmingham Post-Herald (June 17-20), another series on the co-op.

The following were interviewed at Crawfordville: Calvin Turner, O.E.O. director of Community Development; Crawfordville Enterprises plant manager Robert Billingsley of the textilemill; plant manager Joe Strickland of the woodworking shop; co-op staff members Kevin Kane and Mrs. LaDelle Merkerson, and Rev. J. J. Johnson.

Reports on Crawfordville include:

"It works!" *Agenda* (publication of the Industrial Union Department of the AFL-CIO), Jan.-Feb., 1968.

Blackwell, Randolph T., "Some Notes on the Nature and Operation of the Southern Rural Action Project" (report prepared Feb. 1, 1968).

Kurland, Norman G., and Bailey, Norman A., "The Crawfordville Story" (Columbia Forum, Fall, 1968), pp. 28-32.

The National Sharecroppers Fund supports the co-op movement from a New York City headquarters and provides general information on developments in the field. Some articles on the subject:

Rich, Marvin. "Civil Rights Progress Out of the Spotlight," *The Reporter* (March 7, 1968), pp. 25-27.

Trillin, Calvin. *U.S. Journal: Gees Bend, Ala.*, "The Black Women of Wilcox County Is About to Do Something." *The New Yorker* (March 22, 1969), pp. 102+.

"The Great Migration, A Crisis for Both the City and Rural America." *The New York Daily News* (Nov. 20-22).

"Quilting Co-op Tastes Success and Finds It Sweet." *The New York Times* (April 18, 1969), pg. 47.

"Tapping the Green Side of Black Power." *The Wall Street Journal* (June 4, 1968).

The sketch of Charles Evers was drawn from published sources and from observation of his numerous appearances on television programs. Articles included:

Lelyveld, Joseph. "The Mayor of Fayette, Mississippi," *The New York Times Magazine* (October 26, 1969), pp. 54-55+.

Rugaber, Walter. "We can't cuss white people any more, it's in our hands now." *The New York Times Magazine* (August 4, 1968), pp. 12-16+.

CHAPTER 6

In recent years the Census Bureau has issued a series of massi⁄e statistical reports relating to problems of poverty and race and focused primarily on urban conditions. Addressed especially to the black ⁞ircumstances are the following:

The Social and Economic Status of Negroes in the United States, 1970 (*Current Population Reports*, BLS Report No. 394, Series P-23, No. 38). Washington, D.C.; Bureau of the Census–Dept. of Labor, July, 1971.

The Social and Economic Status of Negroes in the United States, 1969 (*Current Population Reports*, BLS Report No. 375, Series P-23, No. 29). Washington, D.C.: U.S. Department of Labor.

Social and Economic Conditions of Negroes in the United States, July, 1968 (*Current Population Reports*, BLS Report No. 347, Series P-23, No. 26). Ibid. Dec. 26, 1969.

Social and Economic Conditions of Negroes in the United States (*Current Population Reports*, BLS Report No. 332, Series P-23, No. 24). Ibid. October, 1967.

"The Negroes in the United States: Their Economic and Social Situation" (*Bulletin No. 1411*). Washington, D.C.: U.S. Department of Labor, June, 1966.

"Job Patterns for Minorities and Women" (*Equal Employment Opportunity Report No. 1.*), Washington, D.C.: Government Printing Office, 1968.

Another report merits special attention though it is now slightly outdated. It distinguishes between general economic progress among urban blacks and the continuing stagnation which occurs in the inner ghetto. The reference:

Characteristics of Selected Neighborhoods in Cleveland, Ohio (*Current Population Reports*, Series P-23, No. 21.) Washington, D.C.: U.S. Bureau of the Census, April, 1963.

Other major census studies include:

Occupation and Earnings of Family Heads in 1969, 1965, and 1959 (*Current Population Reports*, Series P-60, No. 73). Washington, D.C.: U.S. Bureau of the Census, 1970.

Consumer Income, 24 Million Americans: Poverty in the U.S., 1969

(Current Population Reports, Series P-60, No. 76). Ibid., December 16 1970.

Income in 1969 of Families and Persons in the United States (Current Population Reports, Series P-60, No. 75). Ibid., December, 1970.

Special Studies, Trends in Social and Economic Conditions in Metropolitan Areas (Current Population Reports, Series P-23, No. 27). Ibid., February 7, 1969.

Socio-Economic Trends in Poverty Areas, 1960 to 1968 (Current Population Reports, Series P-60, No. 67). Ibid., December 30, 1969.

Consumer Income, Poverty in the United States, 1959 to 1968 (Current Population Reports, Series P-60, No. 68). Ibid., December 31, 1969.

Consumer Income, The Extent of Poverty in the U.S., 1959 to 1966 (Current Population Reports, Series P-60, No. 54). Ibid., May 31, 1968.

Consumer Income, Year-Round Workers With Low Earnings in 1966 (Current Population Reports, Series P-60, No. 58). Ibid., April 4, 1969.

Found useful for either background or specific reference were the following:

Clark, Kenneth B. *Dark Ghetto: Dilemmas of Social Power*. New York and Evanston: Harper and Row, 1965.

Hunter, David R. *The Slums, Challenge and Response*. New York and London: The Free Press, Collier-MacMillan Ltd., 1964.

Frazier, E. Franklin. *The Negro Family in the United States*. Chicago and London: University of Chicago Press, 1939, 1948.

Handlin, Oscar. *The Newcomers: Negroes and Puerto Ricans in a Changing Metropolis*. Garden City, New York: Doubleday and Company, 1959.

McCord, William, Howard, John, Friedberg, Bernard, and Harwood, Edwin. *Life Styles in the Black Ghetto*. New York: W. W. Norton & Co., 1969.

Rainwater, Lee, and Yancey, William L. *The Moynihan Report and the Politics of Controversy*. Cambridge, Mass., and London: The M.I.T. Press, 1967.

Niedercorn, J. H. and Pascal, A. H., "Resumé of the Rand Conference on Urban Economics" (Rand Report P-2991). Santa Monica, Calif. October, 1964.

Niedercorn, John H. "Suburbanization of Employment and Population 1948-1975" (Rand Report P-2641). January, 1963.

Silberman, Charles E. *Crisis in Black and White*. New York: Alfred A. Knopf, Inc., and Random House, 1964.

Taeuber, Karl E. and Alma F. *Negroes in Cities, Residential Segregation and Neighborhood Change.* New York: Atheneum, 1965.

Williams, Walter. "Cleveland's Crisis Ghetto," *Trans-Action* (September, 1967).

The Negro and The City. (Adapted from a Special Issue of *Fortune* on: "Business and the Urban Crisis.") New York: Time-Life Books, Time, Inc., 1968.

The story of the child killed by heroin was from *The New York Times*, January 12, 1970. Sharon's essay was provided to this writer by Francine Krisel, who did much research and reportorial work for this book.

CHAPTER 7

The difficulties facing city government are well stated in:

Lindsay, John V. *The City.* New York: W. W. Norton, and Co., 1969.

Focus on People: A Glimpse at Key Anti-Poverty Programs. New York: Human Resources Administration, undated.

CBS News Special Report: "The Cities." With CBS News Correspondent Walter Cronkite. Telecast June 24-26, 1968.

Moynihan, Daniel P. *Maximum Feasible Misunderstanding: Community Action in the War on Poverty.* New York: The Free Press, a Division of the MacMillan Co., 1968.

One Year Later. An Assessment of the Nation's Response to the Crisis Described by the National Advisory Commission on Civil Disorders. Printed in the United States of America. The staffs of the Urban Coalition and Urban America, 1969.

Powledge, Fred. *Model City.* New York: Simon and Schuster, 1971.

Pascal, Anthony H., ed. "Contributions to the Analysis of Urban Problems, a Selection of Papers from the Rand Workshop on Urban Programs" (Rand Report P-3868). Santa Monica, Calif. August, 1968.

Report of the National Advisory Commission on Civil Disorders. New York: Bantam Books, Inc., Grosset and Dunlap, 1968.

Ruchelman, Leonard I., ed. *Big City Mayors: The Crisis in Urban Politics.* Bloomington, Indiana: Indiana University Press, 1970.

Ryan, William. *Blaming the Victim.* New York: Pantheon Books, 1971.

Supplemental Studies for the National Advisory Commission on Civil Disorders. Ann Arbor, Michigan: Survey Research Center, Institute for Social Research, University of Michigan, June, 1968.

Periodical citations are too numerous and repetitive to justify full listing. Useful detail came from the following articles:

Gans, Herbert J. "The White Exodus to Suburbia Steps Up," *The New York Times Magazine* (January 7, 1968), pp. 28+.

Hadden, Jeffrey K., Masotti, Louis, Thiessen, Victor. "The Making of the Negro Mayors, 1967." *Trans-Action* (Jan.-Feb., 1968), pp. 21-30.

"The Negro in America—What Must Be Done," *Newsweek Magazine* (November 20, 1967), pp. 40-42+.

"The Sick, Sick Cities: Introducing a New Section on Urban Life," *Newsweek Magazine* (March 17, 1969), pp. 40-44+.

Text of the President's Message to Congress on Federal Budget for Fiscal Year, 1972. *The New York Times* (January 30, 1971), pp. 13-14.

"Financial Problems Plague Schools Across the Nation." New York Times (March 15, 1971), pg. 31.

"Bipartisan Efforts to Give the City Greater Realty Taxing Power Are Stepped Up." *The New York Times* (November 25, 1969), pg. 37.

"Model Cities Struggle: Black Jobless vs. Unions." *The New York Times* (April 3, 1969), pp. 45.

Text of President's Message to Congress on Federal Budget for Fiscal Year, 1970. *The New York Times* (January 16, 1969), pp. 19-20.

CHAPTER 8

The Newark investigation was conducted with the aid of Mrs. Helen Smith who contributed greatly in gathering material, conducting interviews and shaping conclusions.

Numerous Newarkers were helpful to the effort. They include Dr. George Sternlieb, who allowed generous use of his housing study, Donald Malafronte and Samuel Shepherd at city hall, and Frank Grant, who helped to open doors on the street. Principal sources include the following:

Official documents and reports

Civic Improvement Training, 1967, A Newark City Report.

Economic Blueprint. (A plan for city development.)

Health Report, 1967, Department of Health and Welfare, Newark.

Model City Report. An application to the Department of Housing and Urban Development for a grant to plan a comprehensive city demonstration program. Trenton, N.J., April 24, 1967.

Newark's Urban Renewal Program. Prepared by the Division of City Planning in cooperation with the Newark Housing Authority, July, 1967.

Report of the Governor's Commission on Civil Disorders, Newark, February, 1968.

U.S. Congressional Record, January 22, 1971. Prepared testimony of Mayor Kenneth A. Gibson, Joint Economic Committee of the 92nd Congress.

City Blacks, Newark, N.J. Washington, D.C.: U.S. Census Bureau. 1960.

Books

Baraka, Imamu Amiri (LeRoi Jones), and Fundi (Bill Abernathy). *In Our Terribleness*. New York: Bobbs-Merrill Co., 1970.

Crews, Harold. *The Crisis of the Negro Intellectual*. New York: Morrow and Co., 1967.

Hayden, Tom. *Rebellion in Newark, Official Violence and Ghetto Response*. New York: Alfred A. Knopf and Random House, 1967.

Jones, LeRoi. *Home, Social Essays*. New York: William Morrow and Co., 1966.

Kaplan, Harold. *Urban Renewal Politics: Slum Clearance in Newark*. 1963.

Nortman, Bernard P. *An Economic Blueprint for Newark*. Newark: Office of Economic Development, City of Newark, 1968.

Smith, Georgina M. *On the Welfare*. New Brunswick, N.J.: Quinn and Boyden Co., Rutgers, 1969.

Telecast

WNET-TV, Channel 13. New Jersey Speaks, February 7, 1971. Discussion by Imamu Amiri Baraka and Steven Adubato.

Periodicals

Anderson, Jervis. "The Voices of Newark," *Commentary* (October, 1967), p. 90.

"Newark," *Atlantic Monthly* (August 1965), pp. 4-8.

Caplan, Nathan S., and Paige, Jeffery M. "A Study of Ghetto Rioters (1967 in Detroit and Newark)," *Scientific American* (August, 1968), pp. 15-21.

Cook, Fred J. "Newark's 'Responsible Militants' Say: 'It's Our City, Don't Destroy It,' " *The New York Times Magazine* (June 30, 1968), pp. 10-11+.

Llorens, David. "Ameer (LeRoi Jones) Baraka," *Ebony* (August, 1969), pp. 75-8+.

Goldberger, Paul. "Tony Imperiale Stands Vigilant for Law and Order," *The New York Times Magazine* (September 29, 1968), pp. 30-31+.

Hayden, Tom. "The Occupation of Newark," *The New York Review* (August 14, 1967), pp. 14-21.

Mann, Eric. "The Newark Community School," *Liberation* (August, 1967), pgs. 26-33.

Mayer, Martin. "The Full and Sometimes very Surprising Story of Ocean Hill, the Teachers' Union and the Teacher Strikes of 1968," *The New York Times Magazine* (February 2, 1969), pp. 18-71.

"Newark: The Price of the Past," *Newsweek* (August 3, 1970), pg. 18.

"The Black Mayors," *Newsweek* (August 3, 1970), pp. 16-18+.

"Ecstasies and Agonies of LeRoi Jones," *Ramparts* (June 29, 1968), pg. 14-19.

Sackett, Russell. "In a Grim City, a Secret Meeting With the Snipers," *Life* (July 28, 1967), pg. 27-28.

"New Script in Newark," *Time Magazine* (April 26, 1968), pp. 18-19.

Wittner, Dale. "The Killing of Billy Furr, Caught in the Act of Looting Beer," *Life* (July 28, 1967), pgs. 21-22.

Newspaper accounts
The New York Times:

April 16, 1971. "Crisis in Newark," Guest essay by Imamu Amiri Baraka.

April 14, 1971. " 'Impossible' School Crisis."

February 14, 1971. "Newark School Strike Splits Blacks."

November 15, 1970. "Business Administrator Faces School Fund Crisis in Newark."

September 20, 1970. "Gibson Finds Corruption Exceeds His Fears."

July 21, 1970. "Young Lords in Newark Accuse Police of 'Brutality' in Parade."

June 21, 1970. "Both Sides in Newark Seek Orderly Shift as Bitterness Fades."

June 16, 1970. "The Rivals in Newark's Mayoral Election Today." pg. 50.

June 14, 1970. "Newark's Mayoral Contest Reaches a Bitter Climax."

May 31, 1970. "LeRoi Jones Defines Role in Newark Race."

May 30, 1970. Interview with LeRoi Jones.

May 17, 1970. "Election in Newark Threatens to Polarize the City." pg. 3.

May 14, 1970. "No. 1 in Newark Vote."

April 1, 1970. "Who Fired Accidental Shot in Newark City Hall?"

March 10, 1970. "Addonizio Opens Campaign, Sure of Vindication."

February 7, 1970. "Newark School Conflict."

December 21, 1969, pg. 1. "Newark Corruption Held a 'Textbook Case' for U.S." pg. 1+.

December 10, 1969, pg. 1. "Riots Brought Newark's Mayor From Obscurity into Spotlight."

August 4, 1969. "Newark Reports a 9.7% Drop In Major Crime Since 1968."

March 18, 1969. pg. 30, "Flight to Suburbs Hurts Newark."

February 21, 1969. pg. 45 "Library and Museum Pawns in Newark Financial Crisis."

February 11, 1968. "Newark Riot Panel Asks Inquiry Into Corruption."

February 4, 1968. "Unemployment High Among Newark Nonwhites."

"The Central Ward's Ominous Message," *The National Observer* (October 9, 1967).

Interviews

Phil Brito, assistant public health educator.

Charles Cobb, Gibson campaign worker at the victory party on election night.

Frank Grant, founder of HOPERS.

Mayor Kenneth A. Gibson.

Aron H. Haskin, health officer, Division of Health, Newark.

Judy Kincher, Afro-American Association.

James F. King, director, Newark Commission for Neighborhood Conservation and Rehabilitation.

Donald Malafronte, former administrative assistant to Mayor Addonizio, former special consultant to Mayor Gibson.

Theodore Pinckney, black activist and political candidate.

Tyrone Roe, Hoper.

Lucius H. Tompkins, black activist in the Miracle Committee.

Samuel Shepherd, administrative assistant to Mayor Gibson.

Mrs. Larry Stalks, former Director of Health and Welfare.

Dwight Watson, Hoper and street veteran.

Thelma Williams, tenement dweller.

Willie Wright, United Afro-American Association.

CHAPTER 9

Black Power literature is enormous and wide ranging; it extends from reform to revolution and from political assertion to cultural withdrawal. This writer is white and makes no pretense of inside insights into black soul. Any writer, however, is entitled to evaluate as best he can the over-all context of the political and social movements of his time. The judgment recorded in this book is an attempt to estimate the black power thrust in various perspectives, both historical and current, and is drawn from a large number of sources including the following representative examples:

Benedict, Stewart H., ed. *Blacklash*. Popular Library, New York. 1970.

Brink, William, and Louis Harris. *Black and White*. Simon and Schuster, New York. 1966, 1967.

Carmichael, Stokely, and Charles V. Hamilton. *Black Power, the Politics of Liberation in America*. Alfred A. Knopf and Random House, New York. 1967.

Cleaver, Eldredge. *Soul On Ice*, Dell Publishing Co., New York. 1968.

Douglass, Frederick. *Life and Times of Frederick Douglass, written by himself*. DeWolfe, Fiske and Company, Boston. 1895.

Essien, Udom, E. U. *Black Nationalism, A Search for an Identity in America*. Dell Publishing Co., New York. 1962.

Marine, Gene. *The Black Panthers*. New American Library, New York. 1969.

Thompson, Daniel C. *The Negro Leadership Class*. Prentice-Hall, Inc., Englewood Cliffs, N.J. 1963.

Young, Whitney M. *Beyond Racism*. McGraw-Hill Book Company, New York, Toronto, London, Sydney. 1969.

X, Malcolm. *The Autobiography of Malcolm X*. Grove Press, New York. 1964, 1965.

CHAPTER 10

Personal viewpoints, based on findings already presented.

Index

Index

DATE DUE

GAYLORD			PRINTED IN U.S.A.